THE SPHINX AND THE COMMISSAR

By the same author:

THE ROAD TO RAMADAN

THE SPHINX
AND THE
COMMISSAR

The Rise and Fall of
Soviet Influence in the Middle East

Mohamed Heikal

1817

HARPER & ROW, PUBLISHERS

New York, Hagerstown, San Francisco, London

FIRST U.S. EDITION

ISBN: 0-06-011804-0

LIBRARY OF CONGRESS CATALOG CARD NUMBER: 78-22440

79 80 81 82 83 84 10 9 8 7 6 5 4 3 2 1

Contents

Illustrations

*These photographs, grouped in a separate section, will be found
following page 128.*

Heikal and Khruschev

Khruschev's first sight of Egypt

Nasser and Khruschev in the Egyptian Museum, Cairo

Khruschev between Gromyko and Nasser

Mikoyan, Heikal, Sadat and Marshal Malinovsky

Heikal and Gromyko

Heikal and Podgorny

Kosygin and Sadat

Boumedienne and Kosygin
  (*United Press International*)

General Hafiz al-Assad, Syrian Defence Minister and Marshal
  Gretchko
  (*Associated Press*)

Marshal Zakharov and General Fawzi

Ali Sabri, Brezhnev and Nasser

Nasser and Brezhnev

Podgorny, Brezhnev, Nasser, Mahmoud Riad and Heikal

Podgorny and Sadat sign the Soviet–Egyptian Treaty

(*Photographs supplied by the author except where otherwise stated*)

Introduction

I HAVE CALLED this book 'The Rise and Fall of Soviet Influence in the Arab World', but readers will find that there is much more in it about the Soviet Union's relations with Egypt than with any other Arab country. This is to be explained not so much by the fact that it was from Egypt that I watched the events of these twenty years as by the central role in them which history and geography inevitably cast for my country. It was appropriate that Egypt should have been the first Arab country to establish relations with the Soviet Union and to have dealings with it. It was inevitable that Egypt should have become in a sense the gateway for the Soviet Union to the rest of the Arab world and to parts of Africa. Correspondingly, it was natural that those who wished to eliminate the Soviet Union from the Arab world and Africa should have started this reverse operation with Egypt.

In preparation of this book I have relied primarily on my own collection of documents and on my memories of the years which I spent close to the centres of power in Egypt, first with President Nasser from 1952 to 1970, and then with President Sadat from 1970 to 1975. I have not, of course, relied exclusively on these sources, but have made use of the testimony of others who took part in the events I have described. If I do not refer to them by name, this is not through any lack of gratitude, but in order to avoid any misunderstanding which might be caused by associating them openly with a book in the preparation of which they have not been involved.

This book should, in fact, be regarded as a personal narrative, rather than as a work of scholarship or research. Those who have been privileged to observe at close range the unfolding of political and diplomatic affairs have a duty to describe what they saw as accurately and dispassionately as they can. This is what I have tried to do.

It has never been my intention to write a book which could be labelled anti-Soviet or pro-Soviet. The only point of view from which I write is that of an Arab, and as an Arab I have always been anxious to see the Arab world achieve a balanced relationship with the Soviet

Union. After all, the Soviet Union is one of the two superpowers; it is geographically near the Arabs, and it represents one of the main ideologies which have shaped the world in which we all have to live. This means that the Soviet Union is not just something peripheral to the Arabs; it is bound to be an essential part of their experience.

It was unfortunately necessary for me to take up a position critical of the Soviet Union at the time when, after the death of Nasser in September 1970, I felt that its influence in the Arab world was becoming too great. This did not, however, mean that I ever thought it would be right to replace the influence of one superpower by that of the other. So in due course I found myself obliged to be critical of what I felt to be undue influence being exercised in the same area by the United States.

At various times I have been the target for fierce attacks by the Soviet press and radio; at other times they have praised me in extra-vagant terms. I have tried not to let any of this affect my account of the twenty years between 1955 and 1975. I believe that the Arab world learned a great deal from the Soviet Union and benefited a great deal from contact with it. I think, too, that the Soviet Union gained much, and learned much, from its contacts with the Arabs. I do not believe, for example, that the Soviets' recent successes in Angola and in the Horn of Africa could have been achieved if it had not been for the lessons they learned in the Middle East during the period which this book covers.

However, whatever successes there may have been in parts of Africa, this does not alter the fact that the great Soviet offensive in the Arab world failed. Not only was the offensive halted – it was obliged to turn back. But this abortive offensive represents only one chapter in the story of relations between the Arabs and the Soviet Union. It does not mean that the story has ended, for it is out of the question that the Soviet Union should ever isolate itself from what goes on in the Arab world. It would be quite wrong, for obvious historical and strategic reasons, if it tried to do so. Accordingly this book should be seen not just as a review of what has gone before, but as a pointer to what is to come. I would like it to be read as a prospectus rather than as an obituary.

Once again I should like to thank my friend Edward Hodgkin for help in preparation of my material.

CAIRO
June 1978

I
Nasser's Advice

THE ROOM in which the Soviet Politburo meets is on the second floor of the Praesidium building in the Kremlin. It is a long room, with windows on both sides, those in front looking over a garden and those on the other side looking over a yard. The only ornamentation consists of large portraits of Marx and Lenin which, side by side, gaze down on the green baize cloth of the conference table, on which are laid out supplies of mineral water, biscuits, chocolates and cigarettes. On a smaller table to one side are arranged books and pamphlets, together with models of rockets, space-craft, and aeroplanes.

It is in this room that formal discussions with visiting delegations from foreign countries are conducted, each negotiating team occupying similar brown leather chairs, one on each side of the table. But today, which is a day in the summer of 1977, no foreigners are present. The nine men now seated at the table are all Soviet citizens. Together they make up a group of the most powerful men in one of the two most powerful nations of the world.

At the head of the table sits Leonid Brezhnev, General Secretary of the Central Committee of the Communist Party of the Soviet Union and, since June, President of the Praesidium of the Supreme Soviet. Ranged at his side are Alexei Kosygin, Chairman of the Council of Ministers, Mikhail Suslov, the party's ideologist, Andrei Gromyko, Minister for Foreign Affairs, Dmitry Ustinov, Minister of Defence, then two of the rising stars in the Soviet firmament, Kyril Mazarov, whose responsibilities include arranging assistance for national liberation movements abroad, and Yuri Andropov, head of the KGB, who sits with his head leaning on one hand while with the other he scratches with his pen meticulous lines on a sheet of foolscap, which later he will tear into the minutest fragments. The group is completed by two of Suslov's aides – Boris Ponomarev, Chairman of the International Department of the Central Committee, and R.A. Ulianovsky, an assistant to Ponomarev who specializes in ideological questions affecting national liberation movements.

These men comprise the standing committee of the Politburo which is concerned with all matters of defence, foreign policy and security. Today it has before it the problems of the Middle East, and its members have been considering one by one the countries there with which they, as a government, have been concerned.

They have found little in their review to comfort them. Egypt, the country with which their association has been longest and most intimate, whose defence forces they modernized and armed, whose High Dam, that miracle of modern engineering, their engineers helped to build, has now turned contemptuously on them while its President daily upbraids them and all their works in the most scathing terms. The Sudan, where once was to be found the most thriving communist party in the Arab world, is hardly less hostile than Egypt. With Syria, another outstanding beneficiary from Soviet civil and military aid, relations are still close, but can hardly be described as easy. Iraq, a country which a few years ago seemed willing and, indeed, eager, to be wholly dependent on the Soviet Union, is now busily engaged in 'diversifying'; in other words, the Iraqi government is looking west for technical aid and awarding its fattest contracts to western firms.

From Saudi Arabia there is obviously nothing to be expected but active hostility. North Yemen had once looked a favourable prospect, when the huge Antonov planes were shuttling backwards and forwards, bringing supplies of arms and even food for the troops of the Yemen Republican Army, but now there is not a single Russian technician left in the country. There had been good grounds for hope in Somalia too, but all has gone sour there, and Soviet fortunes in the Horn of Africa are being ground to nothing by the millstones of war between Somalia and Ethiopia. Only the Palestinians remain more or less faithful, but of what real value are these men with a cause but without a country? How many divisions has the Pope, asked Stalin. How many divisions has Yasser Arafat, his ghost might ask his successors in the Kremlin.

No doubt, even as they contemplate this bleak picture, they are reminded of the numerous occasions in the past when they had serious differences of opinion even with Nasser. They will never forget how Nasser advised Libya's President, Muammar Ghadaffi, to buy arms from the West rather than from the Soviet Union, and how this advice was taken and the Mirages were bought. Nor, though relations with that other staunchly anti-communist Arab country,

Jordan, have improved, can they forget that it was Nasser again who advised King Hussein to continue buying arms from the United States and not switch to the Soviet Union, as he had proposed. 'We must not let the Arab–Israeli conflict become polarized between the superpowers,' had been Nasser's argument; 'this is bound to happen if the Arabs are armed exclusively by Russia and the Israelis exclusively by the United States'. Once again Nasser's advice was listened to, and the approach to the Soviets was not made.

In fact, by this summer of 1977, there can be no escaping the realization that the entire Middle East policy of the Soviet Union is in ruins. There is not a single country in the whole area which can be considered a true friend, let alone a reliable ally. Whereas a few years earlier the Soviet Union had been everywhere regarded as the principal defender of Arab rights, today it is to Washington that all roads from the Arab world lead. To rub salt in the Soviets' wounds is their realization that if, at this particular moment, there is any prospect of their once again playing a significant role in decision-making processes in the Middle East, this will only come about as a result of an American invitation to do so. It is the Americans who see a useful function for their Geneva conference co-chairman to perform, even if the Arabs do not.

Nor is it simply a political disaster that the men round the Kremlin table have to contemplate. The economic cost of failure has to be reckoned up also. A few years earlier Kosygin had stated that Soviet investment in the Arab world amounted to fifteen billion dollars or more; by 1977 the figure must have risen to at least twenty billion dollars. And what dividend – political, military or even economic – is there to show for that vast capital expenditure? Who talks any more about the High Dam or the Euphrates Dam, or the electrification of rural Egypt?

Looking around them, the Soviet leaders can see that there is one service, and one service alone, that they are called on by the Arabs to perform, and this is to act as a supplier of arms. It is really almost as though the whole world has accepted the doctrine which Henry Kissinger once propounded in an interview he gave me: 'All the Russians can give you is arms; we Americans can give you peace.'

But even this role of arms provider for the Arabs has produced more friction than gratitude. Nor is it a role which the Soviets can regard with any relish. They know that the Chinese have mocked them over it. 'What has happened to the first socialist country in the world?' Chou En-Lai asked me when I interviewed him in January 1973. 'It's become nothing but an armaments dealer, mopping up your produce to pay the interest on the arms you've had to buy.'

So it was that in November 1975, when the Egyptian Foreign Minister, Ismail Fahmy, met his Soviet counterpart, Andrei Gromyko, he received an unexpected rebuff. Thinking to be the bearer of good news he told Gromyko that the Kuwaitis would shortly be turning up in Moscow to buy arms, bringing with them $200 million in cash. 'Mr Minister,' said Gromyko bitterly, 'do you really believe, then, what the Chinese say about us?'

But gradually the Soviets themselves began to see the execution of their policies in the Middle East more and more in terms of their ability to supply or withhold arms, thus ironically slipping into the role of arms dealer which they so indignantly repudiated. Once again it was Ismail Fahmy to whom this was to be brought home when he was negotiating with Brezhnev in Moscow in 1977. He mentioned some spare parts and replacements for arms that had been promised Egypt but not delivered; 'no doubt,' he added, 'owing to some bureaucratic hold-up, which you, Mr Chairman, will be able to overcome.' Brezhnev looked at him. 'That was not the result of any bureaucratic hold-up,' he said, 'it was the result of a political decision.' 'Who took it?' asked Ismail Fahmy. 'I did', said Brezhnev. 'The implication of the policies pursued by your government is that in no circumstances is Egypt going to fight. So what do you need these arms for?'

The prospect confronting the men sitting round the long table in the Kremlin is bleak indeed. Ignored, abused, dunned for arms but denied agreed payment for them, the Soviet leaders seem to have no assets left to them. Brezhnev may ask his colleagues for suggestions as to how the situation can be improved, but what consolation can they offer? They are all worried and anxious men. Gromyko is well aware that Soviet defeats in the Middle East have weakened his negotiating position with the United States when it comes to the vital question of detente and SALT. Ustinov is conscious of pressure from the marshals and admirals to safeguard the defence pattern in Russia's southern approaches. Andropov can argue that everything that has gone wrong is the consequence of sinister plots concocted by America and Saudi Arabia, but even if true that would be slight consolation. Somehow the Middle East has proved a minefield in which the Soviets walk at their peril. It is a grenade which has blown up in their hands. The metaphors may vary, but the facts remain the same.

★   ★   ★

The meeting I have sketched does not have a precise date and the tenor of its discussions must, of course, be a matter for conjecture, though it is fairly easy to guess at them. But the existence of the standing committee referred to is a matter of common knowledge, and it is known too that it held, and holds, regular meetings to review the situation in the Middle East. It is known, for example, that it held at least six meetings following President Sadat's expulsion of the Soviet technicians from Egypt in the summer of 1972.

If, as must be assumed, a great deal of bitterness and frustration where the Arab world is concerned was revealed in the course of the committee's discussions, that is hardly to be wondered at. The contrast between Soviet prospects in the Middle East as they were in the summer of 1977, and as they had been 22 years earlier when Egypt's so-called Czech arms deal first sucked the Soviet Union into the area, was almost unbelievable.

Then, it had seemed, they had everything going for them. World War II had destroyed the authority of the two powers which for a generation had dominated the area. France had been defeated; Britain was exhausted and almost bankrupt. The Soviet Union had emerged from the war with military strength and prestige equal to, if not greater than, that of its only rival, the United States. Fresh ideas were circulating through the Arab world; winds of change were blowing. The traditional governments left in power when the war ended were aware of these winds but lacked the skill or the will to do anything to adapt to them.

Inevitably new leaders emerged in the Arab countries more in touch with a world in which radio and air travel were opening up lands which had been inaccessible for centuries, and in which atomic weapons, the cold war, and the United Nations in their different way symbolized the fact that, for good or ill, the world was a very different place from what it had been in 1939. In this changed world the revolutionary might of the Soviet Union was clearly going to have a major role to play.

In Arab countries it was the armies – the only relatively well organized and modernized organizations in still largely backward societies – which were to provide the new leadership. In one Arab country after another – Syria, Egypt, Iraq, Yemen, Algeria, Sudan, Libya – army officers took over. Sometimes their motives were purely selfish, the pursuit of power for its own sake; but at other times they came to power with a programme of reform which they had long been brooding on and which they were determined to implement.

Neither the ambitious nor the idealists were to have an easy road. This was the era of the cold war, when the two superpowers confronted each other, but when the unacceptability of nuclear war made them look for other ways of carrying on the struggle. This was the heyday of propaganda and psychological warfare, and of secret agencies, especially the CIA and KGB. The Third World became a principle field for open and clandestine rivalry between the two armed ideologies, capitalism and communism, which had replaced the simpler colonial rivalries of expansionist Europe.

In this highly charged atmosphere the new leaders of the Arab world were subjected to enormous strains and stresses, whether they liked it or not. The West was the world they knew. Their hatred for western policies was often mixed with admiration for western institutions. They recognized the worth of liberal democracy and would have been happy to see it flourish in their own countries, but thought that it was something for which their people were not yet ready. Besides, it was with the old classes they had forcibly replaced that the West maintained an open or tacit alliance. So, after first turning almost automatically to the West for help, the new leaders found themselves in conflict with it, and with tormented hearts they addressed themselves to the East, to the world of communism.

Their change of front was not accomplished without grave misgivings. All the formative influences in the new leaders' lives – the books they had read, the history they had learned, the films they had seen – had come from the West. The languages they knew in addition to their own were English or French – Russian was, and remained, a mystery to them. It was impossible for them to remain unaffected by all that they had heard about the communist world – the closed society, the suppression of thought, the Stalinist terror. None of them went to Moscow without the fear – the certainty rather – that all his conversations would be bugged. Later, reports of the Twentieth Congress of the CPSU had their effect. The Arabs were determined not to become too involved in this new world that was opening to them. While they felt that the West had much to teach about political freedom, they felt that the East had useful lessons to give where equality and social justice were concerned. But at the same time they wanted to keep their distance.

There is hardly one of the new leaders in the Middle East or black Africa who has not begun his speech of greeting to Soviet hosts or guests with the words 'In spite of ideological differences ...' Most of them, in addition, were well aware that there existed in their own country a communist party which owed more loyalty to Moscow than to themselves.

But the socialist countries had much to offer a nationalist leader. They could, first of all, be of great assistance in the primary task of ending colonial domination by the West. After that they could help in the economic development of his country. Almost always he would find that, whereas the West, with its liberal–capitalist system, had little more to teach him, there was much that he could learn from Soviet experience that had relevance to his own situation. He was attracted by the centralization of authority and planning. He discovered that there were areas inside the Soviet Union with climatic and social conditions similiar to those he was trying to grapple with. Thus almost every Arab visitor to the Soviet Union would be taken to Kazakhstan, there to be told that this was a land where people used to live just as his did now, but which had, as he would see, been transformed out of all recognition.

So these leaders were torn between real attractions. The western doctrine of individual liberty could not be rejected as worthless, but the East was engaged in the construction of an egalitarian society which looked in many ways like the society they were themselves trying to build. The pull of the East was strong – indeed, before long stronger than they really liked. They therefore hoped to be able to cooperate closely with the East but to keep their lines open to the West.

To do this they had to study the ways of the two superpowers, which were very different from each other. The West in its dealings with the Third World countries, tended to think it already knew most, or all, of the answers. It drew confidently on a past colonial experience, which in the circumstances was a poor guide. The Americans, in particular, too readily assumed that if they could get control over the police and intelligence services of a country the rest would follow.

The Russians, who had studied western methods and come to the conclusion that they could improve on them, decided that the best way in which they could gain the influence they sought was to provide equipment for the armed forces and encourage industrialization, which would produce an industrial proletariat. But the Russians were extremely worried when they contemplated the countries with which they were becoming involved and realized how much everything depended on the will and capacity to survive of one man. In virtually every newly independent country they found one man – he might or might not be the same man who had led the struggle for independence – who made all the decisions, particularly in matters of foreign policy and defence. This stage in the transition from a traditional society to a more complex constitutional society may be inevitable, but it carries with it particular hazards.

Aware of these, the Russians were constantly urging this one man to build up an organization which might outlive him. It was their dream that men like Nasser might become their country's Constantine, converting to the new religion of communism themselves, and by so doing opening the way to the conversion of their whole people. It was, after all, a not impossible dream – Castro had not been a communist when power fell into his hands on the first day of 1959, yet he had soon seen the light and carried the people of Cuba with him. Why should not the same story be repeated by a Nasser or a Qasim? This was not to be, though their hopes received encouragement every time a western leader, such as Dulles, tried to ostracize Nasser by branding him a communist.

For the Soviets the new relationship established in Egypt by the 1955 arms deal was an event of the utmost importance. It not only provided the entry into the Middle East which, for strategic reasons, Russia had been seeking for over a century; it also opened the high road to Africa and set a pattern for Soviet relations with movements of national liberation everywhere in the world. So that the setback of 1972 in the Middle East must have had far more than local significance for them.

By the summer of 1977 signs of how far their authority had been eroded were not wanting. There was, for example, that occasion soon after President Carter took office in 1976 when the Secretary-General of the UN, Kurt Waldheim, urged him to make more use of the UN in the pursuit of his international aims. 'There is no need for you to be afraid of the UN,' Dr Waldheim had insisted; 'the automatic Third World majority there which the Soviet Union used to be able to command against you no longer exists.' The Soviet leaders knew this was so. They knew that much of the magic that had once attached to their name had evaporated.

True, from the outset they had had their misgivings. Success had at times come almost too easily, but even when their star seemed most clearly in the ascendant the Soviets had wondered exactly what it was that the Arabs wanted from them. Had they simply been called in as a counterweight to the West? When the Arabs felt the emergency was passed, would their new Soviet friends be placed in the deep freeze? Long before the fiasco of the years following the 1973 war, the Soviets had tried to analyse the Middle East scene and their role in it. With all the resources of doctrine at their disposal they had tried to see the Middle East in its correct ideological and historical setting, so that they might thereby be enabled to pursue policies which were both theoretically correct and practically successful.

Leading Arabs too had done their own share of analysis. They were as anxious to understand the Soviets as the Soviets were to understand them. They realized how much hung on achieving a working relationship with these new and mysterious partners. They, no less than the Soviets, wanted the partnership to be fruitful; they wanted to avoid friction and quarrels if they could.

* * *

No Arab leader had longer or closer relations with the Soviets than Nasser. He had seen them at every level and in all circumstances. He had come to power in the days of Stalin and the cold war; he died in the days of Brezhnev and detente. In between there had been moments of glory and times of tragedy, there had been war and peace, euphoria and near despair. He had had personal contact with Soviet leaders at every level – not simply with the bosses in the Kremlin, but with technocrats like Niporozhny, Skatchkov, Novikov and Ustinov; and with marshals and admirals like Malinovsky, Gretchko, Gorshikov, Patisky, Sokolovsky, Rokossovsky, Yakobov, Rodenko and Zakharov.

Because of Nasser's long and diversified experience of dealing with the Russians many Third World leaders came to ask his advice before their first visit to Moscow. As well as Arabs, men like the Sudan's Nimeiry and Algeria's Ben Bella, it was the heads of newly independent black African states, such as Ghana's Nkrumah, Congo's Lumumba and Mali's Modibo Keita who found what Nasser had to say on this subject particularly useful. When later, as so often happened, Nasser saw them facing difficulties in their dealings with the Russians, trying to keep a balance between East and West, or among their own people, or with neighbouring governments – when sometimes he saw this tightrope act fail, or the leader come to grief – he felt that, as he had learnt the hard way, with no one except Tito and Nehru to consult and discuss things with, there ought to be some method whereby the fruits of his experience could be made available to others.

It was in the evening of May 18, 1964 that the idea first came to Nasser of putting his thoughts on how to deal with the Soviets in written form. The previous days had been historic ones – they had seen the completion of the first stage of the High Dam, and the diversion of the waters of the River Nile, an event which had brought to Aswan tens of thousands of rejoicing Egyptians and a distinguished gathering of foreign guests. Among these were President Abdel Salam Aref of Iraq, President Sallal of Yemen, and President Ahmed Ben Bella of Algeria. But without any doubt the star of the occasion was the Prime Minister and First Secretary of the Communist Party of the Soviet Union, Nikita Khruschev, paying his first visit to an Arab country and to the African continent. It was the High Dam ceremonies which had lured the Russian leader to Egypt, and now the occasion was being converted into a festival of Arab–Soviet cooperation. The High Dam was the greatest engineering feat ever to be seen in Africa. After the West had fumbled and failed it was the Soviets who had stepped into the breach, and with their money and their skills had built the 'new pyramid' which was finally to harness the waters of the Nile and, by providing greatly increased irrigation and electricity, to revolutionize the lives of the peasants and industrial workers of Egypt.

After the exertions, in the stifling May heat, of the actual ceremonies in Aswan, Nasser had planned a few days' relaxation. All his visitors were to move to Berenice on the Red Sea, where the official yacht *Hurriyeh* was anchored, and where a programme of boating and fishing had been arranged for them.

Most of the Arab guests were already on board the yacht by the time Khruschev arrived on the morning of May 15, and came forward to greet him. But, when President Aref of Iraq held out his hand, Khruschev scowled and drew back. 'I'm not going to shake hands with people whose hands are stained with the blood of communists!' he shouted. The reason for Khruschev's outburst was that some days before Baghdad radio had announced that several communists had been shot. Aref tried to explain that these people had been executed, not because they were communists, but because they had conspired against the state. But Khruschev was not to be mollified, and soon Aref showed signs of losing his temper too, muttering protests. 'Brother Aref,' said Nasser in Arabic, 'don't say any more now.'

But the atmosphere was spoiled. Nobody felt in the mood for enjoying themselves. Instead they all sat around in chairs on the deck of the yacht, talking around the old familiar subjects – nationalism, communism, socialism, religion and so on. Ben Bella was particularly argumentative, and so of course was Khruschev. Nasser, as host, tried to prevent the discussion from getting out of hand, but did not find this easy.

At one point, for example, he made a valiant effort to get Khruschev to take a more reasonable attitude towards Aref. 'You were used to dealing with Qasim,' he said, 'so naturally you don't find it easy to deal with his successor, whom perhaps you still think of as Qasim's number two. But remember that people used to say Neguib was the top man in Egypt, and I was just his number two. The same with Ferhat Abbas and Ben Bella in Algeria. You get on well enough with Ben Bella and me now. Why not with Aref?'

'Nah, nah,' said Khruschev. 'It's not at all the same thing. I'll tell you a story. At the time of the war between Russia and Japan in 1905 the Russian fleet was commanded by a prince who was hated by everybody. He was incompetent and a brute. But his second-in-command was liked by everybody, an efficient sailor and a good man. Then the news came that the flagship containing the admiral and his second-in-command had been sunk, and everyone in it drowned. There was general rejoicing in the navy at the thought that the prince was dead, but sorrow that his deputy was dead too. Then came a second message, to the effect that after all some of those on the sunken ship had been saved, and included among these was the commander. But his deputy was definitely drowned. And I'll tell you what the sailors said then. They said, "We might have known it. Gold sinks, but shit floats." '

Then, suddenly realizing that the implications of this story were not particularly flattering to some of those he was with, Khruschev tried to excuse himself. 'Of course,' he said, 'none of that applies to present company.'

But the day was not a pleasant one. Host and guests sat around for about six hours, the conversation flowing on but getting nowhere. The fisherman in their boats waited idly for customers who never came. At last it was agreed that we should all go back. This, the next day, we did.

Three days later, when we were back in Cairo and talking over Khruschev's visit, Nasser's thoughts returned to the Aref incident. 'These people don't know how to deal with the Russians,' he said. 'I would like to write a book about it – an instruction manual, of the sort you get for a new car.' I thought this was a very good idea, and said so: 'Why don't we go to work on it?' In fact we did have one meeting in which we discussed the project, but then we decided that it had better wait until Nasser got down to writing his memoirs – it was always his dream that he would occupy himself with these memoirs when he retired.

Nasser was quite clear in his own mind about the form his projected handbook should take. It would have nothing to do with policy. He was not concerned with whether a country should or should not cultivate relations with the Soviet Union, or how close these relations ought to be. That obviously was not for him to say. All he was concerned about was the question of technique, of style.

Nasser thought he would start by defining the stages through which the relationship between a Third World country and the Soviets must be expected to go, and that he would then proceed to list a series of dos and don'ts which should guide the Third World leaders in their behaviour towards their Soviet counterparts.

Looking at the notes of the conversations which I made at the time, I am reminded that it was Nasser's belief that every Third World leader should expect his relations with the Soviets to go through five distinct phases, though these would not necessarily always follow each other in the same order. He listed them as follows:

1   *Mistrust*

First comes a period of mistrust. Any newly emerged Third World leader is initially regarded by the Soviets with grave suspicion. He will either be ignored, or attacked by the Soviet press and radio. Although the declared policy of the Soviet Union is to support national liberation movements wherever they are to be found, in fact the ideas and emotions which inspire the leaders of such movements are treated with scepticism. In Soviet eyes nationalism has to be seen only in the context of the class struggle and the dynamics of history. If the nationalist movement emerges from the army it is all the more suspect, since they believe most armies have shown themselves to be upholders of the status quo, counter-revolutionary rather than revolutionary, and so potentially fascist. Their thinking has been largely influenced by the long history of right-wing coups organized by the armed forces in Latin America, and by the early army coups in Syria, which they regarded, with a good deal of reason, as being the outcome of rivalries between the big British and American oil companies in the area. (So it was that to begin with they persisted in seeing Nasser as simply a pawn in the struggle between the colonial rivalries of Britain and America in the Middle East. Even after Bandung[1] the Soviet radio continued to describe Nasser as a tool of imperialism. Only more recently have Soviet ideas about armies in the Third World begun to change.)[2]

2 Interregnum

However, eventually something happens to convert phase one into phase two. The Soviets discover that the new leader is in fact opposed to the old colonial powers. Perhaps he quarrels with the Americans and tries to associate himself with some of the progressive Third World groupings – Afro-Asian solidarity, for example, the non-aligned grouping, or the Organization for African Unity. Phase two can be described as an interregnum between the period of distrust and the period of total acceptance. During this interregnum the Soviets assess the leader's record to date. Their radios and newspapers neither attack him nor praise him. He is, so to speak, on trial. It is up to him to prove himself. During this period limited dealings of a practical nature, such as trade exchanges, are possible.

---

[1] The first Afro-Asian conference was held in the Indonesian town of Bandung in April 1955.
[2] In 'Nasser's Handbook' my own comments are included in brackets.

3   *Honeymoon*

Then comes the third phase – the breakthrough. This follows some obviously revolutionary action on the part of the new leader. (In Nasser's case the breakthrough came with the nationalization of the Suez Canal and the events leading up to the Suez War.) It will be greeted at first by a short period – say four or five days – of silence, during which the Soviet leadership tries to subject what has happened to scientific analysis. When this silence is broken, the new leader may find himself overwhelmed by a wave of adulation. He is the hero of the hour, a pet, a superman. He will be cultivated and pampered; nothing will be too good for him. Unlimited political and economic backing will be his, and direct channels of communication with the Kremlin will open for him.

In other words, this is the honeymoon period in relations between the two countries, and like all honeymoons it must come to an end. (Others beside Nasser to enjoy their honeymoon period have been Cuba's Castro, Iraq's Qasim, Algeria's Ben Bella, Zaire's Lumumba, Sheikh Mujibur Rahman of Bangladesh, Agostinho Neto of Angola, Siad Barre of Somalia and Mengistu Haile Mariam of Ethiopia.)

But one consequence of phase three is that the new leader comes to be regarded in the West as a communist, or, at best, as a communist stooge. Because of this, and because also he begins to find Soviet patronage heavy-handed, he tries to assert his independence. He makes a point of stressing the ideological differences which separate him from Moscow. He may even attack the communists within his own borders.

4   *Quarrels*

So the petted superman turns out to be human after all. The Soviets retreat into their shell. This is the fourth phase, and it is critical, since in it the next round of the game will be decided. The new leader will either be dropped completely, or be established on a more realistic footing, according to the degree of the Soviets' disappointment and the amount that they have already invested in his country. (In Nasser's own case the honeymoon ended, and phase four began, after his attacks on the Iraqi communists at the end of December 1958 and his subsequent angry exchange of letters with Khruschev.)

5   *Pigeonholing*

So we come to the fifth and final phase, which could be called the phase of normalization or pigeonholing. (To appreciate what goes on in this phase I think that some understanding of Soviet society is essential. The Russia of the Tsars and the Orthodox Church was a rigidly stratified society in which everyone had an identifiable place. Onto this society has been grafted the Communist Party, with the result that today Russia is perhaps the most precisely organized country in the world. It is the steps in the party hierarchy which really count in Russia, for these determine exactly the sort of life a man and his family can expect.

(The base of the Russian pyramid consists, as it always has done, of the general mass of the people, but from them emerges the Communist Party, itself divided into two tiers, full members and candidate members. Elected from the party members is the All Union Congress, from which in turn is drawn the Central Committee. The Praesidium of the Central Committee, since 1966 called the Politburo, is the highest body in the party, the apex of the pyramid being the First Secretary of the Party.

(On a person's position in the pyramid depends his style of living. A minister will automatically receive a three-room flat in Moscow, a a Shaika car and a dacha in the country. But if, in addition to being a minister, he is a member of the Politburo, he will receive a five-room flat, a Zim car (with curtains) and two dachas, one in the country near Moscow and one by the sea.)

This same precision and sense of hierarchy extends to the Soviet treatment of foreign countries. The Russians grade countries, as they grade party members, because it is alien to their nature to do otherwise. Broadly speaking, Third World countries may expect to find themselves in one of three categories, and it is most important for them that they should be placed, during this phase, in the highest category possible, because it is almost impossible to move from one category to another.

The top category – Nasser called it category A– carries with it a sort of most-favoured nation status. Once in it a country receives a great deal of political support and economic aid, but this is no longer automatic or unconditional, as it was during the honeymoon. In the international field, Soviet support can go as far as threatening to intervene on the country's behalf, whereas during the honeymoon phase the Soviets would have been prepared to back it to the brink.

As far as aid goes, category A has many advantages. In it a country will be sold arms at two-thirds cost price, with the bill payable over

20 years at 2.5 per cent interest, with a period of grace before the interest payments begin. All transactions for a country in category A are carried out at the highest level. Even though requests are sent to Moscow through normal diplomatic channels the answer will come back from the top Kremlin leadership. In cultural exchanges, there will be visits from the top ranking stars of the premier Bolshoi company, who in the 1950s were Galina Ulanova and Maya Plisetskaya. (Nasser was in category A from 1962 to 1965, and again after 1968.)

A country in category B likewise receives reasonable aid from the Soviets. It will be sold arms at cost price, still carrying 2.5 per cent interest, but repayable over 12 years instead of 20 and with no period of grace before the first instalment falls due. Requests for aid initiated by the country will normally be dealt with through the machinery of joint committees, and may very probably be slashed by half. Subsequent negotiations may, with luck, get this raised to two-thirds of the amount originally requested, but never more.

The government of a country in Category C will find that it is dealing entirely with the Moscow bureaucrats. Their decisions are irrevocable, so no amount of pleading will make them budge. In cultural relations the best that can be looked for is a third-class ballet from Baku.

It is not unusual for a country, after the first shock of Soviet disappointment, to find itself consigned to category C. It then depends on what the leaders of the country do, whether it ever struggles up again into category B, or even category A. But nobody should have illusions about the difficulty of the task. It involves getting the whole machinery of party, government and Kremlin leadership moving again. A government may plead to be upgraded, but it will plead in vain until events take a hand and force the Soviets to reconsider.

Perhaps a fourth category – category D – should be added. This is a stage of cold formality and scarcely concealed hostility. (After the row with Khruschev in 1959, when there were delays in the supply of arms and other equipment that Egypt was expecting from the Soviet Union, I remember saying 'We seem to be in category D now.' This too was the category Egypt found itself in when the Soviets were excluded from Geneva after the October war of 1973.)

★   ★   ★

Now we come to what would have been the main part of Nasser's instruction manual – dos and don'ts for Third World leaders about to negotiate with the Soviet Union. This was, he always insisted, something not to be lightly undertaken, and careful attention to his advice might have spared them – perhaps might still spare them – much frustration and disappointment.

DOS

1. Ensure that you negotiate with them in a language that both sides understand, since bad translation can cause endless trouble. The Russians will insist on using their own interpreters who never admit the possibility of error. Their interpreters in the main languages, like English and French, are faultless, but those in less familiar languages, like Burmese, Swahili or Arabic, are to be avoided. (The Egyptians started with Arabic/Russian interpreters who had been taught locally in schools of oriental studies and were terrible. Nasser's first quarrel with Khruschev was largely caused by a failure of translation. So stick to English or French.)

2. Go to Moscow provided with a good stock of anecdotes, jokes, proverbs and folk sayings. These can greatly help in smoothing over difficult moments in the negotiating process. It is important to remember the differences between the leaderships in West and East – whereas those with whom you negotiate in the West usually come from privileged classes, the Soviet leaders have all come up through party cadres and most of them have never been outside the Soviet Union. A man like Brezhnev will spend a great deal of time telling you jokes or proverbial stories or reminiscing about the time when he was a political commissar in the army. You must be able to cap jokes and stories with some of your own.

3. Go well briefed on the history of World War II and the fundamental part in it played by the Soviet Union. It is important that you know details – which general served in which command on which front, and so on. You must resign yourself to hearing over and over again about the experiences of your interlocutors in the 'great patriotic war', which is far and away the most memorable period in the lives of the present generation of Soviet leadership.

4. You will need a strong digestion and a strong head to survive all the toasts that are drunk by the Russians, and not just at formal banquets.

If you do not think you will be able to cope, make your position very clear from the start. Tell your hosts at the outset that you don't drink, for reasons of health or religion.

5. The leader of your delegation must be in full control of its other members. During negotiations the whole delegation will be under scrutiny from the Soviet leaders facing them, who will be trying to discover who ranks where in your hierarchy. In particular they will want to find out who is number two. (There was a time when they decided that number two in Egypt was Field-Marshal Abdel Hakim Amer, Minister of War, and they began referring to 'Nasser and Amer'.) So it is important that the whole delegation should speak with a united voice.

6. It is most important that you should get to recognize the different languages talked in the Soviet Union. We tend to look on it as a monolithic government but there is always an interplay of forces going on inside it in which you may find yourself unwittingly caught up. You will hear different things – or things put in different ways – according to whether you talk with the leadership, with the military, or with the technocrats or bureaucrats. What really matters is what you hear from the leadership; if you place too much reliance on what you hear from others you may be heading for disaster. (For example, when the Egyptian Minister of War was leaving Moscow on the eve of the 1967 war, his Soviet opposite number, Marshal Gretchko, who had come to see him off, said: 'Stand up to them! The moment they attack you, or if the Americans make any move, you will find our troops on your side.' Our ambassador in Moscow later asked Gretchko if he really meant what he had said. Gretchko said: 'It was just one for the road.')

What you hear from soldiers or technocrats or bureaucrats may be perfectly valid, but it may equally be the expression of one opinion in a debate about policy which is still going on. It would be a grave mistake to build too much on it. Yet these people can be used at times as legitimate channels of communication. It is not just in offices that business in the Soviet Union is conducted. Particularly at parties and receptions you may hear many significant indications of the way things are moving. You may, for example, have been trying for some time without success to get wheat from the Russians; then someone at a reception says to your ambassador or to a member of a visiting delegation: 'Perhaps this is the moment when your leadership should ask for wheat' – here is probably a hint that should be taken. But where major policy or planning decisions are involved trust only what you are told by the First Secretary of the Party.

7. You must appreciate that there are some elements within the Soviet leadership which have put their bets on you and will accordingly feel that their fate is to some extent bound up with yours. They have a vested interest in your success, and so will speak up for you even inside the Politburo; if you fail, you fail them too. So try to find out who your friends are, and watch how they are treated. If they show signs of slipping it may be that you are slipping too. (For example, many of us who had been to Moscow watched with anxiety the decline and fall of Alexandr Shelepin, with whom we had had many fruitful dealings, from Deputy Prime Minister through a succession of less and less important posts to Secretary of the Association of Professional Trade Unions. A signal of his impending fall was given when some of his proteges like Garimov, the head of Tass, and Vladimir Semichastny, one of the directors of intelligence, began to fall out of favour. We discovered that it is sometimes from the fate of these proteges that you can learn the relative standing of the men at the top.)

8. The Soviet leadership, as has been seen, finds it essential to fix people firmly in categories. On the whole they will refer in quite a friendly way to those they have got to know through negotiations, but they mistrust those who have been educated in America or who have had anything much to do with international institutions. (Thus they mistrust all those who have had anything much to do with the World Bank or the International Monetary Fund; in other words, they have mistrusted virtually all Egypt's Ministers of Finance and Economics. They have a tendency to over-simplify – to label people as friends or enemies. Nasser once tackled them on this: 'I know you think Ali Sabri is your man, and Zakaria Mohieddin is America's man,' he said. 'But it's not true. It so happens that I sent Ali Sabri to deal with you and Zakaria Mohieddin to deal with the Americans. But they are both my men.')

9. If you want something specific in the way of aid from the Soviets, give them plenty of time. They don't like being surprised by last minute demands. Everything has to be planned, and their planning processes are extremely rigid. So if, for example, you ask for a factory to be

set up, this will have to find a place in their next five-year plan, or, if it is to be supplied sooner, somewhere in the Soviet Union will have to go without.

10. Remember that agriculture is the Soviets' Achilles heel. You can ask them for arms, or for factories, but, unless you are in a real crisis, never ask for wheat. They will almost certainly be unable to provide it. This will make them feel apologetic and embarrassed.

11. Remember that the Soviets assess any political problem with their eyes on the United States. America is an obsession with them. The American element affects every decision, even those decisions which apparently have no connection with the United States. (Their evaluation of each American president colours their policy. Thus, they had an understanding of a sort with Nixon; they looked back to Kennedy with a certain nostalgia; but Johnson really scared them. 'The man would start any adventure,' Brezhnev told U Thant. 'The world must beware of him.')

12. Remember that the Soviets think on a different time-scale from yours. Your problems are probably urgent; they see things in terms of historical and revolutionary processes. When, for example, they were talking about the Arab–Israeli problem with the Arabs, they would often bring up the example of the treaty of Brest-Litovsk as an argument for compromise. Lenin, they would point out, was prepared to yield large tracts of the motherland to the aggressor, and even to allow three new states to be carved out of the Soviet Union, but he saw all this as a temporary sacrifice which could be won back in due time.

13. Always remember that the Soviets look on the prospect of another war with horror. They will never fail to remind you that the Soviet Union lost twenty million people in the Great Patriotic War, and will insist that only those who do not know what war means can contemplate with equanimity the thought of a nuclear confrontation.

14. You must realize that for all their pragmatism, the Soviet leadership is made up of Slav peasants, easily moved to laughter and tears. They are fascinated by the attributes of power. In the West, a politician as a rule becomes gradually acquainted with the secrets of government and the realities of power, but in the Soviet Union the gulf

between the Central Committee and the Politburo is wide indeed. When anyone crosses that gulf the shock of what he learns is enough to throw him off his balance. His new responsibilities fill him with awe.

DON'TS

1. The Soviets will not permit any discussion of their errors or short-comings, past or present. Even Stalin is not permissible as a target. Brezhnev has said: 'I can criticize Stalin, but you cannot.' In a way, criticism raises doubts about the legitimacy of the revolution and the whole Soviet experiment.

2. If you must quarrel with the Soviets, see that your quarrel does not last longer than a year, or 18 months at the outside. When differences arise between the Soviet leaders and the leader of a country which has enjoyed category A status, they are, to begin with, anxious to play these differences down as far as possible. They naturally hope that the quarrel will be resolved, and do not want to expose themselves to criticism on the ground that their judgement has been at fault. But if the quarrel persists, and they come to the conclusion that there is nothing to be looked for from the leader with whom they are dealing, they will eventually give the signal that he is to be regarded as an enemy. This signal will be passed down through every level of the Soviet hierarchy, from the Central Committee to the party rank and file, and once this has happened the process of rehabilitation will have been rendered almost impossible.

3. It is absolutely taboo to equate them with the US as a superpower. ('I must warn you again,' Brezhnev said to me, 'not to write about "the two superpowers". How can you equate us with the Americans?') Anyone who does this will be accused of falling victim to Chinese propaganda.

4. On no account try to defend China. China has become an even bigger phobia than America for the Soviets. They will insist that China is a backward country and demand to know what China has done to help you economically, militarily or in any other way.

5. Don't take offence at what may seem to be their interference in your internal affairs. They are free with advice and warnings – that a coup in your country is likely, that such and such of your fellow-countrymen are reactionary and not to be trusted, and so on. (There

was one occasion when Podgorny asked Nasser to sack me from my job as editor of *Al Ahram*, but neither of us held this against him.)

6. Remember that the Soviets are highly sensitive about the publication of any information concerning themselves. They will not tolerate any violation of the secrecy with which they insist on surrounding all their transactions. They are always shocked when reports of negotiations in which they have been taking part come back to them via a third party. (For example, they were furious with the Egyptians when they found that they had disclosed to the Syrian leadership the special discount which Egypt had been allowed on its arms purchases. The publication of news for the sake of news strikes then as pointless and irresponsible. Brezhnev once asked me why I had reported something in *Al Ahram*. I told him 'It's for my readers.' 'They don't need to know all that,' he said. The Soviet point of view is that what appears in *Pravda* is enough. The purpose of the media is to act as propaganda for communism and the revolution. Normally when Brezhnev spoke to me he would address me as 'Gospodin Heikal', but when he wanted to be particularly friendly he would call me 'Gospodin Propaganda.' This would make me tear my hair, but he meant it as a compliment.)

7. Don't underestimate the Soviet leadership's sensitivities about the status of local communist parties. They themselves will not deal directly with local parties but they are upset if these are the object of attack. They will never complain officially about the treatment to which your communists may be subjected, though they may say something at a party, like 'Why are you treating your communists in this way?'

8. Be careful in your choice of gifts. Never offer them jewels. Cultural objects – antiquities – are best. (When Nasser gave Khruschev a vase from the Sakkara excavations, and told him it was 5,000 years old, Khruschev took it to a meeting of the Supreme Soviet and put it on the table in front of him.)

*   *   *

That was an outline of Nasser's manual. It represented his carefully thought out attempt to provide a basis for reaching understanding with one of the two superpowers on whose decisions the fate of the smaller countries of the world must depend. It has, of course, to be remembered that the only time Nasser and I discussed the manual was in 1964, and Nasser lived for six years after that. Had he been able at some later stage to turn his attention to the manual again he might well have wished to make additions or alterations. But, rather than try to guess what these changes would have been, I have thought it best to present the manual as it emerges from the notes which I made after our discussion in 1964.

Whether any similar manual for the guidance of those who have to deal with the Arabs has been produced by the Soviets we do not know. But we know that they did try with almost desperate earnestness to understand the Arabs. They failed. The Arabs failed. Instead of the 'historic compromise' which is sometimes referred to as a solvent between the points of view of nations we saw a 'historic misunderstanding.'

At the time when the hypothetical Politburo meeting referred to earlier in this chapter took place its members may have had before them the report of an incident which must have seemed to them to sum up the depths which this misunderstanding had now plumbed.

One day early in the summer of 1977 President Sadat summoned the ambassador of South Yemen. He explained to him that there was an island off the coast of South Yemen on which he wished to place a contingent of Egyptian forces for the common defence of the Arab world. The ambassador reported this request back to Aden and in due course received a reply from President Salim Robaya Ali, to the effect that it was impossible to give Egypt the facilities asked for because there were already Soviet experts on the island. 'Your reply', said President Sadat, 'has made my mission easier. Tell your President it's not the island itself that interests me. It's the experts. I want to see Soviet experts out.' When this was reported Aden naturally wanted to know why. President Sadat explained. He wanted, he said, to be able to go to Geneva, for the projected Middle East conference, knowing that the Red Sea was free of any Russian presence. He was sure that the Israelis would claim they had to hang on to Sharm el-Sheikh on the grounds that this was an essential counter to the Russian presence at the other end of the Red Sea, round Bab el-Mandeb. 'I want to deprive the Israelis of this argument,' said Sadat.

When the Soviets heard of this exchange they must have seen it not so much as part of the Egyptian government's preparation for an international conference but simply as one more step in a campaign to drive the Soviet Union out of the Arab world lock, stock and barrel. And once out of the Arab world, why should they not be driven from Africa and the Indian Ocean? What, they must have asked themselves, is the purpose of it all? Who engineered it? How did it come about that they were being hounded into an ignominious retreat?

The answers to these questions are more complex than the guidelines Nasser laid down about the Russians or any guidelines the Russians may have drawn up about the Arabs. The whole story of this strange friendship, this uncomprehending alliance, has to be told if we are to see how and why 1955 led to 1977. The story covers only a little over twenty years – no more than a flicker of time in the immense history of the Middle East. Even in the narrower context of Soviet–Arab relations it represents only one chapter in what is bound to be a long book. But the chapter will have a profound effect on those that come after.

2

The First Red Waves

BEFORE 1917 Russia's drive for a warm water outlet in the south took two main directions – through Turkey and the Straits to the Mediterranean, and through Iran to the Indian Ocean. In all this period the Arab world was treated simply as part of the Ottoman Empire. There was, however, one small incident which foreshadowed what was to come, and which is often forgotten. In 1768 the Mamluk ruler, Ali Bey el-Kebir, proclaimed the independence of Egypt. The Porte ordered the navy to Alexandria, but Ali Bey had some contact with the Russians and they sent him a supply of arms and ammunition as well as provisions. This was Egypt's first arms deal with Russia.

After 1917 Russia continued to be interested in the Middle East, but now the approach was two-pronged; to the same territorial calculations which had dictated policy under the Tsars was added the concern of Russia as the homeland of world revolution. Sometimes over the past sixty years the interests of state and revolution have coincided, but sometimes also they have been in conflict.

From the point of view of Russia as a state the first considerations must be that of geography – of proximity. Whenever Brezhnev or any of the other Soviet leaders talks about the 'legitimate interests' of the Soviet Union in the Middle East he always begins by mentioning the word 'proximity'. Second, there are the natural resources of the area, principally of course oil, and the sea routes (though the Soviets do not openly talk much about the latter). Third, there has been the presence of colonial – or what Soviet leaders would call neo-colonial – forces in the area. Fourth, there is the consciousness of Russia's own Islamic minorities and their links with other Moslems. The Russians know that when the Americans were toying with the idea of an Islamic Pact one of the considerations they had in mind was the influence that such a pact might be expected to exert on Moslems in the Soviet Union.

Revolutionary Russia naturally took notice of what was going on south of its borders. In 1918 the Union for the Liberation of the Orient was formed. By 1919, with the ending of the war in Europe and the

Middle East, Egypt and India were in ferment, and their struggle for independence attracted the attention of Lenin. The Baku Congress of the Peoples of the East met in September 1920, under the presidency of Grigori Zinoviev, and was attended by, among other, 235 Turks, 192 'Persians and Parsees', 157 Armenians, eight Kurds, and three Arabs. Zinoviev called for 'a holy war against English imperialism', and delegates debated how the revolutionary situation in Egypt could be transformed into a general trend, so that the peoples in Africa and Asia under colonial rule could fulfil the role Lenin and Trotsky had laid down for them – to become, with Soviet Russia and the proletariat of the industrialized world, one of the three pillars of world revolution.

This friendly attention from one of the great powers was naturally very welcome, particularly since the Arabs had been favourably impressed by the Bolsheviks' action in releasing to the world the text of the Sykes–Picot Treaty, which they had found in the imperial archives and which gave the first public indication of how Britain and France were planning to divide up the Arab world between themselves. The active support which revolutionary Russia gave to Atatürk was also seen by most Arabs as very much to its credit, for, though he shocked conservatives when he abolished the Caliphate, the masses found Atatürk a nationalist liberator after their own heart.

There is a legend among communist parties in the Arab world that Lenin sent a telegram to Saad Zaghlul, the leader of the Wafd Party which spearheaded the agitation for independence, expressing support for the Egyptian revolution and offering to aid the Egyptian people in their struggle in every way, including the supply of arms. After the Egyptian Communist Party quarrelled with Zaghlul in 1924 its members claimed in their leaflets to have seen this telegram, which had, they said, been sent from Moscow and confiscated by the British censors. But there has never been any proof that such a telegram existed. What is certain is that in March 1919 the First Congress of the Comintern referred to the 'open risings and revolutionary unrest in all colonies', and ended with a call to 'the colonial slaves of Africa and Asia' promising them that 'the hour of the proletarian dictatorship in Europe will strike for you as the hour of your deliverance'. Lenin did make a statement about the necessity for India and Egypt to achieve their independence, and Mohammed Farid, successor to Mustafa Kamil as leader of the Egyptian Nationalist Party, who was then in exile in Switzerland, sent him a telegram of thanks.

When Lenin contemplated the Middle East he was, as Mikoyan was to explain to Ben Bella many years later, much affected by what he had read about Islam while he was in London. On numerous occasions he expressed the opinion that Islam was capable of being a progressive religion: it had once created a social revolution and still influenced the daily lives of its adherents. He looked on Islam and Buddhism as religions of the oppressed, and Christianity as the religion of the oppressor.

Lenin also showed a much more practical understanding of the needs and potentialities of oriental countries. Two remarks of his at the Second Congress of the Comintern illustrate his common-sense approach. First, he rejected the thesis of those who argued that, because underdeveloped countries had no proletariat the best thing for them would be to remain under imperialist domination, which would speed up their industrialization and hasten the day when they possessed a deprived and disaffected proletariat. Lenin argued that backward countries might, if supported by the 'victorious revolutionary proletariat' elsewhere, be able to 'make the transition to the Soviet order, and thence through defined stages to communism, avoiding the capitalist stage of development'. Secondly, he expressed the opinion that revolutions in the East would almost certainly exhibit special characteristics of their own, and it was up to revolutionaries in the West to be on the lookout for these and to recognize them when they appeared.

* * *

In 1919 a distant observer of the Egyptian scene, even one so acute as Lenin, might be excused for thinking that the Egyptian people were poised to follow the revolutionary path marked out by the Russian people, but anyone closer to the scene would have been bound to make a different assessment. To explain why this should be so it is necessary to take a quick look at the social and intellectual forces that had been at work in Egypt and the Arab world.

In the first half of the nineteenth century almost all the Arabs stagnated under the Ottoman rule; only in Egypt and Lebanon were there any stirrings. Some members of the large Christian community in Lebanon, reacting against Ottoman domination, began to cherish the dream of a secular state which would give them a measure of equality. A few of the more enterprising spirits migrated to the freer atmosphere of Egypt, where they took a prominent part in the intellectual life of the country, virtually creating the Egyptian press.

The opening of Egypt to the ideas and inventions of western Europe is usually, and with much justice, attributed to Napoleon and the savants he brought with him when his army invaded the country in 1798. But shortly before Napoleon's arrival there had occurred the incident which many Egyptians regard as their Magna Carta, when the ulamas and merchants of Cairo compelled the two ruling Mamluks, Murad Bey and Ibrahim Bey, to issue a declaration on human rights, taxation, consultation with the people, etc.

After Napoleon came Mohammed Ali, who was determined to build up an army to secure his independence against his nominal suzerain, the Sultan of Turkey. With this in view he sent, during the 1820s and 1830s, hundreds of young men to France to study a wide range of civil and military subjects, including shipbuilding, arms manufacture, engineering, irrigation, textiles and so on. With them went, as imam to look after their spiritual welfare, Rifaa Tahtawi. On his return to Egypt in 1831 Tahtawi, through his direction of the Cairo School of Languages and his translation of French classics, including works by Voltaire, Rousseau and Montesquieu, introduced a generation of young Egyptians to new and exciting ideas. But the West was to become more directly involved in Egypt. The magnificences and extravagances of Mohammed Ali's grandson, the Khedive Ismail, led to the intervention of European powers, at first financially, but in 1882 militarily, and by Britain alone.

By the end of the nineteenth century the impact of the West on the traditional fabric of Egyptian society had given rise to a wide variety of schools of thought. Four main trends can be identified, their influence being by no means confined to Egypt and Egyptians, but spreading through most of the Arab and Islamic worlds. First there were the conservatives, whose attitude towards new ideas was to say that everything was in fact already there in traditional Islam. Secondly, there were the reformists, like Jamal el-Din el-Afghani (who, in spite of his name was probably born in Persia) and Mohammed Abduh, who believed that Islam must reform itself if its influence was to survive. Thirdly there were those, like Ahmed Lutfi el-Sayyid and Taha Hussein, who thought that a compromise between Islamic tradition and European political and educational ideas was possible. Finally there were the secularists, like Shibly Shumail, a Lebanese, who argued that the old must be swept away before the new rational and scientific society could be built.

It was this group which prepared the ground in which the seeds of Marxist thought were later to be sown. At the end of World War I, which with its legacy of shortages, inflation and conscripted labour had caused considerable unrest, a group calling itself a socialist party came into existence in the port of Alexandria, largely through the efforts of a Jewish jeweller, Joseph Rosenthal. The aims and allegiance of the party were at first far from clear, but Rosenthal was in touch with an English Jew, Victor Stein, who was serving in the army of occupation and was a devout communist. Stein helped to push the party in the direction of the Third International, and 1921 saw the creation in Alexandria of an Egyptian Communist Party, with a central committee composed of Rosenthal, Husni el-Orabi, a lonely intellectual, and Anton Maroun, a lawyer, resident in Egypt but of Lebanese origin. A year later Orabi submitted the party's application for membership of the Comintern, and this was granted. It was at about the same time (1921) that the first communist cell was formed in Beirut under the leadership of two Armenians, Artin Madoyan and Hikazan Boyaegian, and given the code name of Spartacus.

One of the great weaknesses of these early stages of the communist movement everywhere in the Arab world was the prominent role played in it by foreigners and members of the minorities, especially Jews. In Egypt this was to a large extent explained by the capitulations which, until their abolition in 1937, gave anyone with a foreign passport (and many Egyptian Jews had these) special privileges. Thus, their houses were immune from search by the police except with the permission of their consul, and they could only be tried in the special mixed courts on which foreign judges sat.

These foreign communists tended to stick together, with the result that there were to be found in Egypt separate cells of Greek communists, Armenian communists, Italian communists and so on. Each cell looked abroad to fellow communists of its own nationality and tended to import from them advice and literature. Naturally enough, this encouraged the fragmentation of the communist movement.

Another weakness, shared by both socialist and communist parties, was that they had no audience. There was practically no industrial proletariat, and the intelligentsia were, on the whole, loyal to the wealthier classes from which they were drawn. The most these activists

could do was produce a few clandestine newspapers or try to achieve
some limited contact with the workers. Newspapers have always been
of great importance in the Arab world, where the written word has,
by tradition, become an almost sacred symbol, Arabic being the original language of the Holy Koran. Newspapers acted as a legal facade for
an illegal political organization, or as a substitute for such an organization, or as a recruiting agent, or as a main channnel for the organization's activities. Both the Egyptian and the British authorities were
well aware of the activities of the socialists and communists and refused
to give them licences. They tried to get round this ban by buying out
people who had a licence to print a paper, but the authorities shut each
paper down as it came out. For example, an item in *Al Ahram* of July 7,
1922 reports that the Egyptian Socialist Party has applied for licence to
produce a paper and that the request has been refused by the ministry
of the Interior. Later the party acquired the licence of an obscure weekly
magazine and produced it with a hammer and sickle on the masthead
and an article about Lenin inside. The magazine was promptly closed
down. When both socialist and communist parties were without
newspaper outlets they turned to printing leaflets in the form of open
letters – to the workers of Egypt, to Zaghlul, to intellectuals and so on
– which they sold for one piastre, then worth little more than one penny.

To begin with the Egyptian Communist Party gave broad support to
Zaghlul and the nationalist movement. Stalin wrote in 1924: 'The
struggle of the Egyptian merchants and bourgeois intelligentsia for the
independence of Egypt is an objectively *revolutionary* struggle in spite
of the bourgeois origin and bourgeois status of the leaders of the
Egyptian national movement, in spite of the fact that they are against
socialism.' However, in the same year Zaghlul, who was by then Prime
Minister, cracked down on the Egyptian Communist Party following
a workers' strike in Alexandria. He may have been influenced in this by
the Palace or the British, but his own convictions were strongly anti-
communist. The party was dissolved, its entire Central Committee
was brought to court, and, in October 1924, sentenced to terms of
imprisonment.

A policy of suppression was continued by the Ahmed Ziwar government, formed after the assassination of the Sirdar (the British general
commanding the Egyptian army) and the resignation of Zaghlul in
November 1924, following a British ultimatum. The new government even tried to prevent all Soviet ships from entering Egyptian

ports, ideas being considered as contagious as disease. When a Soviet ship, the *Shishrin*, arrived in Alexandria in June 1925, guards were placed on board and neither cargo nor passengers were allowed to be landed. (The authorities later relented in respect of the cargo, but not for the passengers.) No communist books were allowed to be sold in Egypt, and *L'Humanité*, which had been coming in since 1919, was banned. So the Communist Party was forced underground. The day of the sentencing of the Central Committee saw the appointment of a new Central Committee, with a Lebanese as First Secretary.

Although Zaghlul was the man who had crushed them, the Egyptian communists felt they had no choice but to back him when he moved into opposition again. They tried to convince the Wafd leadership of the need to create a new political party aimed specifically at the working classes; they argued in the leaflets which they printed around this time that the 1919 Egyptian revolution had been made possible by the participation in it of the workers and peasants but that control of it had been stolen by the bourgeoisie. The communists tried, too, with limited success, to infiltrate Wafdist newspapers. Meanwhile a debate went on inside the miniscule party on two main topics: is the bourgeoisie really capable of confronting colonialism; and is it better for the Party to try to work legally or underground?

While this debate was going on a Syrian–Lebanese Communist Party was formed in Beirut, headed by Yusef Yazbak and Fuad Shamali, who had been influenced by what they saw of the French tobacco workers in Bakfaya, among whom were some party members who spread the doctrine. The formation of the party was attended by a representative of the Comintern, Joseph Berger, and a sub-committee was set up in Damascus headed by a man called Shatila. A year later, on May 1, 1925, a ceremony took place in the Cinema Crystal in Beirut at which the creation of the party was formally anounced as well as the intention to start a newspaper in French to be called *L'Humanité*. There was a call for unity and the two originators of the Spartacus cell, Madoyan and Boyaegian, were included in the new Central Committee of the party, together with Yazbak and Shamali. Significantly there was also a delegate from Palestine on the Central Committee, intended to demonstrate that, in spite of the post-war carve-up by the imperialist powers, Palestine was still regarded as an integral part of Syria. This was a man called Jacob Tepper, belonging to a cell composed entirely of Jewish immigrants from Russia. He was given the code name Abu Zaim.

The Iraqi Communist Party was also formed in 1925, headed by four Jews – Yusef Salman, Sadiq Yehuda, Sassoon Dallal and Yacoub Cojman. There was a communist party in Algeria, but it was entirely French. In fact, when a recommendation came from the Comintern that an approach should be made to the Moslem masses, the answer of the party leaders was that the idea was quite unacceptable since the Moslem masses had no understanding of the situation. The Algerian Communist Party, they said, did not wish to accept the responsibility before history of stirring up the Moslem population. The first agitation among the Algerian Arabs was to come from another direction, when some communists infiltrated the Red Star of North Africa movement which had been created by Messali Haj in Paris.

All these parties were in contact with foreign elements. In Egypt one such was a strange character called Constantine Vance, a Swiss, who introduced himself as a representative of what he called the 'International Press'. He was extremely active and probably an agent of the Comintern. Another agent, who operated for some years at this period, was a man called Bahil Cosi, who used the code name Avigdor and reported to the Middle East department of the Comintern.

Most of the leaders from the Syrian–Lebanese and Iraqi Communist Parties were sent to Comintern cadre schools in the Soviet Union, one of the most promising of these being a young man called Khaled Bakdash, of whom much was to be heard later. In the early 1920s a few Egyptians attended an institution in Moscow called the University of Toilers of the East, a modest forerunner of the present Lumumba University.

In 1931 documents published in Moscow by the Comintern revealed the results of discussions said to have been held with members of the newly created Egyptian Communist Party in which a three-phase strategy for Arab countries had been worked out. The first phase was to be the expulsion of the colonial powers by means of a national liberation movement, leading to independence. Strangely enough the Comintern seemed to have been sufficiently taken in by the 1922 declaration of independence (made unilaterally by the British Government and not, of course, ending British occupation of Egypt) to assert that Egypt had already passed through this phase. In the second phase the task of local communist parties was said to be to convince the people that political sovereignty is not enough, and that genuine independence involves a social revolution as well as a political one; the people must be freed from the yoke of capitalism and landowners as well as from the yoke of the imperialists. The party programme in this phase was to call for the overthrow of the old bureaucracy, and the nationalization of banking, industry and irrigation schemes, and the establishment of a regime of workers and peasants. The third phase would see the seizure of power by the Communist Party and the formation of an alliance with the USSR, with the revolutionary proletariat in other countries, and with those still toiling under the colonialist yoke.

Whoever concocted this programme was living in a dream world. This was in fact a time when the Soviet leaders were having a good deal of difficulty in making up their mind about the correct attitude to adopt towards nationalist movements in the East, such as the Kuomintang, the Indian Congress and the Wafd. By 1923-4 hopes that Eastern as well as European countries were on the eve of revolution had largely evaporated, and Moscow was prepared to support strong nationalist governments like Atatürk's Turkey and Reza Shah's Iran which had been born out of opposition to Western imperialism.

But there was also a tendency to believe that the bourgeoisie could never be anything but a vehicle for a new form of colonialism because it would always be prepared to collaborate with imperialists to get a share of the loot. The communists, both in Moscow and outside, seemed to assume that once a country had got rid of the imperialists there was nothing to stand in the way of the revolution except a flabby bureaucracy and a few unimportant political parties. They underestimated – as for a matter of fact they still do – the strength of the small and middle bourgeoisie and the pull which property and religion exercise on it. They also underestimated the appeal of nationalism for newly independent countries and for countries aspiring to independence.

During the late 1920s the communist parties in the Middle East declined into a state of almost total impotence and insignificance; these were what Egyptian communists refer to as 'the bleak years'. There were quarrels between Stalinists and Trotskyists; their newspapers were almost non-existent – the Egyptian party's paper, *Ruh el-Asr* (*Spirit of Our Times*), committed *hara-kiri* by publishing an article which its editors knew would result in closure rather than admit that it had no funds left with which to carry on. The best indication of how completely at sea the Egyptian Communist Party was at this time is the ludicrous incident when the Labour Movement, with which it was actively collaborating at the time, appointed Prince Abbas Halim leader of the Movement for life. This colourful figure belonged to a rival – and in his view senior – branch of the Mohammed Ali family to that represented by King Fuad and King Farouk. He had been a dashing and courageous officer in the German army in World War I, and used to attend metings of the Federation of Workers, a monocle in his eye, a riding-whip in his hand and accompanied by an enormous German sheepdog.

Apart from its continuing concern with its nearest neighbours, Turkey and Iran, the only other areas where Moscow showed any real initiative during this period were, oddly enough, Saudi Arabia and Yemen. The Soviets offered aid to Ibn Saud, the creator of the Kingdom of Saudi Arabia, after his conquest of the Hejaz and sent him wheat. His son, later King Feisal, visited the Soviet Union in 1931 and negotiated some agreements with the Soviet government. Imam Yehya of Yemen also sent a mission to Moscow, though little is known about what, if anything, it achieved.

★   ★   ★

The dramatic change in Soviet policy during the thirties caused by the rise of Hitler to power, Italy's invasion of Abyssinia, the Spanish Civil War and the threat of another world war, affected Soviet attitudes towards countries of the East as well as towards Europe. In Europe communist policy, directed by the Comintern, advocated collective security and the formation of Popular Front governments embracing all 'progressive forces' – liberals and social democrats as well as, of course, communists. In Asia too there was a call for a closing of the ranks to meet the threat of fascism and war, and as a result communists found themselves summoned to make another somersault. Whereas at the Sixth Congress of the Comintern in 1928 A. Vassiliev had described the Wafd as the 'deadly enemy' of the Egyptian workers and peasants, these workers and peasants were now called on to treat it as an ally.

Those who had to execute the new party line in Egypt were almost entirely foreign nationals or of foreign origin. Thus there was a Cypriot poet, Theodosis Perides, and his wife who were active in Alexandria, and a girl called Anna Caenco who taught history at a Jewish school in the same city and who started a special course in

Marxism. Then there was a Swiss called Jacob Descombes, and a group called 'Bread and Freedom' led by Marcel Israel. Descombes' father was a Swiss contractor living in Egypt who sent his son to Germany to complete his studies, where he came into contact with German communists. On his return to Egypt young Descombes was sent to work for his father's firm in Aswan. The miserable conditions which he found there affected him deeply, but he had no means of communicating with the oppressed workers. When he came back to Cairo he joined, rather surprisingly, a cell composed of Greek communists.

Marcel Israel was the first Egyptian communist to contact communists in other Arab countries. Just before World War II started he went to Lebanon, where he met Farajallah Helou and Nikola Shawi, two leading members of the Lebanese Communist Party at the time. With Shawi he met a member of the French party and he was also introduced to Khaled Bakdash and an Armenian communist. All combined to urge Marcel Israel to intensify party activity among the Egyptian workers and intellectuals.

There was also a Trotskyist group in Cairo, almost entirely composed of Copts. In 1938 Henri Curiel, member of a rich Jewish banking family (to be assassinated in Paris in 1978 by French right-wing extremists), opened a library of Marxist literature in Mustafa Kamil Square in Cairo, which in the 1940s became virtually the headquarters of the communist movement.

The leading part played by Jews in the communist movement was embarrassing both to non-communist Jews and to non-Jewish communists. It gave colour to the accusation that communism was an imported alien doctrine. Moreover, the shadow of Zionist colonialism in Palestine was causing anger and dismay in the Arab world. Jewish communists tried to argue that the Zionist colonists were poor Jews whom the rich assimilated Jews of Europe wanted to get rid of, so that the Arab workers should feel solidarity with them. But wealthy Jews in Egypt were afraid that events in Palestine might stimulate anti-semitism in neighbouring countries, and after the 1939–45 war evidence came out that one of them, Yusuf Kattawi Pasha, had paid large amounts to some members of the Student Federation to prevent them from making any link between the situation in Egypt and what was happening in Palestine.

When the outbreak of war became imminent, there was a frantic scramble by foreign communists to recruit native Egyptians to take their place. Perhaps not surprisingly the first three Egyptian citizens to be thus recruited were all Jews, but they decided it would be tactically better for them to become Moslems, and accordingly effected the change.

In Syria and Lebanon the party managed a good deal better than in Egypt. The Syrian–Lebanese Communist Party reorganized itself with a Central Committee composed of Khaled Bakdash, Ahmed Zaza and Fawzi Zaim for Syria; Rafiq Ridha, Farajallah Helou, Nikola Shawi and Fuad Kazan for Lebanon. The Palestinian delegate, Tepper, vanished from the scene. The French language paper, L'Humanité, was stopped, and an Arabic language paper, Fajr el-Ahmar (Red Dawn), was started in its place.

The Syrian–Lebanese party benefited considerably from the coming to power of the Popular Front government in France in 1936, which was vigorously supported by the French Communist Party, though the communists were not actually represented in it. Communists in Syria and Lebanon were able to operate in the open, and Bakdash even found himself in a strong enough position to confront the authorities in Damascus with the threat of a direct appeal to Paris, should they be difficult. He was, however, sometimes forced by Moscow's new line into positions which were in direct conflict with the general mass of Syrian opinion. Thus he supported the cession by France to Turkey of the Sanjak of Alexandretta (the Hatay) on the ground that France was justified in making sacrifices for the purpose of gaining Turkish support in the coming struggle against fascism. Other Syrians not unnaturally failed to see why this support should be bought at the expense of Syrian territory.

Then came the Nazi–Soviet Pact of August 1939, with another turnabout for the communists, followed by the German invasion of Russia in June 1941, with yet another. So, whereas in August 1939 the communists were praising the Wafd for keeping Egypt out of the war, two years later they were attacking it for doing precisely the same thing. These continual shifts of policy, combined with the nature of the leadership, did nothing to enhance communist prestige.

★   ★   ★

Russia's entry into the war was to have a profound effect on the political scene in the Middle East. The British occupation authorities relaxed their vigilance over left-wing groups in Egypt. They even, as Egyptian police reports disclosed, contacted some communist groups and tried to enlist their support in spreading anti-Nazi propaganda. Strong Marxist elements emerged among some of the Allied troops stationed in the area – the mutiny of left-wing troops in the Royal Hellenic army in Cairo early in 1944 had a considerable impact. But the slogan 'the enemy of my enemy (i.e. Britain) is my friend' had an appeal for many petit bourgeois nationalists who were attracted by Nazi propaganda, and again it was the Jews, shocked by Nazi persecution of their co-religionists, who headed all the principal groups in war-time Egyptian communism.

Henri Curiel's Egyptian Movement for National Liberty, with the code name Hadeto, was less doctrinaire, more flexible and more Egyptian than the others. It drew recruits from the working classes rather than from intellectuals, concentrating particularly on Nubians and Sudanese students. It was from among these that the Sudanese Communist Party under Abdel Khalek Mahgoub was later to be formed. Oddly enough, when Mahgoub, together with his fellow students Abdu Dhahab and Shafi'ah Ahmed, returned from Cairo to Khartoum with the intention of starting up a Sudanese Communist Party, they found a small one already in existence. This was the creation of a British army officer serving in the Sudan who operated under what was presumably the cover name of 'Astor'.

Iskra (*The Spark*), called after Lenin's newspaper of the same name, under Hillel Schwarz was aimed in the first place at the Jewish community and then at Egyptian intellectuals and students. Schwarz, when asked why he did not pay more attention to the workers, countered with his idea of a 'three-stage' revolution – that Marxism should first be introduced to those who could best digest its theory (i.e. the foreign intellectuals), that these would then transmit it to Egyptian intellectuals, who would in turn transmit it to the Egyptian workers.

Jacob Descombes' New Dawn Group (this was also the name of their review, *Fajr el-Jedid*) declared that the communist party must not dissociate itself from the main nationalist party, the Wafd – which, as has been seen, had been the Moscow line off and on since the early 1920s.

But in fact very little was known to the authorities about the communist movement in Egypt, as far as can be seen from a telegram from the British ambassador, Lord Killearn, to the Foreign Office, in April 1945, in which he referred to fears expressed by King Farouk at the spread of communism, which had been reported by Amr Pasha, the Egyptian ambassador in London. 'The Oriental Secretary to the embassy,' Killearn stated, 'has discussed this problem with the Director-General of Public Security, who was astonished, but who assured us that he had no definite information about communist activities.' In this telegram Killearn recommended the appointment of a Labour Attaché at the embassy 'to contact the working class and always be in contact with labour affairs'. If the British embassy thought that such communist activities as there were in Egypt were based on the labour movement, it was sadly mistaken.

In the Middle East as elsewhere the greatest stimulus for communism came from the victories of Soviet arms, but parties operating in the open, like those in Syria and Lebanon, were better able to capitalize on these victories than were the ones which were still underground, such as those in Egypt and Iraq. In Syria and Lebanon where the joint party was now divided into two, communist candidates stood at the 1946 elections, the first to be held after independence, some doing remarkably well. Thus Farajallah Helou got 10,000 votes in Mount Lebanon and Nikola Shawi 7,000 votes in Tripoli, though this was not enough for either of them to be elected. But in Damascus Khaled Bakdash, with 11,000 votes, became the first communist deputy in the Chamber. By contrast the same year in Egypt saw a mass arrest of communists on the order of the Prime Minister, Ismail Sidqi, and in Iraq the attempts of the illegal Communist Party to establish itself in the oil centre of Kirkuk and the port of Basra met with little success.

The charge brought against the Egyptian communists by Sidqi was that they were in collusion with Zionism – a charge made plausible by the equivocal attitude to Zionism which some Jews had adopted. The dilemma in which Egyptian Jews found themselves in the immediate post-war world was particularly acute among left-wing sympathisers.

One of the most important Zionist centres in Egypt between the wars had been the Maccabee club in Zaher, in the Abbasiyah quarter of Cairo. One of the club's officials, Yusuf Hazan, trained young members not only in sport (the Maccabee movement's official function) but also as recruits for Hashomer Hatzair ('The Young Watchman'), a Marxist group favouring a bi-national state in Palestine. But some Egyptian communists felt that even left-wing Zionism could do them nothing but harm, so by 1947 the 'League for Combatting Zionism' had been formed. This body even went so far as to issue a 'Proclamation to Jewish Mothers' which warned them that Zionist propaganda was aiming to take their children to Palestine where they would find themselves surrounded by the enmity of the mass of the population and living under a regime of tyranny and racism. The proclamation ended: 'O Jew, O Jewess, the Zionists want to isolate the Jews from the toiling masses of the Egyptian people. Zionism is the enemy of the Jews! Down with Zionism! Long live the brotherhood of Arabs and Jews!'

In fact by far the greatest mistake made by Arab communists was their failure to understand what was happening in Palestine. This was not just because of the long involvement of Jews in Arab communist parties and their ambivalent feelings towards Zionism; most of the blame must rest with the Soviet Union, which made a totally erroneous analysis of the situation. Stalin seems to have believed that the creation of a Jewish state might help to solve the Jewish problem in Russia and might also inject into the backward area of the Middle East a new progressive element. This thinking was probably influenced by a superficial knowledge of the kibbutz movement, by the number of Zionist leaders who came from Russia, and by the prominent positions held by Jews in the new communist regimes then ɛstablishing themselves in eastern Europe. Moscow saw everything in terms of the struggle between communism and western imperialism. Jewish groups were in arms against British imperialism in Palestine, and it was easy to argue that, when imperialism was swept away, Jewish and Arab proletariats would march forward shoulder to shoulder towards the new red dawn.

As so often before and since, theorizing in Moscow bore no relation to the realities of the situation. When, only a matter of hours after the announcement on May 15, 1948 that Israel had been born, Russia became the second country to recognize the new state, the Egyptian communists obediently issued a statement that the war which was then erupting between Israel and the Arab armies was one imposed by British imperialism on behalf of the Arab bourgeoisie with the aim of suppressing the growing proletarian forces in Palestine (by which presumably the kibbutzim were meant). The communist faithful were also obliged to devote a lot of their propaganda to what was happening in places like Greece and Azerbaijan, all much more remote than the war in Palestine, and to refer to nationalist leaders in Asia like Gandhi,

Nehru and Sukarno who, after all, did seem to be freeing their countries of foreign occupation, as 'accepters of fake independence'. It is not to be wondered at if communists in the Arab world were regarded as no more than the rather inept agents of a foreign power and treated accordingly.

All the same, in spite of its apparently total failure, by 1948 the communist movement had achieved something in the Arab world. It had helped to raise the level of political debate and propaganda, and had benefited the nationalist movement by injecting some social ideas into it. But the communists themselves remained for most of the time a small coterie of squabbling and secretive theoreticians.

★   ★   ★

In the post-war period, Soviet involvement with the Arab world moved onto an official governmental level. When, as a result of Hitler's invasion of Russia in 1941, the Soviets joined the 'free world' alliance, Britain put pressure on the Arab governments to establish diplomatic relations – a prospect which clearly alarmed most of them, particularly the more right-wing and religious regimes, which talked ominously of the contagious dangers of atheism and socialism. However, Egypt opened up relations at legation level in 1943, to be followed a year later by Iraq, Lebanon and Syria. In Egypt the appointment of diplomats was a royal prerogative, and King Farouk chose as Egypt's first minister to Moscow Kamal Abdel Rahim, who was married to a daughter of Mohammed Mahmoud Pasha, a former Prime Minister belonging to one of the leading feudal families. When Rahim had an audience with Farouk before leaving he was told that diplomatic relations with the Soviet Union had only been opened up because of British insistence, and his task would not be to stimulate good relations between the two countries but to block them. On their side, the Russians sent to Cairo as chargé d'affaires a Moslem and an Arabist, Abdel Rahman Sultanov. The first thing Sultanov did after his arrival was to pay a call on the Sheikh of Al-Azhar. Some time afterwards he was invited to address the Society of Moslem Youth. He was asked a number of questions about communism and life in the Soviet Union, to which he replied: 'To all the questions that I have been asked I will give but one answer – read the Koran!'

The Russians showed themselves in their early days very inexperienced in their dealings with the press. They started a regular Tass bulletin in Arabic in 1946, which later, when I was editing *Al Ahram*, they offered to me. I told them I doubted whether I should find it of much value, to which their answer was that it was going to be improved. I asked how much the service would cost, and they said it would be provided free. I told them in this case it would be impossible for me to accept it, because it would be bound to be regarded as propaganda rather than a genuine news service. 'Very well,' they said, 'you suggest a suitable amount for us to charge you.' So in the end a price was fixed, about a fifth of what we were paying agencies like AP or UP.

The Russians proved extremely generous hosts to Arab diplomats. Though this was still the immediate aftermath of war and a time of terrible shortages, each diplomat received seven kilos of proteins, including smoked salmon and caviar, a month. For most Arab diplomats this was their first introduction to these delicacies, and as there were no refrigerators they sometimes had to be consumed in a hurry, with unfortunate consequences. Whenever scarce vegetables were available the Arab diplomats got more than their fair share. Yet they found their life extremely hard. There were none of the distractions they were used to – parties, restaurants, night clubs. There were theatres and ballet, but not many, apart from the first Egyptian minister, Kamal Abdel Rahim, his counsellor, Mohammed el-Kouni, and their wives, took an interest in these. There was nothing to buy, no mixing with the Russians or visiting their homes, no adventures for the young. Worse than anything, there was always the danger that when the diplomat returned home it would be assumed that he must have been contaminated by his sojourn in the communist world and would find himself placed under police surveillance. To forestall this fate the reports sent back from Moscow by Arab diplomats tended to be extravagantly anti-Soviet.

As can be imagined, there was not much business to transact. The counsellor at the Egyptian legation, Mohammed el-Kouni, had some discussions about the problems of Iran, a country in which Egypt naturally took an interest, both because of its Middle East setting and because the Shah was then married to King Farouk's sister. One day in late 1946 el-Kouni, then chargé d'affaires, was asked to call on the head of the Middle East department at the Ministry of Foreign Affairs, who enquired how negotiations with Britain were going. El-Kouni got the impression that he was being given a hint that the Russians thought Egypt should take its case to the Security Council. This was at a time when the Council was discussing Iran's complaint against the Soviet Union, which had refused to carry out its obligation to withdraw its troops from Azerbaijan. The implication was that, though the Russians might not feel any particular enthusiasm for Egypt's case, they could see some advantage if it helped to distract attention from that of Iran – 'help to keep the presure off us and we'll keep the pressure up on Britain'. The Egyptian chargé d'affaires was rather impressed by this argument, but the Minister of Foreign Affairs, Ahmed Lutfi el-Sayed, sent a telegram instructing him not to discuss the subject again and not to send any more telegrams about it. All the same, the Soviets continued to drop hints along the same lines, and the next Egyptian minister to Moscow, Kamel Bendari Pasha (known as 'the red Pasha') took up the idea enthusiastically. When eventually, in the summer of 1947, Egypt did take its case against Britain to the Security Council the Soviets gave it backing of a sort. But the general impression was that they were more anti-British than pro-Egyptian.

★   ★   ★

There was indeed no real community of interest between Egypt and the Soviet Union. When in May 1948 Britain withdrew from Palestine and the first Arab–Israeli war broke out, one of the reasons Nokrashy Pasha, the Prime Minister, gave in parliament when asking for a declaration of war was that Israel was the vanguard of world communism. He cited the kibbutz movement to press his point. Both houses of parliament, in fact, voted for war against Israel 'in defence of Arab rights and against Communist atheism and nihilism'. Some support for this point of view was to be found in the speed with which the Soviet Union hastened to recognize the new state of Israel and the way in which the Israeli forces were enabled to regroup with Czechoslovak arms during the first truce in the fighting. It seems probable that the Soviet Union believed at this time that Israel could become a progressive, and therefore sympathetic, element in an area of generally reactionary and unsympathetic governments. If this was so, it proved to be a colossal miscalculation.

The Soviets viewed with a good deal of suspicion the various minority governments put together in Egypt by the Palace after the disaster of the Palestinian war. This was not surprising. Ibrahim Abdel Hadi Pasha, who became Prime Minister after the assassination of Nokrashy Pasha on December 29, 1948, not only did his best to crush the Moslem Brotherhood, but imprisoned a number of radicals and communists as well. The Wafd, which came back into power under Nahas Pasha in January 1950, seemed an improvement from Russia's point of view when it refused to have anything to do with the Middle East Defence Organization, sponsored by the British, American, French and Turkish governments, and when it refused to participate in the Korean war.

But the situation was rapidly moving beyond the control of the traditional political forces. The King, surrounded by a group of upstart courtiers, had forfeited all respect. Corruption had permeated all levels of public life. There were attempts by groups of peasants to take over some of the enormous private estates, such as those belonging to Prince Mohammed Ali. Bloody clashes between British troops and Egyptian police in the Canal zone led to the burning of Cairo on January 26, 1952. Egypt was clearly on the verge of revolution of some sort, and there were those in authority who were prepared to see the hand of communism at work everywhere. (One high official in the Royal Palace submitted a report to the King which accused the Polish embassy of bringing in lorry-loads of dynamite and other explosives for use by the mob in the burning of Cairo.)

Then, on July 23, the revolution did in fact take place, but it was not one that the Soviets had expected or relished. To them it seemed just another military coup d'état like that of Colonel Husni Zaim in Damascus on March 30, 1949, or the one by Colonel Sami Hinnawi four and a half months later which ousted Zaim – or like any of the Latin American coups d'état on which the two Syrian ones seemed to have been modelled. They thought it might be something to do with Anglo-American rivalries in the Middle East, or even be a cunning American plot to abort a genuine popular revolution.

Soviet suspicions increased when the Free Officers moved swiftly to impose order. On August 13 at Kafr el-Dawar, near Alexandria, the workers, probably prompted by communists, seized control of a textile factory. The two ringleaders were tried by a military court, sentenced and hanged. The only reference to Egypt to be found in the great Soviet Encyclopaedia for 1952 is that 'a regime of reactionary officers linked with the USA attempted savage repression of the workers'. The Polish news agency spoke of the formation of 'a fascist military dictatorship to stifle the growing anti-imperialist movement in Egypt'. To the Soviets andtheir friends the July revolution was clearly the work of the bourgeoisie.

*   *   *

The Nineteenth Congress of the Communist Party of the Soviet Union, held from October 5 to 14, 1952, laid down a new policy directing communists to join democratic parties in popular fronts – success lay in 'raising the banner of democratic freedoms'. Replying to the greetings of foreign delegates, who had expressed their parties' faith in the Soviet Union, Stalin said: 'Before, the bourgeoisie was considered the head of the nation; it upheld the rights and the independence of the nation, placing them above everything else. Now not a trace of the national principle remains. Now the bourgeoisie sells the rights and the independence of the nation for dollars. The banners of national independence and national sovereignty have been thrown overboard. There is no doubt that it is you, the representatives of the communist and democratic parties, who will have to take this banner and carry it forward, if you wish to be the true patriots of your countries, if you wish to become the guiding force of the nation. There is nobody else to raise it.'

Some Arab communists attended the congress, though their identities were never revealed. They all spoke of 'fascism and repression' by the Egyptian Free Officers. The congress provided the first post-war opportunity for representatives of the various Arab communist parties to meet each other. They were able to attend many meetings in the building of the Central Committee and were pleased to find that their opinions were listened to. With the prestige of the victorious Soviet Union to back them they looked forward to a new advance towards power.

Stalin's death in 1953 produced no real change. The Russians opened a cultural centre in Cairo and there were some trade agreements, but communist parties everywhere maintained their hostility towards the Egyptian revolution. When the clash came between Nasser and Neguib in February 1954 the Egyptian communists, like the Moslem Brotherhood, took the side of Neguib.

But slowly the Soviet Union and Egypt began to take a more

realistic look at each other. Nasser's hostility to pacts and in particular to the Baghdad Pact of 1955, brought him into conflict with the West. His retort to Dulles did not go unheeded in Moscow: 'The Soviet Union never occupied our country; it has no imperial past in the Middle East. I don't see why I should turn my country into a base to threaten the Soviet Union with nuclear warheads when they have never threatened us. The communists are at most an internal danger to Egypt, but one that can be dealt with by social reform.'

Nasser went to Bandung in April 1955 and the Afro-Asian solidarity movement was born. Moscow had broken off diplomatic relations with Tel Aviv, following the notorious 'doctors 'plot' of January 1953 against Stalin, and not long afterwards Egypt raised its legation in Moscow to an embassy. The way was being cleared for the start of the big Soviet offensive in the Middle East.

3

The Beginning of
the Great Soviet Offensive

THE DEVELOPMENT OF nuclear arms compelled the Soviet Union to look afresh at the world beyond its southern frontiers. In the old days the Russians had been able to sit tight in their own lands, ready to crush any invader rash enough to attack them. But now things were different. They had to concern themselves not only with countries immediately the other side of their borders, such as Turkey and Iran, but also with Syria, Iraq and even East Africa as well. Egypt was now being asked by West – and refusing – to join an alliance directed against the Soviet Union, thus demonstrating its strategic significance in the cold war. It was with some justice that Nasser used to tell the Soviets: 'We offered you our help before you offered us anything. We stood beside you before you stood beside us. We refused to turn Egypt into a base to threaten you before we had had anything to do with you.'

When the rulers of Russia looked at the world from the Kremlin, they were struck by the growing importance of the Middle East. NATO was now firmly anchored in Europe, and the Truman Doctrine had extended it eastwards to take in Greece and Turkey. After 1954 NATO was duplicated in the far East by SEATO. But in between these two western alliances there was a gap. If the West could bridge the gap by means of a Middle East Defence Organization the chain of alliances would be complete, and the Soviet Union would be ringed round by hostile states.

But the Arab world itself was deeply divided. In Iraq the Hashemite family, together with Nuri Said, the country's most enduring politician who had fought with Feisal and Lawrence in the Arab revolt and who, whether in or out of office, continued to direct policy along staunchly pro-British lines, were convinced that the only salvation for the Arabs lay in their joining a western sponsored military pact. They thought this would both provide the most effective means of preventing further Israeli expansion and be the only way of ensuring for the Arabs the arms which they needed. But in Egypt and Syria contrary ideas were gaining ground.

After Bandung, much was heard of the virtues of non-alignment. The Soviets liked this coming from Nasser, but disliked it from Tito. A non-aligned Nasser would mean a diminution of strength for the West in a part of the world which it regarded as essential to its security; a non-aligned Tito meant a loss of strength for the communist bloc. So in Egypt's case non-alignment was patriotic; in the case of Yugoslavia it was treason. The Americans, of course, saw things exactly the other way round, and sometimes when I have been in Moscow and heard Gromyko talking about non-alignment I have felt that if I closed my eyes I could be listening to Dulles. Superpowerdom imposes its own logic; it requires an arsenal and an ideology – long-range missiles and long-range ideas.

★   ★   ★

The background to the so-called Czech arms deal has been repeatedly told, but the stages by which it was actually arranged make a rather strange story. Nasser wanted to make an official visit to India on his way to Bandung, where, in April 1955, the first Afro-Asian conference was to meet. As he did not trust any of the regular airlines (the British and American governments had been making every sort of threat to prevent him from attending the conference) he hired an Air India plane for the whole of the journey to and from Bandung. The plan was to spend two days in Delhi, go on with Nehru to Rangoon, spend a night there, pick up U Nu, and then for all three prime ministers to go together to Bandung. It was not known that Chou En-Lai was already in Rangoon, and that he had decided to accompany U Nu to the airport to meet our plane. So it was with considerable astonishment that Nasser looked out of the window of the plane after it had landed in Rangoon and saw Chou as well as U Nu coming forward to greet him. Nehru performed the introductions, and the Egyptian party all went to the former Governor's mansion which was now used for the reception of official guests, and in which the delegations from Egypt, India and China had each been allotted one floor. Nehru asked Nasser if he would like to have a meeting with Chou straight away. This was arranged, and in the course of their discussion Nasser maintained that Egypt felt itself threatened by attack and that he was having great difficulty in securing the arms he needed for Egypt's defence. 'I don't know whether the Soviet Union would be prepared to sell us arms,' he said. Chou offered to get in touch with the Russians. 'I think they would be prepared to give a positive answer,' he said.

Chou wrote a report on his conversation with Nasser for Mao, who recommended that it should be sent to Moscow through the Soviet ambassador in Peking, who should also be informed of Nasser's request. The report is a shrewd analysis of a man and a situation. A copy of it was sent by the Chinese to Cairo after their quarrel with the Soviet Union had broken out, with the aim of disproving the Soviet accusation that China believed aid should only go to communist countries, and not to the Third World.

The text is as follows:

1. When Nasser talked to me about his ideas I found that there was one idea which absorbs him completely – the idea of Arab nationalism. I gained the impression that he is convinced this idea can generate new forces which will play a vital part in liberation movements in the Middle East.

2. I think Nasser is a firm believer in the policy of non-alignment, and as a long-term strategy, not as a short-term tactic, and that it can bring him material advantages, economic or military, from a number of sources. If his disagreement with the West were no more than tactical it would not have reached its present pitch.

3. Nasser asked me if the Soviet Union would agree to sell him the arms which he was unable to get from the United States and which he badly needs if he is to break out from the monopoly over arms supplies which dominates his part of the world, and if he is to be able to meet the armed raids over Egypt's frontier to which he is subjected. My reply to him on this point was that I thought the Soviet Union would examine with a favourable eye the possibility of meeting his requirements, but that I could not give a definite answer until we had sounded out the Soviet leadership through the proper channels.

4. From my talk with Nasser I concluded that we must expect a major collision in the Middle East between what he calls the new forces of Arab nationalism and the colonialists and reactionaries who oppose it.

5. It is impossible for the socialist camp to adopt the role of a spectator in the inevitable battle in the Middle East. As I see it, our position obliges us to assist the nationalist forces in this battle for two reasons – because their victory would be in the interest of the socialist camp and because it would thwart all attempts of the western imperialists to complete the encirclement of the eastern camp. My conclusion is that the logic of history points to the nationalist movement as the coming force in the Middle East, and that we should make our approach to it as friendly as we can. There is a great difference between approaching it early in the day, when we can help it to achieve its objectives, and adopting a policy of wait and see, thus leaving its leaders to fight their battles alone and only approaching them after their victory has been won. The advantages likely to accrue to the socialist camp from an immediate approach should not be underestimated.

There was no immediate reaction from Moscow to Nasser's request. But after six weeks Daniel Solod, the Soviet ambassador in Cairo, came up to Nasser at a reception being held in Sudan House (this was in the days before the Sudan had established an embassy) in honour of Ismail el-Azhari, the Sudanese Prime Minister. 'Mr Prime Minister,' he said, 'I have instructions to transmit to you an answer to the question which you put to our friends.' Nasser understood, and made an appointment for the next day.

It was agreed at their meeting that a committee should be formed consisting of General Hafez Ismail, Chief of Staff of the Egyptian Army, Ali Sabri, director of the President's office, and Colonel V. Nimechenko, the Soviet military attaché. The strictest secrecy was to be observed, so, after an initial meeting at army headquarters, it was decided that somewhere less conspicuous would be preferable, and subsequent meetings took place at a house in Maadi, a Cairo suburb, belonging to some of Ali Sabri's relatives. When negotiations had reached an advanced stage the two delegations, supplemented on the Russian side by two generals, adjourned to Prague. It was at this point that the Russians, anxious not to do anything that might prejudice 'the spirit of Geneva' (the optimistic mood which followed the four-power summit at Geneva in July 1955), suggested that the transaction should be nominally concluded through Czechoslovakia.

Then in July Moscow sent Dmitry Shepilov, editor of *Pravda*, to

Cairo to make his own assessment of Nasser – was he the sort of person who would stand firm in a crisis, or would he back down if pressure from America and Britain became too strong? Nasser and Shepilov got on well together, and Shepilov reported to Moscow that Nasser was unlikely to be scared out of going ahead with the deal and so leave his new friends in the lurch. On his side, Nasser made his position quite clear – he told Shepilov he was not a communist, and referred to the case of some Egyptian communists who were even then being sent for trial. Shepilov told him that the Soviet Union had nothing to do with local communists; what Nasser did with his communists was a purely domestic Egyptian affair.

The whole arms transaction was, in fact, kept so secret that Egypt's new ambassador to the Soviet Union, Mohammed el-Kouni, who was due to take up his appointment, knew nothing at all about it. Solod, assuming that he must have been briefed, made an oblique reference to the arms deal in a conversion with el-Kouni, who, being an intelligent diplomat, gave no indication of not understanding what was referred to. When he got to Moscow el-Kouni, still officially in the dark, met Vladimir Semyonov, the assistant to the Minister of Foreign Affairs, who mentioned the arms deal to him, adding that if he looked at history he would observe that the Soviet Union had helped every country struggling for its independence. If Egypt cooperated with the Soviet Union, Semonov said, the Soviets would do for Nasser what they had done in the past for Atatürk. El-Kouni sent a report of this conversation back to Cairo by bag in his own handwriting, not trusting a cipher telegram. For reasons of security he received no reply to this message.

★　★　★

All the same there was a leak. The Americans somehow got wind of what was being prepared, and a member of their Cairo embassy staff, John Eichelberger, called me up on the telephone at three in the morning of September 27 to tell me that Kermit Roosevelt was due to arrive in Cairo at four the same afternoon, bringing with him a special message for Nasser. That was not in itself surprising. Kermit Roosevelt had a long experience of Middle East affairs, and had been a frequent visitor to Cairo. Only two months after the 1952 revolution he had turned up there as President Truman's special envoy, entrusted with the task of evaluating the aims of the revolution and the personalities of its leaders. A few months later he was again in Cairo to prepare for the visit of the new Secretary of State, John Foster Dulles. Though this was not to be understood in Cairo until a good deal later, Kermit Roosevelt was on both these and subsequent occasions a representative of the CIA.

In these early years after the revolution Nasser believed America to be capable of playing a useful and constructive role in the Middle East, for alone among the major powers she seemed potentially able to influence events in the right direction. Russia was preoccupied with other matters; China too remote; Britain and France still fighting for what was left of their colonial heritage. But it was reasonable to suppose that America might be able to help Egypt in a number of ways. Since the American government seemed to favour regional rather than bilateral pacts, it might be persuaded to put pressure on Britain to withdraw its occupation forces. The Americans might also be willing to come up with economic aid and to supply arms. American pressure on Britain to withdraw was, in fact, to some extent forthcoming, though the looked for economic and military aid was not. But up to this time, in the summer of 1955, Nasser had without doubt been justified in encouraging the maintenance of contacts with the Americans at every level.

Now, however, it was clear that what brought Kermit Roosevelt to Cairo in such a hurry must be foreknowledge of the arms deal. It had to be expected that he would do everything in his power to prevent the deal from going through. By then no shipment of arms had actually reached Alexandria, but Nasser decided that the only course for him to pursue was to make news of the deal public before Kermit Roosevelt arrived, and so present him with a *fait accompli*. 'I'm not going to let the Americans ask me questions,' he said, 'and if they do ask me questions I'm not going to let them make me lie. Whatever happens we are going to be subjected to tremendous pressure, and the best way to counter that is to mobilize Arab public opinion behind us.' Nasser asked his secretary if there were any invitations for him for that day which would provide a forum for what he had to say, but was told there were none. Then he noticed in one of the papers that an exhibition of photographs organized by army public relations was due to be opened in Cairo, and Nasser let it be known that he intended to be present. The organizer of the exhibition was pleasantly surprised by this unexpected honour, but there was no time to make proper preparations. So Nasser made his dramatic pronouncement about the arms deal to an audience of seventy-two people, mostly photographers.

Kermit Roosevelt was still in the air when the announcement of the arms deal was made. I saw him soon after he landed, and he told me that he had brought with him what amounted to an ultimatum. This threatened that, if Egypt persisted in the arms deal, technical aid under Point Four and economic aid would be cut off, diplomatic relations would be severed and there might even be a move to intercept the shipment of Soviet arms on the high seas. I told Roosevelt that if he confronted Nasser with these terms the result would be a catastrophe; the ultimatum would simply explode in Roosevelt's face. I pointed out that his instructions had been drafted before the arms deal was announced, and that now that the deal was a *fait accompli* the sensible course would be for him to ask for fresh instructions. I was helped in my argument by Eric Johnston, Eisenhower's special envoy in the Middle East, who happened to be in Cairo at the time and who urged caution.

I reported what had happened to Nasser, who felt that, while of course there could be no question of letting Roosevelt deliver his ultimatum, it would be wrong to humiliate him by refusing absolutely to receive him. So it was arranged that he should meet Nasser privately for dinner at my house, but that there should be no talk with him about the arms deal until fresh instructions had come from Washington. This was done.

Roosevelt's request for fresh instructions appears to have greatly irritated Dulles, who felt that his emissary was weakening under pressure. Dulles determined to stiffen Roosevelt's resolve by sending to Cairo as reinforcement George Allen, the Assistant Secretary of State for Middle East affairs, bearing with him a written ultimatum along the same lines as the one Kermit Roosevelt had failed to deliver. However, Kermit Roosevelt and the American ambassador in Cairo, Henry Byroade, went to the airport and got into touch with George Allen on his plane, warning him not to give any statement to the press on landing. After they had talked to him they managed to persuade him how dangerous it would be to deliver the ultimatum, and he agreed to suppress it.

Not all those involved managed to control their emotions so effectively. The Egyptian ambassador to Washington, who happened to be in Cairo at the time, stormed into Nasser's office exclaiming: 'Guatemala, Mr President! Guatemala!' (The anti-Arbenz coup, organized by the CIA, had been carried out only three months previously.)

The Russians were taken by surprise by the September 27 announcement. They were unaware of the reasons which had led Nasser to shatter the screen of secrecy behind which they so much preferred to operate. Some of their ships, loaded with arms, were still in the Mediterranean. What was to happen if the Americans tried to stop them? It was not much consolation for them when Nasser said this was a problem which they and the Americans would have to sort out between them. Probably it would have been better if they could have had advance notice of what Nasser was going to say, but the time was too short to allow this.

To complicate matters, a sailor from a Russian ship which had docked in Alexandria disappeared just after Roosevelt and Allen arrived. Every effort was made to find him, and the Egyptian authorities were as surprised as anyone when he turned up in the States shortly afterwards, asking for political asylum. Apparently he had been smuggled by car from Alexandria to Cairo, sent under diplomatic seal to Athens and so to Washington.

It was difficult to persuade the Russians that nothing had been known at the Egyptian end about all this, particularly in view of measures which were being taken against some Egyptian communists at this time and which gave more satisfaction to the Americans than to the Russians. But there was a considerable outcry in some of the more conservative Arab countries, on the grounds that Nasser had bought infidel arms and so had allied himself with atheist communism. One of the methods chosen to combat these charges was to give maximum coverage in the press and radio to the trials of the communists in Egypt. Nasser insisted that he was importing arms, not ideologies. The Russians were quite unable to understand either the extensive coverage given in the Egyptian press to the trials, or the emphasis placed on the non-communist nature of Egyptian ideologies.

★   ★   ★

The arms deal transformed the situation in the Middle East. It was no longer possible for the area to be regarded as a Western preserve, forbidden territory for intruders. The breaking of the West's arms monopoly was a signal to all Arabs that an alternative policy was available, and a very attractive one it looked to many of them. Soon Syria was negotiating with the Soviet Union for arms, and when in December General Templer, Chief of the British General Staff, arrived in Amman in an effort to persuade Jordan to join the Baghdad Pact, he was greeted by riots which were brought under control only after a new government had been formed which promised that in no circumstances would Jordan make pacts with foreigners.

The Americans showed themselves more resilient than the British. Casting around for some way by which to recover from the arms deal disaster, Dulles's thoughts turned to the High Dam. The idea of building a High Dam at Aswan, which would greatly extend the land under irrigation and provide Egypt with much needed electrical power for industry and agriculture, had been one of the first matters to which the new revolutionary regime had turned its attention. Now Dulles calculated that, though the West might have lost the hold over Egypt which came from acting as an arms supplier, it could perhaps win back a grip over the economy and finances of the country by providing the necessary credit for this ambitious and costly project. So he sent a message to Nasser through Eugene Black, the head of the World Bank: 'I want Nasser to understand that the Russians can help him with weapons for death, but we alone can give him and his people life.'

Discussions with the World Bank about financing the dam had in fact been going on since 1953, and when, shortly after the arms deal had been concluded, Shepilov had mentioned to Nasser that Russia had a great deal of experience with big dams, and that this experience would be put at Egypt's disposal if it was needed, Nasser had thanked him but said that he would prefer to do the dam through the West and leave the Soviet Union to help with industrial projects. As a result of this conversation Shepilov stated in public that the Soviet Union would be helping Egypt to build up its industry and was not interested in the High Dam. This statement encouraged Dulles to assume that in no circumstances would the Russians be prepared to become involved with the dam – a fateful misunderstanding, as was soon to be proved.

One of the reasons for American miscalculations was the failure to appreciate that Nasser and the Egyptians saw the Soviet Union as coming to them with clean hands, free of the taint of any imperialist past. Dulles once warned Nasser about what Russia had done in eastern Europe. 'But how can they get at us?' said Nasser. 'They went into eastern Europe because they had common frontiers with the countries there, so they could send their army in. But the Red Army is a long way from Egypt. My problem with communism is an internal one. If the internal front is solid behind the national cause we have nothing to fear.'

★   ★   ★

So the year of Suez opened. By the beginning of 1956 the Russians had good cause to be optimistic over the way things were developing in the Middle East. 'The new period in world history predicted by Lenin,' said Khruschev in his speech to the Twentieth Congress of CPSU in February, 'when the peoples of the East will play an active part in deciding the destinies of the world and become a new and mighty factor in international relations, has arrived. Although these countries do not belong to the socialist world system they can draw on its achievements in building up their independent national economies and in raising the standard of living of their peoples. Today they have no need to go begging for modern equipment from their former oppressors. They can obtain this from the socialist countries, free from any conditions of a political or military nature.'

Following the Congress Egypt began to experience the benefits of grade A treatment. Galina Ulanova paid a week's visit to Cairo; there was a festival of Egyptian films in Moscow; and at an evening of Egyptian culture Yevgeny Yevtushenko read a poem extolling the glories of the land of the Nile. More than 2,000 Egyptians went to Russia over the year as members of one delegation or another, and an agreement on atoms for peace was reached whereby Egypt received its first reactor.

The attitude of the Soviets at this time provided an interesting study. There was no need for them to force the pace because they had been so to speak, sucked into the Middle East by events. It was not they who had started the great offensive but Egypt who had forced it upon them. Egypt needed their arms; Egyptians admired what they had done in the way of planning, of developing backward areas and of mobilizing the people behind a national effort. They, on their side, were fascinated by the way in which Nasser, by turning to the Soviets for aid, had become the idol of the Arab masses everywhere and a legend in his own lifetime.

For the West, and particularly for Britain, the start of 1956 offered much less comfort. On March 1 the young King Hussein of Jordan summarily dismissed Glubb Pasha, the British commander of the Jordanian army. By an unfortunate coincidence news of this dramatic event broke just after the British Foreign Secretary, Selwyn Lloyd, had come away from a dinner in Cairo with Nasser at which some effort had been made to explore the possibility of improving relations between the two countries. Selwyn Lloyd jumped to the conclusion that Glubb's dismissal had been engineered by Nasser and that its timing had been intended as a deliberate snub. The ensuing fury of the British Prime Minister, Sir Anthony Eden, and the Conservative Party was directed not so much against Hussein as against Nasser. When, six weeks later, Bulganin and Khruschev visited London they found Eden, as Khruschev was often to tell us, in a state of mind which made him quite incapable of coming to terms with what was happening in the Middle East.

During this London visit Eden put forward proposals for a limitation on arms supplies to the Middle East, and also suggested that Russia should subscribe to the tripartite declaration of 1950 by which Britain, France and the United States rationed arms supplies to both sides in the area. This proposal found his guests in a mood of indecision. They had not yet made up their minds on the attitude they should adopt towards the Arab–Israeli dispute. They knew they had gained influence in the Middle East, but they were uncertain how much; in particular they were unable to decide how strong the national movement was outside Egypt. They were tempted to use their influence as a bargaining counter with the West, which could perhaps best be done by joining the three western powers as arbiters of events in the Middle East, but equally they were tempted to work out their own policy towards the governments and peoples in the area. The impression in Cairo at this time was that the Soviets were leaning towards the se ond alternative.

Nasser himself was still not fully convinced that the Russians would continue to support him. It was because he thought the possibility of a Russian understanding with the West, particularly over the matter of arms supplies, was still on the cards, that he decided he required another escape route. So in May he recognized the Peking government. Since mainland China was not yet a member of the United Nations, this would provide Egypt with, so to speak, a back door for the supply of arms, if that became necessary. Nasser's action angered Dulles almost as much as the sacking of Glubb had angered Eden. The Suez storm clouds were gathering.

★   ★   ★

American contacts with Egypt over the High Dam continued to worry the Soviets. They feared that the Americans might be using finance for the dam as a means of getting back into Egypt's good books. Every time someone like Eugene Black, or Robert Anderson or John McCloy turned up in Cairo they became intensely suspicious. What, they wanted to know, was he up to? Yet by the early summer of 1956 they felt instinctively that the policy decision not to go ahead with support for the High Dam had already been taken in Washington.

Nasser arrived in Yugoslavia on a ten-day official visit on July 12, 1956, and before he left Egypt he too had come to the same conclusion. But he still ruled out any discussion on the subject with the Russians. This, he thought, would be practically as well as morally wrong. The Americans would almost certainly get wind of it and would come to the conclusion that Nasser was trying to blackmail them into supporting him, which would finally rule out any remaining chance of American backing.

A statement announcing the withdrawal of America's offer to make a major contribution to the financing of the High Dam was handed to the Egyptian ambassador in Washington on July 19, the last day of Nasser's Yugoslav visit. By the time Nasser got back to Egypt, he had already decided that his answer would be the nationalization of the Suez Canal Company, but before he made this public he wanted to find out about the state of British forces in Cyprus, Malta, Libya and Aden. He thought it very probable that, if their troops in the area were available in sufficient strength and preparedness, the British would attempt an immediate military intervention, but that if they were not, he would be afforded some time for political manoeuvre. So he made enquiries, especially from Makarios and Grivas, who had a debt to repay for the assistance Egypt had given to the Eoka guerrilla fighters in Cyprus. He had not received this information by July 23, the anniversary of the revolution, which would have been the natural occasion for an announcement of this importance, but at the reception at the Egyptian embassy in Moscow on that that day, which was attended by the entire Politburo, Shepilov told the Egyptian ambassador: 'You can count on the friendship of the Soviet Union.'

Another occasion was provided three days later, when Nasser was to make a speech in Alexandria to commemorate the departure of King Farouk from Egypt. It was then that he told a crowd of 250,000 in Liberation Square, and a much vaster crowd who heard the speech on the radio, that Egypt would build the High Dam herself and pay for it out of the revenues of the Canal. 'We have taken this decision to restore part of the glories of the past,' he told his audience, 'and to safeguard our national dignity and pride.'

The speech was greeted in Moscow by absolute silence. On July 23 the entire Politburo had been in the Egyptian embassy; on July 26 no member of the embassy staff could contact even a third grade civil servant in the Minsitry of Foreign Affairs. It was not that the Soviets felt aggrieved at Nasser's failure to inform them in advance of what he was going to do – many months later, after the Suez war was over, Shepilov did reproach the Egyptian ambassador in Moscow that 'at least you, our friends, should have consulted us' – it was simply that they were trying to evaluate what had happened. In twenty-four hours the collective mind of the Politburo was made up. Statements were issued giving warm support to Egypt and stern warnings to the West.

Although naturally an immediate start was made on contingency plans to meet armed attack, the assumption from the outset of the crisis was that it would take at least ten weeks for Britain to prepare for military action. It was also calculated that as the weeks went by British and French fury would cool and the risk of invasion would grow less. This view was shared by the Russians, the Yugoslavs and the Indians.

The main object was therefore to buy time. The Egyptian government was careful not to ask the Russians what they proposed to do if Egypt was attacked, fearing that their answer might well be to propose joint military planning, the preparation of bases for their forces on Egyptian territories, the recruitment of volunteers and so on. Egyptian delegates to the first London conference, which opened on August 16, were careful not to give the impression that their policy was being coordinated with the Russians. And indeed there was no coordination. Had there been, the Russians might well have advised Nasser to draw back, or to agree to some unacceptable compromise. Besides, had any hint of such coordination become known it would have been used by Eden to support his claims that Nasser was the catspaw of world communism. Nasser's first intention had been to go to the conference himself, and to appear there as prosecutor rather than defendant, but he changed his mind after a broadcast by Eden on August 8, which seemed to present the matter as a personal struggle between the two men ('Our quarrel is not with Egypt, still less with the Arab world. It is with Colonel Nasser').

It was after the London conference had ended, with an eighteen-power declaration which authorized the Menzies mission to go to Cairo to explain its proposals to Nasser, that the Egyptian ambassador in Moscow sent back a report of a party which he had attended at the Romanian embassy. On this occasion Khruschev had greeted the British ambassador, Sir William Hayter, with the words 'Here comes the imperialist!' He asked Sir William why Britain wanted to reimpose its domination on a small struggling country like Egypt. Sir William answered that Britain was only trying to safeguard its interests in the Suez Canal. 'What about the interests and rights of the Egyptians?' Khruschev insisted. 'Even if you have interests, do you need to mobilize armies and threaten war to protect them? Don't forget that if a war starts because of what you are doing, all our sympathies will be with Egypt. A war of Egypt against Britain would be a sacred war, and if my son came to me, and asked me if he ought to volunteer to fight against Britain, I would tell him he most certainly should do so.'

At this point, the ambassador reported, Khruschev saw the Pakistani ambassador, Akhtar Hussein, standing behind Sir William Hayter. 'So far we've been talking to the imperialists,' said Khruschev, 'now let's have a word with their lackeys.' Akhtar Hussein looked surprised. 'Mr Chairman,' he said, 'I don't know what imperialists you're talking about.' 'I'm talking about the imperialists you're supporting in London,' said Khruschev. Akhtar Hussein said he supposed Khruschev must be referring to the proposals submitted at the conference by Pakistan, but explained that these had only taken the form of a draft resolution. 'But don't you see that this could be a violation of Egypt's sovereignty?' said Khruschev. 'Can't you be honest with yourselves and admit the truth?' 'Mr Chairman, what is the truth?' asked Akhtar Hussein. 'Truth is relative. We all seek truth, but we need knowledge to be able to recognize it. May I suggest, Sir, that we drink a toast to the knowledge which enables us to see the truth?' 'No,' said Khruschev, 'I'm not going to drink with you. We have a saying in Russia that a man who loses his fortune can recover it, but that the man who loses his honesty has lost it for ever.' Here Bulganin, fearing the argument was in danger of getting out of hand, stepped in: 'Let us drink a toast to the people of Pakistan,' he said. 'All right,' said Khruschev reluctantly. 'To the people of Pakistan! But I'll only drink half a glass. I'll keep the second half until the people of Pakistan have secured their government's withdrawal from all military pacts!'

A lot of time was spent in Cairo analysing this report, trying to decide what Khruschev really meant by Soviet sympathies being with Egypt, by a 'sacred war', by volunteers and so on.

⋆   ⋆   ⋆

Shukri Kuwatly, President of Syria, was supposed to start on a state visit to Russia on October 30 (Nasser himself had originally been due to go there in August but for obvious reasons his visit had been cancelled). The Israeli attack on Egypt began on October 29. That day Kuwatly telephoned to Nasser to ask if there was anything he could do. Nasser told him that though the situation was obscure he thought it was under control; if it should get worse, it would be useful if Kuwatly was in Moscow. So Kuwatly went off, arriving more or less simultaneously with the Anglo-French ultimatum.

Immediately on arrival Kuwatly asked to see the Soviet leaders, and a meeting was quickly arranged with Bulganin and Khruschev and some other members of the Politburo. But as he said he wanted to talk about the military situation Marshal Zhukov was called in too. Kuwatly was in a highly emotional state. He insisted that Egypt must be helped.

'But what can we do?' asked Khruschev.

'Is it for me to tell you what to do?' shouted Kuwatly. 'Egypt is being attacked, and Egypt believed you were going to come to her aid. If you do nothing your position in the Arab world will be utterly destroyed.'

Khruschev repeated, 'But what can we do?'

'Why don't you ask Marshal Zhukov?' said Kuwatly.

So Zhukov produced a map of the Middle East and spread it on the table. Then, turning to Kuwatly, he said 'How can we go to the aid of Egypt? Tell me! Are we supposed to send our armies through Turkey, Iran and then into Syria and Iraq and on into Israel and so eventually attack the British and French forces?'

At this Kuwatly became still more excited. 'Marshal Zhukov, Marshal Zhukov,' he cried, 'do you want me, a poor civilian, to tell you, the great marshal, the conqueror of Germany, what should be done?'

Khruschev folded up the map and told Kuwatly, 'We'll see what we can do. At present we don't know how to help Egypt, but we are having continuous meetings to discuss the problem.'

★   ★   ★

As long as the struggle was one in which a small country was ranged against the armies of two still powerful empires Nasser was certain of the sympathy of the world. He had been encouraged by the demonstrations in Trafalgar Square and elsewhere. So, though he would be grateful for any aid the Russians could give, he did not want to coordinate action with them. On November 2 there was a diplomatic reception in Moscow at which both the Egyptian ambassador, el-Kouni, and Khruschev were present. Khruschev spoke to el-Kouni, and all the other guests watched the faces of the two men closely to see if they could detect from their expressions what was being said. In fact the message Khruschev had to convey was far from cheering. 'We are full of admiration for the way in which you are resisting aggression,' he said, 'but unfortunately there is no way in which we can help you militarily. But we are going to mobilize world public opinion.' El-Kouni tried to look much more cheerful than he felt. He sent Cairo a telegram reporting Khruschev's remarks and Kuwatly's meeting with the Politburo.

In the early afternoon of November 6 el-Kouni was called to the Ministry of Foreign Affairs to see Shepilov. He was met at the entrance by Semyonov, the Minister's aide. Semyonov was trembling. This was hardly surprising as events were moving to a climax. By then, British and French forces had landed in Egypt; indignation against the invasion was mounting throughout the world and China was demanding a tough line. At the same time Russian troops had moved in to crush the

Hungarian uprising. It was known that the Politburo had been in continuous session.

All Semyonov could say to el-Kouni was, 'what you are going to hear from the minister will please you.' When el-Kouni reached Shepilov's office he was handed the texts of the two Russian ultimatums to Britain and France. 'We have taken a very firm position, Mr Ambassador,' he said, 'and we shall stand beside you to defeat aggression.'

Later the same day el-Kouni was summoned by Khruschev, who also read to him the texts of the ultimatums. 'This will make them stop,' he said.

'You know, Mr Chairman,' said el-Kouni, 'you nearly broke my heart when you spoke to me at the reception four days ago.'

'I meant to give you a misleading message,' said Khruschev, 'because I knew you would report it back to Cairo in cipher. We think the Americans and British have broken your ciphers and we wanted them to think we were not going to intervene. So we had to use you as a tool in this deception. Please forgive me.'

There was naturally a great deal of speculation by diplomats in Moscow as to what might be done. Would the Russians attack the invading forces in Port Said and Malta with rockets? They could hardly launch an attack on the United Kingdom itself, but perhaps the British and French navies in the Mediterranean might be targets. Or could there be a limited Russian intervention in Iran, as a diversion? What was generally agreed was that if the Russians were bluffing, and did nothing, their reputation in the Third World would be destroyed for at least ten years. Although ultimately what forced the British, French and Israeli governments to halt their aggression was American and not Russian pressure, Russian attitudes made a significant contribution to the final result. When Britain and France realized that they would have to surrender to one of the two superpowers, they preferred that it should be to the Americans.

Yet Egypt's relations with the Russians were not simple. There was still the necessity to avoid becoming dependent on them. So, while it was encouraging that hundreds of young men should call at the Egyptian embassy in Moscow offering their services as volunteers, when a resolution came up at the UN condemning Russia's intervention in Hungary, Egypt's delegation was instructed to abstain. This decision was a very hard one to make, and though the Russians were clearly annoyed by Egypt's action they made no formal protest.

The high point of the Egyptian–Russian honeymoon was seen at the Moscow celebrations on November 7 marking the anniversary of the October Revolution. One of the main slogans on this occassion was 'Warm greetings to the Egyptian people who are courageously defending their homeland, sovereignty and independence!' Khruschev told the Egyptian ambassador that day: 'You have cut off the British lion's tail and we have drawn his teeth! Now he can neither roar nor bite!' Egypt was now a legend in the Soviet Union, and one which brought immediate practical benefits. Nasser was told that all the arms lost at Suez would be replaced – the aeroplanes free of charge and the rest at half their cost price.

★   ★   ★

But new problems quickly began to rear their heads. The Russians – partly no doubt in an effort to cover up their actions in Hungary – intensified the propaganda line that it was their ultimatums alone which had caused Britain, France and Israel to break off their action, whereas people in Egypt not unnaturally felt that if they had surrendered at any time in the eleven days between the beginning of the invasion and the Russian ultimatums all would have been lost and there would have been nothing Russia or anybody else could have done about it. Egyptian communists too tried to make capital out of the situation. Even before the invasion took place a National Guard of civilian volunteers had been formed, and this had played a big part in the resistance at Port Said. Some communists, including writers and other intellectuals, had joined this body and tried to give it a Marxist flavour. The Soviet consul in Port Said was to be seen all over the place, escorted by communist members of the National Guard. Much to the chagrin of the army it appeared as though the National Guard was putting itself forward as the force which had been the true saviour of the nation. So it was decided that the National Guard would have to be dissolved.

The communists distributed leaflets protesting against the dissolution, urging that the National Guard should have been maintained as a weapon for organizing the masses in popular resistance to the invader. A few communists were arrested. This upset the Russians, though they did not complain. But when Khruschev met our ambassador he said, 'I'm not talking to you officially, but as one human being to another. These people you have arrested took part in the national resistance. So why do you treat them in this way?'

There were other irritants. The Suez Canal was cleared of its wreckage and reopened to shipping. The Russians claimed that they had a special position which entitled them to pay transit dues for their ships in Egyptian currency, but they were told that they would have to pay in foreign currency like everybody else. Then they organized a festival of Soviet films in Cairo and sent a supply of films which were nothing but blatant communist propaganda. So some of the films had to be cancelled. Nikloy Mikhailov, the Minister of Culture, was sent to Cairo to repair the damage, but this he was unable to do.

At the same time the Egyptian government was trying to improve relations with the Americans, in recognition of the part they had played in defeating the aggression. This was something the Russians were well aware of, and they did not like it a bit. When the American government formulated the Eisenhower Doctrine, which, under the pretext of offering help against 'international communism', was a blatant attempt by America to replace Britain and France as the dominating influence in the Middle East, and pressed acceptance of the 'Doctrine' on the Arab world, Egypt naturally opposed it, but in such a way as to avoid a direct quarrel. The Americans were still trying to get the Israelis out of Sinai and Gaza (which were not finally evacuated until March 1957), but they were also putting pressure on Egypt. They stopped the CARE programme, which had provided a meal for children in many primary schools, as well as all programmes for economic and technical aid; they refused Egypt's request to be allowed to buy medicine with the frozen Egyptian dollar balances, and to sell Egyptian wheat. But Egypt's answer to this pressure was much more muted than the Russians would have liked it to be.

The fact is that Suez had had such an enormous impact in the Arab world and Africa that the Russians could not afford to show themselves in any way critical of Egypt. Moreover, they themselves were fascinated by the whole Suez affair and were trying to analyse what exactly had happened. As they saw it, Western influence in a vital strategic area had been shattered, and apparently shattered by a national liberation movement led by non-communists. Bulganin told the Egyptian ambassador: 'You should now consolidate your position. The Third World is obviously going to be liberated whatever the imperialists do. If one Suez can change the balance of power in the world to the extent that it has done, much time is going to be saved in the onward march of the liberation movement.' This remark of Bulganin's was in a reality a deviation from orthodox communist thinking. The Soviets remained hostile to what they considered 'adventures', but they had to admit that an 'adventure' had produced a shift in the Middle Eastern scene which could only be described as revolutionary.

Some of this change in Soviet thinking was reflected in the paper presented by R. Ulianovsky, the party ideologue for national liberation movements, to the twentieth Congress of the CPSU in February 1956. 'To a large extent,' he reported, 'the future of the world revolutionary process will depend on the way in which the countries of the Third World solve the social and political problems now confronting them. In our time the countries which had been, as Lenin put it, kept by the colonialists out of history for centuries, have ceased to be simply objects used by the policies of others and have instead become active participants in the making of policy. The prestige of socialist ideas and practices is growing rapidly in these countries.'

But though the Russians were undoubtedly impressed by what they had seen of the strength of a national revolutionary movement in action, and the enthusiastic response it had evoked almost everywhere, they could see dangers ahead too. Everything seemed to them to depend on one man, and this was something contrary to their most sacred beliefs. So they were eager to give advice. They emphasized the need for what they called 'the unity of all nationalist forces' (which could of course have brought the communists back into prominence) and to be always on the alert; the masses, they said, should be organized and mobilized; the masses should be armed. The Egyptian answer to this was to remind them that Trotsky had given up reliance on the militias and had brought in Czarist generals to head the Red Army. Then they warned Egypt to have as little as possible to do with 'the new imperialists' who, they thought, would try to interfere in Egyptian affairs by manipulating 'the traditional bureaucracy', by which they meant the public servants trained in the West or in a colonial atmosphere, of whom they were profoundly suspicious. They were very generous with their advice on all matters.

4
Storm over Iraq

BY THE BEGINNING OF 1957 the Arab world was divided into two fairly clear-cut ideological camps. On one side were reactionary rulers closing their ranks and strengthening their ties with the United States. Among these was Lebanon, whose government alone among Arab countries had refused to break off diplomatic relations with Britain and France as a result of Suez, and the Hashemite kingdoms of Iraq and Jordan, now reconciled with the Saudis. King Saud of Saudi Arabia went to Washington where he was flattered by the suggestion that he should become Pope of Islam, and came back more or less accepting the Eisenhower Doctrine. On the other side were the rising forces of nationalism which had at last found a worthy hero in Nasser.

Syria was destined to become the battleground between these two camps. Once again the world was to witness the traditional conflict between Egypt and Iraq over Syria – a conflict which goes back to the first centuries of Islam and beyond. The Syrians were understandably nervous. To the north was Turkey, more or less hostile; to the east Iraq, like Turkey a member of the Baghdad Pact; to the south Israel and Jordan. Off the Syrian coast cruised the American Sixth Fleet. The internal position of Syria was hopelessly weak. Although Shukri Kuwatly had been brought to the presidency through Egyptian influence, real power was in the hands of a small group of officers, almost all of whom were admirers of Nasser but who were quarrelling among themselves. Now pressure was being brought to bear on them from every side. Russia had supplied Syria with arms, and achieved some influence there as a result. The Americans claimed that these arms were more than Syria needed for her own defence; therefore they must be intended for use against Iraq and Jordan. Some colour was given to American suspicions when on August 6 the Syrian Defence Minister, Khalid el-Azm, signed in Moscow a wide-ranging agreement covering economic and technical aid as well as arms. A week later three American diplomats at the Damascus embassy were declared *personae non gratae*. On August 17 General Afif el-Bizri, a known communist, was appointed Chief of Staff and a purge of senior officers, most of whom were in favour of closer ties with Iraq and Jordan, was carried out. Nor did it go unnoticed that anyone who visited the office of Colonel Abdel Hamid Sarraj, then the director of military intelligence and probably the most powerful figure in the country, would find on his desk a small statuette of Nasser.

American alarm grew, and its manifestations contributed to a heightening of the tension. It was rumoured in Washington that Loy Henderson, one of the State Department's leading Middle East experts, was to leave on August 24 on a fact-finding mission. He was scheduled to go to Ankara, where he was to meet the Kings of Jordan and Iraq as well as the Prime Minister, Adnan Menderes, and then to Beirut. A message was sent through the Egyptian ambassador in Washington suggesting that if Loy Henderson wanted to find out facts about what was happening in Syria he ought to go to Damascus. But a stop there was not included in his itinerary, and after his return it was announced (September 5) that there was to be an immediate airlift of American arms to Jordan, Iraq and Lebanon.

But in fact, so far from hatching the 'Communist takeover' of Syria so widely reported in the western press, the Soviet leaders were extremely puzzled as to what policy they should adopt. They were hesitant to put all their money on the nationalist forces, especially as these seemed to be at loggerheads with the local communists. But it was impossible for them to cooperate with the western powers, though on September 3 Moscow repeated the proposal, which it had put forward twice earlier that year, for a four-power declaration renouncing the use of force in the Middle East. Once again this proposal was rejected by the West.

Nasser found himself in a difficult position. The concentration of Turkish and Iraqi troops on their borders showed that the threat of an invasion of Syria was a real one, and having been through much the same experience himself he could distinguish the extent to which all the talk about Syria's being in imminent danger of a communist take-over was simply alarmist propaganda. Yet he could not help sharing some of the acute nervousness which was agitating Syria, and he knew that if the Arab masses in Egypt and elsewhere, whom he now regarded as his 'constituents', began to believe Syria was about to go communist they would blame him. So he decided that the best encouragement he could give to the nationalist officers and Baathist politicians with whom he was in touch was to send two brigades of Egyptian troops to the Syrian port of Latakia. This he did without consulting the Russians, who were not particularly happy about it.

On July 3 Moscow announced the purge of an 'anti-party group'. Shepilov, who had negotiated the 1955 arms deal and whom Egyptians regarded as their friend, disappeared from the scene together with Molotov, Malenkov and Kaganovich. So, at the end of October, did Marshal Zhukov, who had come to be looked on as the man who would intervene on Egypt's behalf if it was attacked. These changes, combined with the continuing crisis in Syria, made Nasser feel the need for direct consultation with the Soviet leaders. It was impossible for him to go himself, so he arranged to send Field-Marshal Abdel Hakim Amer, Commander-in-Chief of the Egyptian armed forces, as his special representative to the celebrations that were to take place in November in honour of the fortieth anniversary of the October Revolution. Many senior officers were to be included in the delegation, and at the last minute Nasser decided that I should go too, so that I should be able to give him what he called 'a journalist's account of the situation'. He used to say that Amer was incapable of telling a story: 'If you asked him what was the story of Joseph he would tell you "he was a boy who got lost and then was found".' Nasser had been hearing so many conflicting reports about the Soviet Union – what life was like there, how they ran things, what were their real intentions towards the Arab world – that he wanted to get the evidence of a friendly eye witness. He wanted full details, not a bald statement in the Amer–Joseph style. The Russians were considerably surprised at this addition to the delegation.

★   ★   ★

This was the first time I had been to the Soviet Union, and for me it was a tremendously exciting experience. Soon after the plane landed at Venukovo airport I noticed a young man calling out my name, so I went up to him and he told me (in English) that we were to go together to car number four. It was a long way from the airport to the centre of Moscow; the road was flanked by numerous building projects and the whole scene was covered in snow. As I gazed out of the car window I exclaimed in Arabic, to see whether my companion knew the language or not: 'So this is Moscow – ah, wonderful, wonderful ...' The answer came in Arabic: 'So you like Moscow?' I told him I did, and asked him who he was and how he came to know Arabic. He told me that his name was Stepanovski, that he worked in the Ministry of Foreign Affairs, and that he had been given a crash course in Arabic. By 1955, as I subsequently learned, there had been 500 from the army and Ministry of Foreign Affairs learning Arabic at the Moscow Academy of Sciences Institute. His Arabic struck me as very strange; he had obviously been taught the grammar well but his pronunciation made me suspect that he had been taught the spoken language by Kurdish refugees from Iraq.

The car took us to the Hotel Ukraina overlooking the River Moskva. Mindful of the reporting job I had been given to do by Nasser I decided I would have to make something of a nuisance of myself. So I addressed myself confidentially to my guide. 'Mr Stepanovski,' I said, 'I have a problem. This is my first visit to the Soviet Union, but I am not a member of the military delegation. I feel that all my life I have been subjected to western propaganda about Russia and communism – by my reading, education, and so on. So I want to discover the Soviet Union for myself. I must ask you not to come with me. If you are always by my side I shall feel that you are spying on me. And I don't want to stay in this hotel with the delegation, because I feel this will restrict my movements – perhaps even that my hotel room will have been bugged. Nor do I want to be an official guest of your government because in a way this could be taken as a form of bribery. I want to pay my own hotel bill, and I don't want an official car.'

Poor Stepanovski went quite white. To this day I can see the look of total consternation on his face. 'Please don't tell me all this,' he cried. 'Colonel Chouvilski is the man who is looking after the delegation, and you belong with the delegation even though you aren't military. You will have to deal with him.' We were still standing in the hotel lobby, and now moved to a room near the manager's office where the colonel was installed. 'What's the problem?' he asked.

'Colonel Chouvilski,' I said, 'I come to you with a human problem. I am a victim of American propaganda. This I confess. I want to see things for myself.' I then told him what I had already told poor Stepanovski.

'Quite impossible!' exploded Chouvilski. Then followed half an hour of argument, after which Chouvilski said he would have to refer to higher authority. Meanwhile the rest of the delegation were wondering what on earth was going on. When I told them some thought it a good joke, but some were afraid it might prove an embarrassment for them. In the end a compromise of a sort was reached. Chouvilski swore that there were no other hotel rooms vacant in the whole of Moscow, so I would have to stay where I was and would have to let the government pay the bill, but, though Stepanovski and the car would be in attendance all day, I need not make use of either unless I wanted to.

That night we were guests at a dinner in the reception salon of the Ministry of Defence. Marshal Malinovsky presided and all the marshals of the Soviet Union were present – Gretchko, Sokolovsky, Rokossovsky, Timoshenko, Rodenko. It was an impressive turnout; I sat next to Rodenko, a marshal of the Air Force. Toasts began to be offered. I swallowed one vodka and immediately felt as if I was dying. Rodenko was looking all round him exchanging toasts and shouting '*dadna!*' I waited till his back was turned, filled my glass with water, and called to him 'Marshal – *dadna!*' We toasted each other two or three times and his face was beaming with happiness. But then he caught me with the water-bottle. He removed the water, brought a clean glass, filled it with vodka, and said sternly in English 'Drink!' I said, 'I'm sorry. I can't.' Rodenko banged on the table and shouted in his indignation. I was afraid I might be accused of letting the side down, but in fact everyone was enjoying themselves so much that it didn't matter.

The next morning I went down to the hotel lobby, where I found Stepanovski waiting for me. I asked him if he would be good enough to take me somewhere. He said he would be delighted, and asked where it was I wanted to go to. 'I want you to take me to the censor's office,' I said. Stepanovski blanched again. 'There is no censor,' he said. So I tried another tack. 'Very well. But will you do me a favour? Will you give me a cup of tea?' 'Of course,' said Stepanovski. 'But in your own house?' Stepanovski said this would be quite impossible. I suggested this must mean that housing conditions in Moscow were as bad as American propaganda made out. He insisted that this was not so. 'We have a two-room flat,' he told me. 'My wife and two children live in one room, and my mother-in-law and her son in the other.' I said I thought this did not sound a very good arrangement. 'How do you live in Egypt?' asked Stepanovski. I told him. 'But are you a capitalist?' asked Stepanovski, puzzled. I told him I was not a capitalist but a working man. Stepanovski was clearly interested and wanted to pursue the discussion. I asked him what his dreams were: 'Don't you dream of having a house with a car of your own?' He looked me straight in the face and said: 'No, my rank is too low for me to have a car. But I'm planning to have a motor-cycle, and one day I'll have one.' 'But you don't even *dream* of having a car?' 'No, a motor-cycle is the right thing for my rank.' 'Stepanovski,' I said, 'what sort of a system is this which rations the hopes and dreams of its citizens?' Almost with fear in his voice he turned on me: 'Why are you talking to me in this way?' he shouted.

That night there was a big reception in the White Hall to celebrate the fortieth anniversary of the Russian Revolution. Many guests had been invited, including Mao Tse-Tung who was on what turned out to be his last visit to Moscow. The Egyptian delegation was there too, the centre of a great deal of attention. As usual at these Russian receptions a lot of excellent food and drink was provided. Grigory Zaitsev, who was then head of the Middle East department in the Ministry of Foreign Affairs, cornered General Hafez Ismail, who ranked third in our delegation, and tackled him rather aggressively about Egyptian policy. 'All your talk about non-alignment is nonsense,' he said. 'Either you are with us or with the Americans. If you can't be on the side of the imperialists you must be on our side. Join us, and we can give you everything you want. And I don't mean short-term loans or long-term loans. No. Egypt will be a country like our country, and everything will be given to you free – industrialization, development projects, dams, agriculture, everything!'

Hafez Ismail made no comment, but made a report on the conversation which he gave to the head of the delegation. Amer raised the matter with Khruschev, asking if this really represented Soviet policy. Khruschev said it did not. There would be an official investigation, he said, and if it was found that Zaitsev had spoken in these terms he would be punished. The punishment cannot have been severe, because after the 1958 revolution in Iraq he was sent as ambassador to Baghdad.

As a mark of the special favour with which the Egyptian delegation was regarded, Khruschev asked Amer whom he would like to talk to – something the Russians never normally do. But in fact Khruschev arranged everything himself – the delegation was to discuss political matters with Bulganin, Gromyko and Khruschev himself; trade with

Mikoyan and Pervykhin, responsible for external cooperation; military matters with Marshal Malinovsky, the Minister of Defence, and his deputy Sokolovsky.

The delegation had come with Egypt's proposed five-year plan as part of its luggage, and in the course of discussions it was agreed that the Soviet government would contribute $150m towards this plan. There followed a curious little incident which throws some light on how the Soviet system works. The day after agreement had been reached on this aid total Amer talked to Nasser on the telephone, and the day after that he saw Khruschev again. 'You talked to Gospodin Nasser yesterday?' said Khruschev. Amer said he had, and that Nasser had asked him to thank Khruschev very much for the agreement that had been concluded. 'But you aren't very enthusiastic about it?' said Khruschev. 'I think perhaps Nasser is not very enthusiastic.' Amer insisted that Nasser was, on the contrary, very grateful. 'But perhaps he expected more?' Khruschev went on. 'Well, all right. We have made a decision to increase our contribution to $200m.' This was done, and since Nasser had expressed regret when speaking to Amer that the amount was not greater the only conclusion to be drawn was that the delegation's telephone conversations were carefully monitored.

Khruschev spent a lot of time in these discussions attacking the Americans. He said they only wanted governments which would be traitors to their peoples and hand over all their national resources to the foreigners. The Soviets, on the other hand, wanted to see governments which would represent the will of the people and would help these to develop their own resources for themselves. He strongly criticized the American role in the Suez war – something which had always amazed Russia. He claimed that the British and French would never have acted as they did unless America had given them the green light to go ahead, but that America had failed to foresee the consequences of Anglo-French action. 'We intervened,' he said, 'and you resisted. That upset their plans, and by then it was too late for America to rescue Britain. But America helped the aggressors in the same way that the rope helps the man who is being hanged.'

Khruschev made fun of all the American talk about a Middle East 'vacuum'. 'Where's the vacuum?' he said. 'It's all in their heads. The Middle East is the cradle of the world's civilization, but in all the struggles going on in that area today you can smell the reek of oil. The Americans are threatening Syria. They asked Jordan and Iraq to attack Syria – we have documents to prove this. The only thing that stopped them was that they were afraid of the reaction there might be from nationalist officers in the Jordanian and Iraqi armies. So they turned to Turkey. But we sent the Turks an ultimatum. We had learned a lesson from Suez, so we didn't wait for the Turks to start aggression but sent them an ultimatum straightaway.'

Shortly before our delegation arrived in Moscow Aneurin Bevan, after seeing Khruschev in Moscow and Eisenhower in Washington, had put forward the idea of a four-power conference on the Middle East. This had aroused Nasser's suspicions, who saw in it a threat that the big powers might try to arrange things between themselves behind Egypt's back, so Amer had been instructed to question Khruschev about the Bevan proposal. Khruschev admitted that he had told Bevan the Soviet Union would be ready to take part in such a conference. 'People in the Middle East see the idea as another Yalta,' said Amer. Khruschev told him not to worry. 'It's better that we should go along with them,' he said. 'It may help to reduce tension in the area. Mind you, we know they are only trying to deceive us. We are quite aware that they have no intention of allowing us any role in the Middle East – or anywhere else for that matter – unless we completely change our skins; and that is a day which they will no more see than a man can see his ears.'

★ ★ ★

I had asked for an interview with Khruschev, but it was not till our last day in Moscow that I was told I was going to be given it. I was asked to prepare questions, but instead I produced five points for discussion because I wanted our talk to be as free-ranging as possible. I duly presented myself at the building behind Maxim Gorki Street which houses the Central Committee. There I found the colonel who holds the key of the lift which takes a visitor straight up to the office of the First Secretary – the office which had once been Lenin's. Khruschev was seated at his desk – or rather Lenin's desk, as he was always proud to point out – on which was a Soviet flag and a model of the TU 154 jet liner, then in process of development. On a table were chocolates and refreshments. A secretary and a Russian–English interpreter were the only others present.

We all sat down. Khruschev, who had been leafing through some typewritten Russian papers looked up. 'Your questions are inadequate,' he said. 'I know,' I said, 'they were only meant to be points for discussion.' Then I pointed to the papers he was holding; 'Are these all to do with my questions?' I asked. 'No,' said Khruschev. 'This is information about you.' 'My God,' I said, 'what does it say about me?' 'It says you are a friend of Nasser's,' said Khruschev, 'and any friend of Nasser's is a friend of mine.' 'Good,' I said, 'but that information would only take about three lines. What else does it say?' 'It says that you don't like communists,' said Khruschev. 'That's not true, Mr Chairman,' I protested. 'I may disagree with communists sometimes, but I don't dislike them. Many of my friends are communists.' Khruschev returned to the charge. 'But why don't you like communists?' he asked again. I tried a new line. 'May I talk freely?' I asked, and on being given permission I told the story of Stepanovski. ' I can't understand any country which restricts the hopes of the individual,' I said. 'You don't understand us at all,' said Khruschev. 'You come here, and you take a quick look. But you forget that we lost twenty million people during the war. You forget that all our homes were destroyed. It was our people, our armies, not American help, that fought the war and won it. We have got to have priorities in what we do. If you make a proper judgement of our country you must take into account all we have done since the war.'

Before the interview began I had asked for, and been given, permission to smoke, and now was smoking a cigar. Suddenly Khruschev turned on me. 'Are you a capitalist?' he demanded. 'Why are you smoking a cigar?' 'Because I like cigars,' I said. But Khruschev seized my cigar and crushed it out in the ashtray. I protested. 'A cigar is a capitalist object,' said Khruschev. 'You aren't a capitalist because you're a friend of Nasser. Right. Now let's carry on.'

The next time I interviewed Khruschev, in 1958, I left my cigar outside. Khruschev asked me where it was; 'I want to crush it again,' he said. But in 1963, when I was again in Moscow, Khruschev one day presented me with a box of really good cigars. 'Mr Chairman,' I said, 'I'm shocked. Don't you remember what you did to my cigar? Why have you changed?' 'I haven't changed,' said Khruschev. 'It's the cigars that have changed. Since the revolution in Cuba these cigars have become Marxist-Leninist cigars.'

The substance of my first interview was published in *Al Ahram*, and as a result I was furiously attacked in *Pravda* – not for anything that had been reported in the interview but for something I had said in my introductory remarks. There I had referred to Khruschev as 'the Red Tsar'. I agree that this was tactless, and it proved enough to bring down the wrath of the Soviets on my head.

★   ★   ★

There was one incident in the course of the Amer mission which might have had serious consequences, but which fortunately did not. The villain of the piece was vodka, and this has been the undoing of a great many Arab missions to the Soviet Union. All too often the second day of the visit has seen half the mission knocked out by a surfeit of vodka and caviar. On this occasion the delegation was taken on a tour round many parts of the Soviet Union, and while in Kiev a party was arranged for us at a restaurant, our table being outside on the pavement. The commander of the Soviet Black Sea fleet was there, and was placed next to Admiral Suleiman Ezzet, the Commander in Chief of the Egyptian Navy. Both admirals had had a good deal to drink, but Suleiman Ezzet had already shown himself more than capable of holding his own with his hosts. In Moscow he had been challenged to a drinking match with Marshal Timoshenko – and won! He downed 27 vodkas, and never turned a hair, remaining as rock-like at the end as when he had started.

Apparently in the course of conversation the Russian Admiral said to Admiral Ezzet, 'someone on your staff is a spy for the Americans,' citing as evidence the fact that the Americans knew that the first Soviet submarine had already arrived in Alexandria. The Russians, we were to discover, were obsessed with the idea that information was being leaked to the Americans and were continually giving us confidential warnings about people they thought, often on the flimsiest evidence, were responsible for this.

Ezzet felt that he had been insulted. He stood up, pulling the Russian admiral up after him onto the dance-floor of the restaurant. The rest of us had no idea of what was up, when suddenly there was the sound of a blow and we saw the Russian admiral stretched face downwards on the ground. Ezzet, immaculate in his white uniform, standing over him. We crowded round, asking what had happened. 'He called one of my officers a spy,' said Ezzet. 'I can't allow that.'

Another Russian admiral and a lieutenant quickly appeared on the scene and removed the commander of the Black Sea fleet. The party continued, but the atmosphere was understandably somewhat strained.

*   *   *

In spite of the Amer mission the situation regarding Syria remained dangerous and a source of potential disagreement between Egypt and the Soviets. The Syrian Communist Party was the strongest in the Arab world, legally recognized, with elected deputies in parliament and led by a veteran communist, Khaled Bakdash, who commanded wide respect. The other parties – Shaab, Qutla Destouri, Baath and so on – were now all dependent on officers from the armed forces. These had all discovered how easy was the path to power through a military coup – a few tanks at dawn and Damascus had changed hands.

Looked at from Cairo, it could be seen that the communists were busily exploiting the situation, and it was known that the Russians regarded Syria as, so to speak, a second line of defence, should Egypt become unreliable. So Nasser sent a warning to President Kuwatly and his intelligence chief, Colonel Sarraj, about the serious consequences that could arise from the irresponsible behaviour of the Syrian Communist Party. He pointed out that if the Arab masses got the impression that the nationalist movement was being taken over by the communists it would lose their sympathy. But if Nasser's message was received in Damascus it had no effect.

So there was a feeling in Cairo that some new contact would have to be made with the Americans. When I got back from Moscow, Nasser asked me to go and see the American ambassador, Raymond Hare. The message I was to give him was this: 'We consider your alarm over a possible communist takeover in Syria exaggerated, and that it is itself a contributing factor in the present uncertainty. You are making things more difficult by your daily threats against Syria through Turkey and Iraq. In any case this is our responsibility, so please – hands off!' (This warning was necessary since American agencies, including the CIA, had undoubtedly been mixed up in some of the local conspiracies. They had also persuaded King Saud to try to bribe some of the traditional Syrian politicians into taking action.) This message did have some effect; certainly the level of American intervention was reduced.

Sentiment in favour of Arab unity had always been particularly strong in Syria, which could with justice claim to be the birthplace of the idea, and with Nasser now an active champion of unity a first practical step towards its realization seemed to be opening up. During the Suez crisis the Syrian parliament had passed a resolution advocating unity with Egypt. A delegation was sent to Nasser, who told them that the proposal required study. Now, a year later, the Syrian parliament proposed that negotiations for unity should start immediately. For officers in the Syrian armed forces the tension had become unbearable. Damascus was ringed by camps from which groups of officers of different affiliations eyed each other with nervous suspicion. Some of them found it impossible to sleep for days on end, for fear that while they slept a rival group might seize power. So the only solution for them too seemed to be a call on Nasser to take over, and at a meeting of representative officers from all groups this was decided upon. Without informing the President of the Republic, and leaving Colonel Sarraj in charge in Damascus, these officers took a plane to Cairo, where they met Nasser. He was then in favour of federation, but the officers argued strongly that, without a complete union and a totally new form of government, the present uncertainties in Syria would continue.

Nasser was persuaded by their arguments but put forward three conditions – that the Syrian army should become entirely divorced from politics; that the officers who had up to then been playing leading political roles should resign from the army, and that all political parties should be dissolved. The Syrian officers returned to Damascus, where Nasser's conditions were accepted. The union was proclaimed on February 1, 1958.

* * *

Not everyone, naturally, was happy at the prospect of unity. The Baath was divided. While conscious of the urgency of the situation and the danger of a coup, many Baathists, especially Salah Bitar, one of the founders of the party, preferred the idea of federation. But Michel Aflaq, the party's leading theoretician, argued that union would be itself a creative act which would solve many problems. The communist party, which towards the end of 1957 had given support to unity in the belief that this was something Nasser could never accept, now came out against it. Khaled Bakdash, feeling that it would be impolitic actually to vote against the union, left Syria for eastern Europe on February 4.

He found the Russians in a state of complete bewilderment. They had been regarding with understandable satisfaction the growing importance of the communist party inside Syria, and now the party was dissolved, its leader in virtual exile, and Nasser installed in Damascus instead. Once again they misunderstood the nature and the strength of Arab nationalism. They interpreted the creation of the United Arab Republic entirely in terms of Egyptian expansionism. For them the only real unity has always been the unity of the working class. They do not think in terms of nation states but of peoples and nationalities. The idea of the Arabs as a nation struggling for political unity was meaningless to them.

But it was impossible for the Russians to ignore the evidence that what was happening was something very real and very significant. They witnessed the scenes of unbounded joy which greeted Nasser when he visited Damascus late in February; they saw the delegations which went to Damascus to greet him and the scenes of rejoicing all over the Arab world. Nasser himself was astonished at the degree of euphoria which marked his appearance in Damascus. Every space in the city up to the slopes of the hills surrounding it seemed to be filled with cheering crowds. As Nasser came off the balcony, where he had been acknowledging the cheers, he turned to me and said, 'Well, what do you think of it?' 'Mr President,' I said, 'I'm thinking of two things: first, that perhaps I ought to perform for you the function which one of their attendants used to perform for Roman emperors, and remind you that you are a human being. Secondly I am wondering how it will all end.' Though I had always been a firm believer in the necessity for Arab unity, I was worried about how the temporary considerations which had influenced the February decision might affect the grand historical design.

The Russians watched these developments, and though they did not understand them there was little that they could do to influence or oppose them. So they were obliged to give the union their reluctant support, even though it was followed by the arrest of communists in both Syria and Egypt. One thing however was clear – it was high time that Nasser and the Soviet Leaders should meet face to face. So preparations began for his first visit to the Soviet Union.

*   *   *

As usual, when the Americans got wind of the visit they tried to sabotage it. They sent a message to Cairo to the effect that they were still interested in taking part in the High Dam, that perhaps this could be arranged through West Germany, and so on. But this was a waste of their time. The visit began on April 28, 1958, and lasted three weeks, including visits to Leningrad, Baku, Kiev, Stalingrad, Sverdlovsk and (so that he could see the Moslem parts of the Soviet Union) Tashkent and Kazakhstan. To say that the Russians accorded a specially cordial welcome to Nasser would be an understatement. He was the first of the new generation of Third World leaders to be received, and nothing was omitted which could do him honour. The entire leadership was at the airport to greet him; Kosygin, then deputy premier, was assigned to be his constant companion; he was the guest of honour at the Kremlin saluting base for the May Day parade; a special performance of Khachaturian's latest ballet, Spartacus, was put on for him at the Bolshoi theatre, and each night in the Kremlin he was invited to a special late showing of films dealing with subjects designed to impress the visitors, such as military manoeuvres, atomic explosions, and missile attacks on warships.

The Russians wanted Nasser to see the development that had taken place in the backward areas of the Soviet Union, the advances made in Soviet industry and technology, and their military strength. They wanted him to realize that in this they were a match for the Americans. They also wanted him to realize that they were not persecutors of religion. (They themselves were still mystified by religion. On one occasion, in Khruschev's dacha, while discussions were going on, Nasser looked at his watch and said, 'It's time for the communal Friday prayer.' 'That's all right,' said Khruschev. 'We've told the mullah to wait until you're ready.' 'But the time for the Friday prayer is fixed,' said Nasser, hurrying off to the bathroom to wash. When he came back Khruschev was waiting for him with a clean towel and a puzzled look on his face.)

What the Russians wanted to learn from Nasser was what his social programmes were and what were his relations with the Americans. They also wanted to learn from him about Arab unity and the Arab–Israeli conflict. They did not bring up the question of the arrest of communists in the UAR, though Nasser himself did. 'You mustn't believe people like Khaled Bakdash,' Nasser told Khruschev. 'They put you in a difficult position because they take a wrong line.'

'That is entirely your affair,' said Khruschev, 'we don't want to interfere.'

The visit was an exploratory one, each side trying to take the measure of the other. But Nasser and Khruschev quickly established a good relationship. There was only one hitch; this occurred when, at an informal dinner in Khruschev's dacha outside Moscow, Nasser made the mistake of asking after Shepilov. 'Where is he?' he said. 'Can I see him? After all, I negotiated the arms deal with him.' Khruschev did not give a direct answer, but instead launched into a long dissertation about the top leadership in post-war Russia. This was probably intended both to explain to Nasser how things were arranged in the Kremlin and to convince him that, though not directly answering his question about Shepilov, Khruschev was not holding anything back from him. The evening before he had urged on Nasser that the two of them needed to be completely frank with each other. Now he was showing frankness on his side.

'Individuals aren't important in the Soviet Union,' said Khruschev. 'There is always a consistent policy that is worked out collectively and which is unaffected by the comings and goings of individuals.' 'But the Soviet Union under Stalin was very different from the Soviet Union under you,' said Nasser. 'No,' said Khruschev. 'It's true we changed the policy, but it wasn't a change suggested by any one man; it was rather a change dictated by new conditions. Even so the old policy still has its supporters. After Stalin we faced an extremely dangerous situation. The war had changed so many things; it had even changed the party. The Soviet Union lost twenty million dead. Do you realize that in a few years' time we are going to face problems in industry and agriculture caused by the loss of the generation that was never born because the men who should have fathered it were in the army or dead?

'Malenkov was a bad choice to succeed Stalin. He took over all Stalin's posts, but he confessed to the Central Committee that he wasn't big enough for all his responsibilities. Some of the others failed to realize how the war changed things – Beria, for example. The war had changed the whole concept of internal security. You couldn't apply to men who had been defending the revolution and the party and the state against the Nazis the same methods that had been used while the danger of invasion still threatened. The revolution was strong, and the war had made it stronger. We brought Beria before us; we tried him, and we confronted him with all his errors. Some of them were offences against the nation.

'Do you see that general there?' Khruschev went on, pointing to one of the the other guests, General Kyril Moskalenko, commander of the Moscow garrison. 'Beria tried to resist us, so we decided to place him under arrest. He tried to get in touch with some of his people, to get them to act on his behalf, but General Moskalenko came in and arrested him.

'We needed a good filter after Stalin, but it was difficult to decide on the size of the filter. You've mentioned Shepilov. Do you know that some of these people tried to liquidate me? Last July I was away from Moscow. These people came together – Molotov, Kaganovich, even Shepilov, whom I considered a friend. When I got back to Moscow I found a message at the railway station asking me to go to an emergency meeting of the Politburo. I found to my astonishment that all the members of the Politburo were there. Molotov spoke first. He said: "Comrade Khruschev, the Presidium has decided by a majority that you are not fit to be First Secretary of the Party." I said: "Can I know why?" They said I had deviated from Marxist–Leninist thought. Molotov started saying I was destroying the central administration which was essential for central planning. I told Molotov and the others: "Comrades, the Soviet Union now has 200,000 industrial units. They can't all be managed from Moscow." Molotov said that centralization was important; it had been Lenin's way of breaking down the barriers between the minorities and the different nationalities. "But," he said, "the policy of decentralization which you are pursuing is going to pro- duce local governments which will encourage chauvinist nationalisms." I told Molotov that times had changed; the Soviet Union couldn't be entirely governed from Moscow. "We live in the atomic age," I said, "suppose Moscow was destroyed? What would happen then?"

'Molotov also accused me of making mistakes in foreign affairs. He thought we should go back to traditional policies – first, that is, we should draw a line in Europe beyond which we should allow no retreat. Second, we should refuse to discuss anything affecting the countries on our side of that line. Third, we should stop what he called "adventurism", in which he included our interest in your part of the world, Mr President. I told Molotov that to adopt a purely defensive position in Europe would be a mistake, because there are so many currents flowing over Europe, and the socialist movement in western Europe is becoming very important. Offence is the best form of defence. I said we needed a new, active diplomacy, because the impossibility of a nuclear war meant that the struggle between us and the capitalists was taking on new forms. I told them: "I'm not an adventurer, but we must aid national liberation movements, and if imperialism controls somewhere like the Middle East it could liquidate the national liberation movements there and bring back to power the reactionary forces which would be ready to play their part in a policy of encirclement of the Soviet Union."

'Unfortunately, Molotov thought it was my policies that had led to the trouble in Hungary. Hungary had experimented with decentralization and new liberties. Molotov thought that my tolerance of your friend Tito had encouraged the Hungarians. But I told him that it was impossible to keep the socialist camp isolated from other socialist trends in western Europe, and in the national liberation movements. We had to meet them half way. I was sorry about the way we had to put a stop to things in Hungary, but there was no alternative.

'Molotov wanted us to concentrate on heavy industry. I told him that this was an old idea, and that in the aftermath of the war we had to make a switch to consumer goods because it was very important that people who had defended the party, the country and the revolution should have access to them.

'Shepilov was very low. Do you know what he said in this meeting of the Politburo? He said I behaved in an undiplomatic way. He said that when I met the President of Finland I was scratching my armpits as if they had been invaded by an army of fleas, and that this was most unbecoming in the First Secretary of the Communist Party of the Soviet Union.

'In the end I told them that I couldn't accept the ruling of the Presidium; it was the Central Committee that had appointed me First Secretary of the Party, and it was the only body which could take a decision. The Central Committee met, and all of them backed me.

'Zhukov was a good soldier. There can be no denying what he did in the war. But the trouble is that he was a typical bonapartist phenomenon. His head was turned, and he began to see himself as an important politician, especially after Eisenhower in Geneva began having meetings alone with him. Zhukov realized his mistakes. He confessed his errors, and said henceforth he would follow the party line.'

We stayed in the Soviet Union till the end of May. Some deals for economic cooperation were settled, but the bases for these had been agreed before Nasser left Egypt. He had not wanted to bring specific requests with him – he wanted it to be a meeting at which they would be able to talk politics rather than discuss the supply of arms or industrial equipment. But Khruschev wanted to tell Nasser personally what had been arranged, as one leader to another, and not leave it all to the bureaucracy.

★   ★   ★

Shortly after the creation of the UAR an incident occurred which nobody paid much attention to at the time but which was to prove the forerunner of great events. Two Iraqi officers got into touch with Colonel Sarraj, chief of security in Damascus, arranged a secret meeting with him in Deraa, and there explained that they were forming a free officers' movement in the Iraqi army. 'We want to do what you did,' they said. 'We want to join the ranks of Arab unity and get rid of the Hashemites. How should we organize ourselves? How should we plan a coup d'état? What guarantees can the UAR give us if we start a revolution?'

Sarraj took these questions to Nasser, who brushed them aside, thinking it possible that they came from *agents provocateur*. He told Sarraj to meet the officers again and tell them that the best way of ensuring the success of their plans would be to keep their secret to themselves, and that it was wrong for potential revolutionaries to start asking for guarantees. If they believed in their cause they should be prepared to take risks. After this no more was heard and the incident was forgotten. The names of the two officers were Abdel Karim Qasim and Abdel Salam Aref.

On July 14, 1958 Nasser was in Brioni. He had begun an official visit to Marshal Tito of Yugoslavia on July 2, and was due to leave on his return to Cairo at 4 pm on July 14. He would be travelling in the official yacht *Hurriyeh*, with an escort of two Egyptian destroyers. The sea was thought to be a safer means of transport than the air because it was believed that on the eve of the Suez war the Israelis had managed to bring down a plane flying over the Mediterranean by some secret weapon.

But at dawn on the 14th the communications centre on the *Hurriyeh* began to receive messages from Damascus via Cairo to the effect that while the control towers at Damascus and Baghdad airports had been exchanging messages the operator in Baghdad had reported that something was happening in the town – tanks were out, and it looked as if there had been a coup. Nobody liked to disturb Nasser because the information seemed so uncertain. But after I had listened to the first news bulletin on the BBC's overseas service, which confirmed that there had been a coup, I went to the Villa Brionca, woke Nasser up, and together we listened to radio news bulletins and to the reports now beginning to come in from Baghdad via Cairo. By eight or nine o'clock it became clear that the Iraqi army, led by Brigadier Abdel Karim Qasim, had taken over.

The situation was full of potential dangers. It must now be assumed that the Baghdad Pact had collapsed and that the forces of Arab nationalism were controlling the land routes through the Middle East as well as the sea routes through the Suez Canal – as well as Iraq's oil. We learned that America had declared a state of emergency all over the Mediterranean. But what would Israel do?

Nasser naturally wanted to get back to Cairo as quickly as possible. To go in the *Hurriyeh* would take three days. A Viscount aircraft was available, but that would take eight hours to cross the Mediterranean – a dangerously long time. By 4 pm Nasser had decided that he would have to go by sea. Tito announced that he would provide an additional escort of two Yugoslav destroyers, which would accompany the president's yacht not only in Yugoslav territorial waters, but as far as Alexandria. Meanwhile Nasser issued his first statement giving the Iraqi revolution his full backing. He also sent a personal telegram to Qasim. By nightfall we heard rumours of an imminent, American landing in Beirut and of a landing by the British in Amman.

The *Hurriyeh* had not long started on its return journey, and was steaming through the Adriatic, its lights and those of its destroyer escort blacked out, when a message for Nasser from Tito was picked up: 'Suggest convoy stops: am sending boat with important message.' Almost immediately a boat appeared out of the darkness and a naval officer climbed aboard. His message was that Tito strongly advised against Nasser's continuing his journey by sea; he thought the situation was becoming much too dangerous. He recommended that Nasser should proceed to the nearest Yugoslav port, and said that it might prove possible to arrange for a high-speed plane to take him home. This was followed by another message from Tito, saying that he had been able to make the necessary arrangements – the plane would be waiting at Pola airport. He suggested that for reasons of speed Nasser should transfer to one of the destroyers and make for Brioni. 'To facilitate your communications,' Tito added, 'I have requested the Yugoslav navy to place at your disposal two seaplanes. These can provide a link between the communications centre of the yacht and your destroyer.'

Nasser called Dr Mahmoud Fawzi, the Foreign Minister and myself to the cabin he was occupying. He said he felt there was a smell of collusion in the air (it was, after all, less than two years since Suez). British planes, as we were soon to learn, were at that moment over-flying Israel, with Israeli consent, on their way to Amman. The expected American landing in Lebanon must be the prelude to some bigger initiative, but what? What could we expect Turkey to do? (It must be remembered that the Council of the Baghdad Pact was in session in Ankara; the Regent Abdul Ilah and Nuri Said having been murdered just as they were about to leave for it.) In view of all these circumstances Nasser had come to the conclusion that he ought to seek a personal meeting with Khruschev without delay. But first he wanted to know what we thought. We asked for half an hour to think about it, after which time we gave him our appreciation of the situation. The arguments for and against going were nicely balanced, so the final decision had to be his alone. 'All right then,' he said, 'I'm going.' So a message was sent to Cairo for onward transmission to Khruschev in the most secure cipher carried on the yacht: 'Before returning Cairo I wish to see you in any place that suits you. Am now on my way to Brioni. Hope to find message from you awaiting me.'

When the destroyer entered Pola harbour it was met by the Yugoslav Foreign Minister Popovic in a small boat bearing Khruschev's answer. He was, he said, expecting Nasser in Moscow, if that was a suitable meeting place; otherwise he would go anywhere Nasser suggested. We all proceeded to Tito's office, where we found most of his senior colleagues gathered – Rankovic, Kardelj, Goshniak, the Minister of War, Popovic and others. All agreed that the situation was extremely dangerous. To them Nasser explained his reasons for seeking a meeting with Khruschev.

The TU-104 sent by Khruschev was waiting on a remote corner of the airfield, its huge bulk looming up impressively in the darkness. None of us had seen so big a plane before. Only five of us climbed aboard – Nasser, Dr Mahmoud Fawzi, Hassan Sabri el-Kholi, Nasser's secretary, one of Nasser's bodyguards, and myself. All the rest of our original party, including our wives, remained on the *Hurriyeh*, not knowing what had become of us.

The Russian pilot approached Nasser, saluted, and said in English: 'Your orders, Sir?' Nasser told him we were to go to Moscow. I think the pilot had been expecting to fly to Cairo and was a good deal surprised by the change.

The flight took only two and a half hours, so we were at Venukovo airport by dawn. We taxied to the end of the tarmac, an emergency ladder was let down, and we could see three Zim cars waiting for us. These turned out to contain Kosygin, Mikoyan, General Serov, at that time Director of Military Intelligence, and Sobolev, Khruschev's special Arabic interpreter. We drove to a small palace in the country near Moscow, called Kaichova. Arrived there, Mikoyan looked at his watch and said: 'It's now six o'clock. Get some rest, and then we will start to talk. Khruschev will come here – it's better for security. Would ten o'clock be all right for a start?'

This was agreed. But now followed one slightly comic complication. It was necessary for us to get into touch with our ambassador because only a few people in Cairo, including Marshal Amer, knew where we were and they had been told to communicate with us through the Egyptian embassy in Moscow, using our most secure cipher, these messages to be deciphered only by Hassan Sabry el-Kholi. So at 6.30 the Ministry of Foreign Affairs rang up our ambassador, el-Kouni, telling him that his presence at the ministry was required immediately. As there would be no embassy car available at that hour, a special car for the minister would be outside the embassy in five minutes. El-Kouni thought something terrible must have happened – perhaps there had been an ultimatum by the West. Hurriedly putting on a few clothes, he got into the waiting car, but was surprised to find that he was not being driven in the direction of the ministry – in fact the car seemed to be taking him out of Moscow. El-Kouni knocked on the glass partition separating him from the driver; the driver gestured but made no answer. El-Kouni thought he must be the victim of a kidnapping, but he could not think who was doing it or why. The car was being driven very fast, and all attempts to communicate with the driver failed. Finally the car swept into the grounds of Kaichova palace where el-Kouni saw Dr Fawzi and myself walking, deep in discussion. He got out and came over to us: 'Either I'm mad, or the Russians are mad,' said el-Kouni. 'Or we are mad,' I added. Just then Nasser came out of the building, and el-Kouni had the biggest shock of his life.

At ten o'clock Khruschev duly arrived. Nasser was waiting for him at the front door, but Khruschev knew his way around and came in through a door at the back, so we found him behind us. 'I'm very glad you came,' he said. 'We were worried. We didn't want you to go into the Mediterranean in a small ship. The Mediterranean is full of people who would like to make you food for the fishes.'

As Khruschev talked it became clear that the Soviet leadership was fascinated by what had happened – but also scared. And once again the achievements of Arab nationalism failed to fit in with any conventional Marxist analysis. 'The imperialists know that their real battle is with you,' he said. 'For them you are the symbol of the Arabs' struggle! Let me drink a toast (at 10 am!) to your success. No! Today I won't drink any vodka. Today I am a Mussulman! From now on no drinking. I drink a toast in fruit juice to the Arabs' struggle, and to the health of the leader of all the Arabs!' This last was a significant phrase, and one deliberately chosen. It transpired that the Soviet leaders had met and decided to make Egypt the coordinating centre for all their dealings with the Arabs – a resolution which they found themselves unable to keep.

* * *

The discussions began, and I took notes. Nasser described the situation as he saw it. He thought it unlikely that the Americans and British would be satisfied with simply landing a few troops in Beirut and Amman; this would have to be the prelude to something bigger. 'That is why I came here,' he said, 'because I want to know exactly what your position is.'

Khruschev replied. 'First of all,' he said, 'I want you to know that we are strong – stronger than the Americans imagine. This fleet they are deploying in the Mediterranean, with a crazy admiral in command, can easily be destroyed. We have weapons that can turn the American Sixth Fleet into coffins of melting iron for its sailors. But the real problem is not one of weapons; it's one of peace or war. The situation is a highly dangerous one, and I think that the people with the strongest nerves will be the winners. That is the most important consideration in the power struggle of our time. The people with weak nerves will go to the wall.

'We are now involved in a game that is being played at a very high speed, and in which everyone has to act quickly, without being able to judge what the other players are going to do. It is like playing chess in the dark. The confidence of the West is shattered. The Iraqi revolution took them completely by surprise. Dulles never understood anything. He is always talking about democracy and religion, but he doesn't know anything about religion. If the God he worships is really there, I think I am closer to that God than this pseudo-priest.

'Now the Baghdad Pact has disappeared at a stroke. Can we imagine a Baghdad Pact without Baghdad? Can we imagine Baghdad ranged against the Baghdad Pact? This consideration alone is enough to give Dulles a nervous breakdown. I want you to know what Eden told Bulganin and me when we were in London in 1956. Eden said that if he saw a threat to Britain's oil supplies in the Middle East he would fight. He was talking quite seriously, and what has just happened shows this. Nothing we said could soothe his fears. I asked him to use his intelligence. What can the Arabs do with their oil, I said. The Soviet Union doesn't want Arab oil. We produce more oil than we need. We aren't potential buyers of the Arab oil; it's you who are the natural buyers. Mind you,' added Khruschev – but to us, not to Eden – 'there's a difference between a buyer and a thief. The Western powers don't want to buy the oil; they want to steal it. Now, the revolution in Iraq is a threat to that oil. I don't know anything about the new leaders in Iraq, but it is most important that they should reassure the West that its supplies of oil will not be interrupted. You must play your hand very cautiously. Remember, this is a game of nerves. We live in a difficult age. The possibility of a nuclear war is always there, but the moments of greatest risk are in the first shock of new events. If you can get through this period all right, you will be safe. The West must be made to believe that you are ready to come to an understanding with them. In your hour of victory you must show yourself flexible.'

Nasser said he wholly agreed with Khruschev's analysis. 'But,' he said, 'it's important that the West should feel that the Soviet Union is prepared to take up a strong position. Would you, for example, consider putting out a statement to the effect that the Soviet Union is prepared to intervene if the West invades or threatens invasion?'

'That would complicate matters,' said Khruschev, 'because it would raise the temperature, and at this point suddenly raising it could produce unforeseeable consequences. Already the temperature is near boiling-point. We shouldn't do anything to aggravate it.'

'But they must feel that you are prepared to be firm,' said Nasser.

'They will feel it all right,' said Khruschev.

Discussion continued along these lines for some time, and then at about 11.30 Khruschev had to go to a meeting of the Politburo. He said he would be back for lunch with us, but in fact it was not until three that he reappeared. Then he informed us that it had been decided to increase the scale of the Warsaw Pact manœuvres due to take place near the Bulgarian–Turkish frontier. He said that a lot of publicity would be given to these manœuvres the next day, and he thought this would have its effect. Marshal Gretchko would be in command of half a million troops, though of course it must be made plain that these were only manœuvres. The new rulers of Iraq, he emphasized once again, would have to play their part by giving the West suitable assurances.

Khruschev had obviously been enormously struck by the upsurge of nationalist fervour in Iraq, and by the crowds of demonstrators there acclaiming Nasser almost like a demigod. 'These people are your men,' he said. He asked if we knew the new Iraqi leaders. Nasser said that they had already made contact with us: 'We understand from Cairo that they have asked us for military aid. We can easily give them all they want because in Britain's former canal base there are a lot of arms and ammunition of the right sort for the Iraqi army. So we've started an airlift for them, and we've already got a liaison mission in Baghdad.'

Khruschev asked Nasser a great many questions about conditions in Iraq and other Arab countries – about language, religion, customs, and about the Hashemite family and its religious status. Finally he asked the direct question which had obviously been all the time at the back of his mind. 'Is there,' he said, 'a chance of you and Iraq joining together?' 'I don't know,' said Nasser. 'But I do know that Iraq is going to face a lot of difficult problems, and unity shouldn't add a complicating factor to those problems. Iraq is very different from Syria, and there are enough problems between Egypt and Syria. I think there will probably be some sort of link between the UAR and Iraq, but the exact nature of the link will be determined by many circumstances, and it would be wrong to try to define it before I have been in touch with the new leaders in Baghdad to review the position.'

Khruschev was particularly impressed when he heard that some of Nasser's supporters had taken over the headquarters of the Baghdad Pact. 'So now we are taking all the documents we found there back to Cairo,' said Nasser. Khruschev's eyes bulged, and Serov's mouth watered.

The atmosphere became more relaxed, with an exchange of jokes and stories. Nasser had said he wanted to stop in Damascus on his way back to Cairo because this was obviously the centre of the storm, and Serov was waiting for a reply from the Russian ambassador in Tehran who had been instructed to wake up the Shah if necessary, and ask, in Khruschev's name, for permission to be given for a Soviet plane to overfly Iranian territory. This came through at about 10 pm, and we flew south to Baku. The airport there was an extraordinary sight; the manœuvres had already begun, and there must have been 500 to 600 planes arranged wing to wing on the tarmac. As we were breakfasting a general in the Soviet Air Force came up and showed us a copy of the communique about the manœuvres which had been issued, and which was couched in suitably dramatic terms.

In Damascus Nasser emphasized the need for victory to be tempered with magnanimity. The Soviet Union was behind us, he said, and he did not wish to quarrel with anybody. But almost immediately he ran into trouble. Abdel Salam Aref, Qasim's deputy, had come to Damascus to see Nasser, and inevitably the question of unity came up. Although both Qasim and Aref were believers in the general concept of Arab unity, the application of the idea had already become a source of friction between them, Aref speaking strongly in its favour and Qasim preferring a looser federation. Nasser told Aref the debate about unity was an artificial one. He was not urging a federation or a total union or anything else. This was something, he said, that could properly be left on one side for the time being.

*   *   *

In spite of the understanding Nasser had reached with Khruschev, sources of friction between Egypt and the Soviet Union began to arise almost immediately. The Americans sent the Assistant Secretary of State, William Rountree, on another fact-finding mission to the Middle

East, and as usual this made the Russians suspicious. More serious was their demand for copies of the documents that had been found at the Baghdad Pact headquarters in Baghdad. For three days there was a debate as to whether or not to hand these over, but finally it was decided that this could not be done. The issue was really a matter of principle. If the Americans discovered that all their secrets had been turned over to the Russians they would accuse Egypt of being a Soviet puppet, and all future relations with Washington would be soured. So the Russians were told that, though their request could not be granted, they would be informed of anything in the documents which was felt to be of vital concern to them. They were not happy over this decision, and sent a senior diplomat, Nuritdin Mukhitdinov, to Cairo in an effort to clear the air. In this he succeeded, inasmuch as during his visit an agreement was reached for construction of the first phase of the High Dam.

As ambassador to Baghdad the Russians sent a senior diplomat, Grigory Zaitsev. Here things seemed to be going very much their way. They had made direct contact with Qasim and had found in him someone who appeared to be an alternative to Nasser. Perhaps he would even prove to be Nasser's superior, for he seemed to be relying heavily on the communists. His government consisted of an alliance between the National Democratic Party, the Kurdish Democratic Party, and the communists, all of whom opposed the idea of an organic linkup between Iraq and the UAR. By February supporters of unity had been ejected from the government.

Sensing that things were not going well between Egypt and the Soviet Union, the Americans were naturally eager to profit from the situation. When I met Raymond Hare, the American ambassador, at the beginning of November, he asked me if there was anything his government could do. I reported this back to Nasser who told me to ask if they would sell us wheat. This I did, and within twenty-four hours we received a favourable reply. In the coming six years Egypt was to receive $500m worth of wheat from the United States.

This deal with America was of course known to the Russians, and it was used by the communists as further evidence of Nasser's unreliability. Delegations from the Arab communist parties were in Moscow for the annual November celebrations. Why, they demanded, should the Soviet Union continue to support a man who flirts with the Americans and imprisons communists, while there is another charismatic leader in the Arab world who has shown himself willing to work closely with the communists?

After the November celebrations were over the banned Syrian Communist Party issued a statement calling for the dissolution of the UAR and its replacement by a looser federation. As this was a call for the destruction of the state it was in effect a treasonable statement. Many communists were arrested in both parts of the UAR, and in a speech at Port Said on December 23, the anniversary of the final withdrawal of the Anglo-French invasion forces two years before, Nasser obliquely attacked the communists and their backers, reminding his audience how the Arabs united to defeat the Tartar hordes coming from the East which had conquered Baghdad and threatened Syria.

So the honeymoon with the Soviet Union was at an end, and the quarrels began.

5

The End of the Honeymoon

MANY FOREIGN DELEGATIONS, including some from communist parties in Arab countries, had stayed on in Moscow after the November celebrations, preparing for the Twenty-first Congress of the CPSU which was due to be held at the end of January 1959. On January 8 there was a meeting, sponsored by the Italian communists, of those underground Egyptian communists who had escaped arrest, at which it was decided that all their groups should merge in a united Egyptian Communist Party. This was the first time there had been only one communist party in Egypt, and the announcement of the decision was made in Moscow with some pride. But unity lasted less than a year.

In his lengthy report to the Twenty-first Congress Khruschev hailed the success of the national liberation movements in the Arab world, mentioning both Nasser and Qasim by name. But he added: 'The Soviet Union never interferes, and has no intention of interfering, in the internal affairs of other countries. We cannot remain silent, however, in the face of the campaign being conducted in some countries against progressive people under the spurious guise of anti-communism. Since there have recently been statements against communism in the UAR, and accusations have been levelled against communists, I, as a communist, think it necessary to declare that it is wrong to accuse communists of helping to undermine and divide the national effort in the struggle against imperialism. Quite the contrary. There are no people more resolute and loyal in the struggle against the colonialists than the communists. We do not deny that we and some of the leaders of the UAR have divergent ideological views. But in questions of fighting imperialism, of consolidating the political and economic independence of the countries which have cast off the yoke of colonialism, in fighting the war danger, our positions coincide with theirs.'

Then Khruschev turned to and answered a phrase of Nasser's which had obviously irked him. Nasser was determined to show everybody that, by accepting Russia's assistance for constructing the

High Dam, Egypt had in no way surrendered its independence: 'We are ready for cooperation with the Soviet Union,' he had said, 'but we shall no more sell our freedom for roubles than for dollars.' On which Khruschev commented: 'They say they don't want to sell their independence for roubles. Let me remind them that we didn't impose our aid on them.'

Nasser replied immediately. Speaking from the balcony in Damascus from which the creation of the UAR had been announced a year before he said: 'Yes, there is an ideological difference between us. We have never denied this, but also we never thought that it would hinder our cooperation. We always thought that friendship between us would be a good example of peaceful cooperation between two countries of different ideologies and different sizes, one a superpower and one small. We always agreed with the Soviet Union that the principles of the *pancha sheela* [the five principles adopted by the Colombo powers before the Bandung conference as a code of behaviour governing international relations, the most important of which were respect for the national independence of states and non-interference by one state in the internal affairs of another] were to be respected. But what we have heard of Khruschev's speech yesterday is a deviation from them. He has tried to interfere in a very important matter. Four months ago, in the Polish embassy in Moscow, Khruschev said that if I put communists in prison in Egypt that was entirely my affair. We didn't start a crusade against the communists – we tried to stop communists from sabotaging the union of Egypt and Syria. Even if Mr Khruschev is a communist this doesn't give communists any special sanctity. If Mr Khruschev wants to be reminded of communists who by his own criteria were very bad men I need only recall the names of Stalin, Malenkov, Beria, Kaganovich, Zhukov, Molotov, and finally Bulganin himself. What is Mr Khruschev trying to tell me? That it is not permissible to attack communists? We don't dislike them – some of my best friends are communists. Marshal Tito is a communist; I respect him. Chou En-Lai is a communist; I respect him. Mr Khruschev himself is a communist; I respect him. . . .'

★   ★   ★

It was in Iraq that the dispute between Nasser and Khruschev on the role of communist parties was to be put to the test. At the beginning of 1959 the Iraqi Communist Party was becoming increasingly wild in its actions. It is a characteristic of communist parties everywhere in the Third World that, when a political opportunity seems to be opening for them, they rush in impetuously in an effort to exploit it up to the hilt. Like the Syrian Communist Party, the Iraqi communists felt, with some reason, that in the long run circumstances were against them, and that their only chance of success lay in the immediate seizure of power. So they tried to make Qasim their captive, wholly dependent on them for survival. They intensified their propaganda throughout the country, even to the extent of printing forged documents in their party newspaper. The most elaborate of these was supposed to be a directive to all ranks of the Egyptian army, including a speech by Nasser. It read: 'General Commander of the Armed Forces. Office of the Commander-in-Chief. Special Order No 44. Directive by President Nasser. We are meeting today to review our plans whereby Egypt can realize its objective of creating one country from the Gulf to the Atlantic. The aeroplanes which are capable of reaching Tel Aviv in one hour are also able to reach Tripoli, Khartoum and Riyadh. I hope that I shall not be obliged to achieve our ends by violence, but, as you know, we have built up our armed forces and put all our resources behind them so that they may be made the instrument for the realization of Arab unity under the leadership of Egypt. Our armed forces were not created simply to parade through the streets of Cairo. Those who think that unity can be achieved by words or by persuasion are mistaken. All those who cherish such an illusion should open their eyes and consider the state of Egypt's armed forces. I am convinced that other Arab countries and their leaders will day by day become more accustomed to recognizing our armed forces as the weapon by which unity can be achieved, and that in this way our forces will be able to impose their protection on the lands beyond our frontiers.'

This document which was probably forged by the intelligence service of Israel or Britain, since it had turned up once before in Jordan at a time when Egypt's relations with that country were at a low ebb, was broadcast by Baghdad radio, and reproduced in the Soviet trade union newspaper, *Trud*.

The Iraqi communists realized that the main obstacle to the success of their plans was the army. Though they had had some success in infiltrating it, the main bulk of the officers were nationalists, who either wanted Iraq to be genuinely independent or supported Arab unity. It was not the troops in and around Baghdad that the communists had to fear, so much as those in the provinces. On December 23, the day of Nasser's speech in Port Said, some army units in Mosul had arranged a tea party to commemorate the Egyptian victory of 1956. The local communist party secretary, by name Kamal Kazinji, chose the occasion to distribute leaflets attacking Egypt, but the military police stopped his car and confiscated the leaflets. He went to the Officers' Club to protest, and there he happened to meet Colonel Adbel Wahab Shawwaf, brother of the Minister of Health and commander of the Fifth Brigade, which was part of the Second Division. Colonel Shawwaf looked at the leaflets, which advocated a federation between Egypt and Syria to replace the existing union: 'So you want to break up the UAR do you?' he asked. Kazinji agreed that he did, whereupon the officers kicked him out. (In the chaotic days which followed he was shot dead in a latrine by a nationalist NCO who had told him 'I'm taking you where you belong.')

Communists in Mosul as well as in Baghdad were busily infiltrating all the organizations they could – student unions, peace groups and bodies calling themselves 'Democratic Youth', 'The League for the Defence of Workers' Rights', and 'The League for Constitutional Democracy'. Now communists began to attack what they described as 'militarism in the north', and to mention by name the Second Division and the Fifth Brigade. An open letter to General Qasim in the communist newspaper demanded a purge of 'disloyal officers' in these units.

Then, towards the end of February 1959, it was announced that a demonstration by 'partisans of peace', sponsored by the communist party, was to be held in Mosul on March 6. Four trains, supplemented by buses hired from the Rafidain Company, were to proceed from Baghdad to Mosul in what was called 'a march of peace', but reports reaching Mosul suggested that the trains were filled with arms, and the communists themselves talked of 'invading' Mosul. The commander of the Second Division contacted military intelligence and asked, without success, to speak to Qasim, to warn him that the situation was highly explosive.

Colonel Shawwaf came to the conclusion that he might be compelled to act. He got in touch with Colonel Sarraj in Damascus and asked if he could send in Syrian troops through Deir el-Zor. Sarraj explained that this was impossible, so Shawwaf asked for a mobile broadcasting unit. This was sent, and on March 7 'Proclamation No 1', declaring the Baghdad regime illegal and calling for the formation of a new Revolutionary Command Council, was issued. But Shawwaf had miscalculated. He had thought that no army units would be prepared to move against him, and he had forgotten that the commander of the Iraqi Air Force was a communist. Qasim brought the Air Force into action, and luckily for him one of the first bombs dropped scored a direct hit on army headquarters in Mosul, wounding Shawwaf. He was taken to hospital, where, on March 9, one of the male nurses, a communist, stabbed him to death with a bayonet.

The nationalist forces in the north were left in complete disarray; some fled, some surrendered. There was nothing the UAR could do to assist them, and the communists moved in to exact their revenge. Full rein was given to the violent forces which are never far below the surface in Iraq. It is estimated that between six and eight thousand people were killed in Mosul, hundreds of them in a particularly revolting manner, being compelled to dig their own graves and then shot.

In spite of this the Soviet Union continued to give Qasim its full support, and on the occasion of the signing in Moscow on March 16, 1959, of an agreement with Iraq on economic and technical cooperation, Khruschev took the opportunity to needle Nasser. 'What will our relations with Egypt be now?' he asked. 'I think they will be the same as they were before. After all, when we built up our friendly relations with the UAR we were well aware of President Nasser's anti-communist views. True, we thought that more tolerance and more attention to the democratic demands of the people would be shown by the national liberation struggle because it requires the union of all anti-imperialist forces, but instead, unfortunately, measures are now being taken to suppress their freedom-loving aspirations. We would like to state, as friends, that if this policy is continued it will inevitably fail. Nasser wants to annex Iraq. As I see it he is a hot-headed young man who has taken on more than he can manage.'

Once again Damascus was the scene for Nasser's answer. 'Abdel Nasser is not the only one who is passionate and hot-headed,' he told the crowd there on March 22, 'but the whole Arab people ... without this hot-headedness our country would have been turned into rocket bases against the Soviet Union and into western bases against the socialist and communist world. With that same hot-headedness we shall face the new danger, just as we faced dangers in the past. We shall achieve victory against the new agents of communism.'

This was hard-hitting stuff. But Nasser was careful not to refer directly to the Soviet Union, only to *agents* of communism. He realized that if he was to assert his independence this would inevitably involve him in a clash with the Soviets, but never for a moment did he lose sight of his ultimate goal, which was to put relations between the UAR and the Soviet Union on a steady basis of normality, with as high a grade of treatment for the UAR as possible. His aim was to make the Soviets treat him as an equal partner, not to force a break with them. 'Always maintain your objective,' he used to say; that was the useful lesson his study of military history had taught him.

So now the measures which he took against the Soviet Union were always discreet. Thus, he allowed an Arabic version of a book *Life* magazine had produced on Russia's suppression of the Hungarian uprising to be printed in Cairo, but no publicity was to be given to it inside Egypt. He succeeded in making the Soviet leaders appreciate their need for cooperation with the independent Arab movement, without exasperating them.

But during the May Day Moscow celebrations of 1959 there was no mention of Nasser in the slogans or speeches. The only reference to Egypt was the slogan 'Long live friendship with the *people* of the UAR!' The Russian leaders were still trying to digest what had happened in Iraq. The massacres in Mosul had produced so strong a reaction against Qasim that his position was much weakened – a weakening highlighted by the nearly successful attempt on his life carried out in the main street of Baghdad by a group of Baathists on October 7.

★   ★   ★

Nasser's two closest political friends, Nehru and Tito, were uneasy at the way things were developing between the Soviet Union and the UAR, and tried to mediate between them. Tito was never really acceptable to the Russians as an intermediary, but he was worried lest Nasser's policy towards communism might impair a friendship which he had come to value. Nasser explained to him that he was in no sense conducting a campaign against communism in general, or against people for holding communist beliefs, but that he was obliged to take action against any group which engaged in conspiracies. All the same, Tito clearly felt some embarrassment. Nehru was the statesman in the best position to talk to both sides, and he brought the matter up with Khruschev when the latter was on a visit to India in February 1960. Khruschev insisted that the Soviet Union was not making any demands on the UAR – or on any state for that matter. 'We intend to go on conducting our relations with the UAR on the basis of equality and respect for sovereignty,' he told Nehru. He obviously saw that the quarrel with the UAR had alarmed all the other non-aligned countries.

In spite of attempts at restraint on both sides, new occasions for friction continued to arise. There were at this time a large number of Egyptian students in the Soviet Union, mostly on courses of engineering and other technical subjects. It had been agreed that in no circumstances were they to be subjected to any form of indoctrination. Now complaints began to be received by the special department in the Egyptian embassy dealing with students that they were being made to attend lectures on communist doctrine. Also, some of the privileges which they had enjoyed in happier times were being withdrawn. Girls studying nuclear physics, for example, had previously had separate rooms; now they were being put two or more in a room, and had been moved into the same building with the boys.

The Minister of Education complained about this to Nasser, who told me to go and see Raymond Hare, the American ambassador, and ask him if he could find places in the US for all our students in the Soviet Union, so that we could do a complete switch. It was now October. The academic year in the US had already begun. I explained the position to Hare, who asked me how many students were involved. When I told him there were 250 he put his head in his hands and groaned. 'We would like to do it,' he said, 'but how can we?' Anyway, the message went off to Washington, and three days later the reply came that places for all 250 had been found, enabling each of them to go on with his or her chosen course of study. So a special airlift of students from Russia was arranged, and they arrived in the US in a blaze of publicity. This was obviously an extremely bitter pill for the Russians to swallow, but they made no official protest or comment.

* * *

Both sides were in fact looking around for ways of patching up the quarrel. Ignatiy Novikov, the Russian Minister of Power Stations, came to Egypt in January 1959 for the start of the first phase of the High Dam, and Khruschev made him the bearer of a polite but reserved letter to Nasser, simply saying that the minister would be at Nasser's disposal for the discussion of any matters he wanted to raise. With the letter came a modest gift – a box of chocolates and a jar of caviar.

Nasser always made a point of meeting any Soviet minister, and he was anxious to have a talk with Novikov before the official ceremony at Aswan. So a meeting was arranged which was also attended by Musa Arafa, the Minister of Public Works responsible for the High Dam, at which the letter and gifts were handed over. Nasser told Novikov that he considered the Aswan ceremony such an important occasion that he had had a gold medal struck to commemorate it. 'I want to send one to Mr Khruschev,' he said, 'so that he can wear it on the day of the ceremony.'

Nasser then asked Novikov how he thought the work on the High Dam was going. Novikov told him he thought that the division which had been made between the first and the second phases of construction was largely artificial, and would only create trouble and add to costs: 'For example, we are proposing to move large quantities of rock in the first phase, but in the second phase, when the coffer dam is being built, we shall have to bring them all back. If the two phases were combined we could move the rock straightaway to where it is wanted.'

Egyptian experts had already seen this problem and calculated that it would add between 25 and 30 per cent to the cost of the first phase. So Nasser told Novikov they too had always thought the separation into two phases was artificial. 'But would Mr Khruschev be willing to discuss the second phase now? I am making this request officially.' Novikov was taken by surprise, and said that he would have to get into touch with Khruschev.

January 9 was the day of the Aswan ceremony, and Novikov had received no reply to Nasser's request. He stayed on in Egypt waiting for it. The Politburo met on January 17, and on the next day Novikov came triumphantly with the message that the Soviet Union had agreed to finance the second phase of constructing the High Dam. Khruschev suggested that, as time was short, this decision should be embodied in an exchange of letters between him and Nasser. A few days later

Khruschev was at an embassy party in Moscow. 'We have forgotten our quarrels with Egypt,' he said. 'It was all a misunderstanding and a waste of time.'

* * *

But misunderstandings were not at an end, though the next source of trouble was not the Soviet Union but Bulgaria. In January 1960 Sofia broadcast a special announcement, underlined by dramatic music: 'A great Egyptian nationalist and fighter for peace and freedom, Brigadier Yusuf Mansour Siddiq, has died in gaol after being subjected to unheard of tortures at the hands of the police.' The item was rebroadcast several times. Nasser read about it, checked, and found it was completely untrue. Brigadier Siddiq had, in the early days of the revolution, been a member of the Revolutionary Command Council, though after he confessed to being a communist he had been asked to resign. However, he continued to draw his pension, and had remained on friendly terms with Nasser. Nasser rang him up. 'Do you know what Radio Sofia is saying about you?' he asked. Brigadier Siddiq said he did not, so Nasser said he would send him a transcript. 'Why don't you tell them it's not true?' Nasser suggested.

The next day the brigadier went round to the Bulgarian embassy. The ambassador was away, but the chargé d'affaires was there, and to him the brigadier submitted a letter backing up the physical evidence that he was alive and untortured, asking for the broadcasts to be stopped since they 'do not help relations between the people of Bulgaria and the people of the UAR'. There were plenty of photographers present to record the brigadier's visit to the embassy, and next morning the story was all over the papers.

* * *

However, neither side wanted to make too much of the incident, and relations with the Soviet Union had improved sufficiently for a UAR delegation to be invited for the Moscow May Day celebrations of 1960. It was headed by Anwar Sadat, at that time President of the People's Assembly. Khruschev received the delegation in his office on May 3; Sadat made a polite speech and Khruschev's reply began equally politely. He spoke of his pleasure in being able to take part in both phases of the High Dam, a project which would prove 'a great blow to American imperialism. We have proved that small countries can achieve great things without the participation of the imperialists.'

Then he launched out into a sweeping attack on everything American – the Soviet man had circled the world; the American man was still waiting his chance. The Soviet system was more advanced than the American, and in 1970 the Soviet Union would catch up America. 'America is very rich: they are capitalists. But where do they spend their money? We aren't as rich as America, but we spend more on education than the US does. In our country everybody is educated on an equal basis. Those who want to learn should be able to do so without paying anything. We give them a place in a university with free accommodation. This is only done in communist countries. We want to take you along with us to our victory, but you don't want communism. All right; we aren't angry. The future will show you that we are right.'

At this point Sadat tried to put in a few words about the right of every country to choose its own path, but Khruschev was not to be halted; all the frustrations and arguments that had been building up inside him came pouring out. 'We follow that principle too,' he said. We always say that you can't drive people to paradise with a stick. We respect other people's principles and systems. You have liberated yourselves, and I see your chests bursting with nationalism, but nationalism isn't the summit of happiness. Perhaps you think I want to change you from Arab nationalists to communists. I don't want to do that, but I can see from some of your faces that some of you will in future become communists ... You Arabs started to understand – you said you wanted socialism, but you don't understand what that is. If we look at things scientifically, socialism is the first phase of communism, and that means you aren't even in the first phase. You don't understand what you're talking about. You want to build socialism; so how can you say bad things about communism? You are still in the ABC stage of political science. You aren't even at A – socialism is the A of the ABC of the organization of human society. If you say you want socialism how can you say you're against communism? You are getting yourselves into a very awkward position. You are falling into an imperialist trap. I am warning you, speaking quite frankly – communism is sacred. We want to be friendly with everyone, but choosing other systems we leave to other people.'

There was a good deal more in the same vein. Sadat was taken by surprise and the meeting ended on a sour note. When a full report of what Khruschev had said reached Cairo, Nasser was furious. 'If we let this go without answering it,' he said, 'he'll think we've taken it lying down.' So it was agreed that Sadat should send a reply, and that I should prepare a draft for it.

Sadat's reply pointed out that there had been no chance at the Moscow meeting for the UAR delegation to explain its point of view, and in any case it had not wanted to turn the meeting into an ideological debate, 'but we think your frankness demands equal frankness in return.' Sadat pointed out the good relations Egypt enjoyed with a number of communist countries, the admiration felt for great leaders of communism – Marx, Lenin, 'and you, with all you did for your country.' 'But you must not forget,' he went on, 'that the October Revolution has been in power for 43 years. We only started an Arab revolution eight years ago, and most of this time has been taken up in confronting imperialism, facing economic and psychological wars, and even armed intervention . . . Arab nationalism, in which we believe, does not have a narrow sectarian outlook. It has nothing to do with territorial expansion, but is a movement by people who share the same history, who talk the same language, and so are united in their feelings and thinking. I hope that when you said you did not want to convert us from Arab nationalists into communists this was something that will apply to the future as much as to the present. Like you we feel that in the end history will decide between our different ideologies . . . . One of the things about our own revolution of which we are particularly proud is that even in bad times it kept its reputation clean. It has not been a revolution of purges and massacres, executions and concentration camps.

'Regarding the merits of communism – we do not believe that the historical process of mankind up to now has shown that there were only two stages, with capitalism representing the beginning and communism the end. This would leave us with no way forward. But we think there are many roads which have been opened by the creative ideas of peoples with different ideologies and experiences . . . We believe too, Mr Chairman, in moral factors, including religion. We consider that development must take note of moral as well as material values. But as far as Arab nationalism is concerned we do not see any reason why this should conflict with our belief in peaceful coexistence

... We reject capitalism, not just because we hate it, but because we think it does not suit the nature of our people, or their hopes and needs. But if we reject capitalism this does not mean that communism is the only choice left for us; though it has succeeded in other conditions this does not mean that it would necessarily succeed in conditions here. Our people will never let themselves be limited to two choices only. We believe the horizon of man's hopes is wider than this narrow vision, and that our people do not need to cut themselves off from the rich intellectual heritage of the whole world. On the contrary, we think that they can share in it and contribute to it.

'In sum, Mr Chairman, you are making the same error as the capitalists make when they claim that there is no alternative to capitalism but communism – the error which they use to justify waging war against us on the ground that the road to independence must lead eventually to communism.'

★   ★   ★

The General Assembly of the United Nations in the autumn of 1960, which was attended by an unprecendented number of heads of state and government, including Khruschev, Castro, Macmillan and Nasser, provided another opportunity for remedial diplomacy. Nasser was anxious that the dispute with the Soviets should not linger on. We had made our point, and the important thing now was to get back onto as mutually beneficial a level as possible.

But Khruschev was in a strange mood in New York. Events in the Congo cast their shadow, and Khruschev had a feeling that many of the Third World leaders – men like Modibo Keita and Sekou Touré as well as Tito, Nehru and Nasser – were showing signs of forming too much of a bloc of their own and not giving sufficient support to Soviet attitudes. Nasser met Khruschev twice, once in New York and once in the Long Island country house belonging to the permanent Soviet delegation to the UN, but these were unsatisfactorily meetings, much of the time being wasted on raking over old arguments. Nasser told Khruschev that he disapproved of the shoe-banging episode at the UN – a message which Khruschev also received from Nehru and Tito.

6

Normalization

1961 WAS THE YEAR of the breakup of the United Arab Republic, but it was also the year which saw many positive developments at home and abroad. A five-year plan had been inaugurated in July 1960, and it led directly to the socialist legislation of July 19 and 20, 1961, which included sweeping acts of nationalization and further measures of land reform. There were further developments in the fields of education, health and social insurance. Internationally, the UAR, as a result of developments in the Congo and elsewhere, became identified as one of the leaders of the so-called 'Casablanca Bloc' of radical African states, which were generally in opposition to the conservative 'Malagasy Bloc' states still under the influence of their former imperial master, France.

So both internally and externally Egypt seemed to be moving in a progressive direction, and as usual there were those who, through ignorance or malice, interpreted this as meaning that Egypt was falling under the influence – or into the arms – of the Soviet Union. So we felt it necessary to make clear the distinction we drew between socialism, which we practised, and communism, which we rejected. After a number of discussions on this subject I was asked to draft a summary of our conclusions and produced a seven-point statement, which was approved and subsequently published:

1. It is essential to avoid bloodshed in the social struggle. If the social struggle is allowed to escalate during a period of tension, when the two superpowers are ranged against each other, each with its supporters inside developing countries, it will be difficult or impossible to avoid civil war. A progressive main stream must be established with sufficient authority to ensure the orderly execution of the desired social and economic changes, however radical these are.

2. Private ownership remains important, though strict bounds must be set to it.

3. Assets subject to nationalization should not be taken over without reasonable compensation being offered to their former owners.

4. Stress must be laid on the role of the individual in society, not simply on the role of the state.

5. The communist – or rather Stalinist – doctrine that it is legitimate to sacrifice three or four generations in order to build happiness and prosperity for future unborn generations must be rejected. The Egyptian people have the right to an immediate recompense for their past sufferings. Russian arguments in favour of a concentration on the development of heavy industry cannot be fully accepted. The current five-year plan, therefore, while including provision for heavy industry, lays emphasis on increasing the supply of consumer goods, for the production of which Egypt is already equipped. This will simultaneously meet the requirements of the people and avoid the danger of inflation.

6. We must not be tied down to a narrow choice between two ideological doctrines, forged in the nineteenth century and now assuming the proportions of holy writ, though lacking the spiritual authority of the Koran or the Bible.

7. We believe that it is possible, once the former exploiting class has been isolated, to form a popular alliance between the remaining classes which can, by evolutionary stages, effect the transfer of wealth from the minority to the majority.

This statement may or may not have helped to explain things to the Soviet leaders; there was certainly a great deal to mystify them in what was going on in Egypt. The July laws, which they had looked on with approval, had been one of the causes of the breakup of the UAR. Following the breakup, reactionary forces took over in Syria, but the Syrian Communist Party, always hostile to the union, joined with the separatists, so we had the strange sight of Khaled Bakdash, the communist, hand in hand with people like Maamun el-Kuzbari, the feudalist. The Iraqi Communist Party, too, welcomed the demise of the UAR, as Qasim himself was becoming increasingly dependent upon a strange alliance of opportunists. By contrast Egypt's answer to the breakup was the arrest of a large number of 'reactionaries and feudalists' and the sequestration of their property, and preparation for a new political organization from which 'reactionaries' would be excluded. Intrigued by what was going on the Soviets sent a number of people to investigate, including Satiakov, the editor of *Pravda*, and I myself invited Alexei Adzhubei and his wife Rada, Khruschev's daughter, to come and see for themselves, which they did.

Khruschev had strong family feelings, and these could sometimes get him into trouble, as a story from about this time illustrates. El-Kouni was due to leave Moscow after a very successful term as ambassador there, and in the course of a farewell audience Khruschev said to him, 'I am watching with admiration what is being done in Egypt, though I don't altogether understand the way in which you are doing it. Where exactly do you stand ideologically? We can't make President Nasser out.' Then he became more confidential. 'By the way, Mr Ambassador,' he said, 'I have a question I want to put to you, and to you alone. You must not repeat it to President Nasser. Why does Nasser criticize members of my family?' El-Kouni was shocked and said he could not believe this. Khruschev said he had heard reports that the Egyptians thought Adzhubei drank too much and asked for favours. El-Kouni said he knew that the Adzhubeis had been the guests of a close friend of the President's, and had seen Nasser several times, but he couldn't believe that he had criticized them. 'All right – forget it,' said Khruschev. 'But promise me not to tell Nasser.' El-Kouni promised, though obviously he had to report the conversation. It came out later that what had happened was that some members of the Politburo, annoyed at the growing responsibilities given to Khruschev's son-in-law, had attributed to Egyptian sources criticisms of him which they wished to make themselves.

*   *   *

Through most of 1962 relations between Egypt and the Soviet Union continued fairly fluid. The Soviets were impressed by the National Charter of Socialist Principles, which was presented to the Congress of Popular Forces by Nasser in a five-hour speech on May 21. In this speech he spoke of the dire need to create a new Vanguard among the popular forces, henceforward to be represented in an Arab Socialist Union. Soviet theoreticians, such as Ulianovsky, thought they could discern in the Vanguard the nucleus of a new progressive party.

But, though the Soviets were still uncertain which pigeonhole to place Egypt in, they continued to give it special consideration. Throughout the summer Cairo received a steady flow of communications from them, providing information about all happenings that might be thought to be of interest to Egypt. But in the autumn came the Cuba crisis, and all else was forgotten. When at last they were able to divert their attention from Cuba, and take a look at what was going on in the Middle East, they found a new problem confronting them – Yemen.

The Soviet Union, as has been seen, had had some early but tenuous relations with Yemen. Now this tip of the Arabian peninsula, backing onto the world's largest oilfields and opening onto the sea routes to India, was clearly of more significance than it had been in the twenties. The revolution which overthrew the monarchy in Sanaa and touched off the civil war took place on September 26, 1962. By October Egypt was deeply involved on the republican side, and as soon as the Soviets were again able to pay attention to such matters they found a request from Cairo for transport planes to make possible the airlift of troops to Yemen which the republicans stood in urgent need of. Only three days after this request was made the huge Antonov troop carriers – equivalent to the American C130s – started to arrive in Cairo.

Little more than four months later another Arab regime – and one which concerned the Soviet Union more closely – was in its turn to be violently overthrown. General Qasim died in the ruins of the television building on February 8, 1963. A junta of nationalists and Baathists seized power, and proceeded to take a bloody revenge on the communists.

It was all very bewildering for the Russians, and observers in Cairo watching their ideological machinery turning over, trying to process the new facts which were being fed into it, found themselves in their turn seeking answers to some fundamental questions about Russian intentions. What did they really want? Was it simply to be able to exert influence in the area, or to liquidate the influence exerted by the West? Did they aim at consolidating a territorial position in the Middle East, or simply at using any position they might have there as what later came to be called 'linkage' in their negotiations with the West? It was impossible to come to any firm conclusions.

*   *   *

As usual at a time of crisis, Cairo received a visit from Ulianovsky. Talks with him showed that he and other theoreticians had been paying more attention to Africa, and he was much taken by the idea that there were now 60 to 65 underdeveloped countries, either already members of the UN or about to join it, which could play a highly significant role. These countries were linked by common hostility to the imperialism from which they had escaped and were, as he and his colleagues saw it, bound to follow the non-capitalist road to development. This later became a most useful expression. It fitted countries like Egypt, which had shown that they had no intention of becoming communist, and it received the sanction of orthodoxy from the doctrine dating back to Lenin's time, which laid down that the peoples of the East could move direct to socialism without passing through the phase of capitalism.

Between them these countries could claim 65 per cent of the world's population, but only ten per cent of the world's production, 25 per cent of its trade turnover, 40 per cent of its agricultural and animal production, and 12 per cent of its reserve currencies, including gold. The productivity of the workers in these countries was only eight to nine per cent of that of workers in industrialized countries, and their income only ten per cent. The external debts of these countries amounted to ten billion dollars and were still increasing. The industrialised countries invested seven to nine billion dollars in them annually, but drew from them in profits from investment 17 to 22 billion dollars. The raw materials and the labour forces in these countries were exploited by others; their agriculture remained backward; the technological revolution was passing them by.

The conclusion which Ulianovsky drew from all this was that a genuine revolutionary situation existed in a majority of Third World countries, which the Soviet Union should not ignore. It was a situation which must produce anti-imperialist nationalisms, but these would have to respond to the social demands of the people. The resulting regimes would have to have a progressive outlook, with development channelled through the public sector. But there would have to be an important role in them for the bourgeoisie as managers. Thus a new form of social development, quite distinct from previous forms, was to be looked for. It would be non-capitalist, based on a working class in the countryside and in an industry still in the process of formation, and inevitably supported by certain elements of the bourgeoisie. The task of the socialist countries (in other words, of the Soviet Union) must be to make this process irreversible. How could this be done? First, the Soviet Union must always encourage the non-capitalist road to development; next, it must try to help the nationalist leaders and make them understand that there is no alternative to cooperation with the socialist camp.

Of course, Ulianovsky's analysis went on, there are difficulties. Many of the new nationalist leaders are of the personal, charismatic type, easily removed from the scene. Again, some elements of the bourgeoisie are bound to abandon public sector development to become business partners of world capitalism, and spread their corruption through even the best bureaucracies. Then there are other influences – religious, tribal, family – which have to be taken into account, and which are capable of using the slogans of socialism and exploiting them for their own benefit. It will not always be easy to distinguish between the true and the false regimes. But communists must take all these factors into consideration and learn to profit from them. They must work among the people, and persuade them that they, the communists, represent the most nationalist, the most democratic and the most revolutionary forces in society. Now is the time for all communist movements to aim at working with – even merging with – the nationalist forces, and by so doing convince them that hostility to communism and persecution of communists weakens the struggle for national and social freedom, and that any dispute between nationalists and communists can only result in making both the victims of the imperialists and reactionaries.

Communists, Ulianovsky continued, must understand that students are an extremely important and active element in these emerging countries, but that, because of their lack of experience, they are always liable to misdirection by forces ready to exploit their readiness for revolutionary action, their patriotism and their eagerness for quick results. Abuse of student potential can easily obstruct progress. The communists must therefore make every effort to encourage student participation, thus securing for them experience and responsibility.

Finally, concluded Ulianovsky, the problems faced by these new regimes include a lack of clear programmes for the social transformation of their countries, a tendency to appease imperialism, and the practice of a narrow nationalism which, especially among peasants and illiterates, can easily be perverted into anti-communist channels. This is something of which communists must beware. The experience of communist parties in Africa, Asia and Latin America has shown that it is essential for the working class not to isolate itself from the non-proletarian elements of society, but rather to establish the strongest possible ties with them.

Ulianovsky, who was preparing his report for the forthcoming congress of the Soviet party, described Egypt as 'a leader of the anti-imperialist struggle for the peoples of Africa and Asia'. So, theoretically at least, Egypt was back in official favour. It had become one of the shining examples of the 'non-capitalist road to development', and the Russians were continually bombarding Cairo with advice as to what should be done next.

The Soviet Union was very active at this period in all Third World countries. Instructions had gone to local communist parties that, in line with the Ulianovsky report, they should associate themselves with the nationalist forces, and Moscow backed this up with its advice on the formation of national fronts. The governments of Egypt, Syria (where there was a series of coups following the breakup of the UAR) and even Iraq were treated to lectures on the merits of the Ulianovsky programme. Certainly, they were told, leadership should be in nationalist hands, but behind the leadership should be a broader-based political alliance, including of course the communists. It must be admitted that there was some reciprocity in all this. It was at about this time that delegations from the Arab Socialist Union began to be welcome visitors in cadre schools in the Soviet Union, and even to be received by the Central Committee.

★　　★　　★

But these developments had an upsetting effect on those Egyptian communists who were still in prison. Their outlook on events had preserved a pristine simplicity. When, towards the end of 1961, the estates of so many wealthy Egyptians were nationalized, they regarded this as simply a quarrel between two rival bourgeois groups – the Banque Misr group, backed by the elements which promoted the 1952 revolution, was, as they saw it, liquidating the Abboud Pasha group. But then the ideas outlined in the Ulianovsky report were smuggled into their prisons, and they learned that they were expected to line up by the side of the nationalist movement. At once Egyptian gaols became a hive of self-criticism, and by the time the National Charter had been published in May 1962 and the new constitution came into effect, most of the communists had been released.

But, though they tried to adjust to the new circumstances, the Egyptian communists never really understood them. They continued to mistrust the concept of the ASU, which they regarded as an attempt to 'nationalize the class struggle' and so freeze it. They failed completely to understand the nature of Arab nationalism and how it is that every Arab leader must always be talking to a wider audience than his own people. They did not grasp how it was that the bourgeoisie in countries like Egypt, Syria and Iraq had been able to fill a large part of the gap left by the departure of the imperialists. They underrated the social, cultural and intellectual legacy which religion has left to the Arabs. They mistook the significance of the Arab–Israeli conflict and the complications arising from it. And they always felt that, however apparently cordial relations between Arab nationalists and the Soviet Union might be, there was an instinctive anti-communism lurking not far beneath the nationalist surface. Yet they themselves had their suspicions of the Russians, who seemed to them to be more concerned with their responsibilities as a superpower than as agents of the revolution. In the wake of the Cuban crisis everyone was obliged to make a reassessment of Soviet intentions. Nasser was one of many Third World leaders who was told by Castro that the Russians had not consulted him about their decision to withdraw their missiles from Cuba and that the first he knew of it was when he heard it on the radio.

Nothing had happened to change Nasser's view that the Soviets seemed incapable of understanding the meaning of Arab unity, or the nature of the Arab-Israeli struggle, or why it was that Egypt could never become communist, and that it was essential to go on trying to explain the Egyptian point of view on these matters to them. Now that relations with the Soviet Union seemed to be going so well, it would, he felt, be beneficial to make some dramatic gesture to emphasize the fact. The first phase of the High Dam was due to be completed in 1964, and many events seemed to be combining to highlight Cairo's position as the capital of the Third World. January 1964 was to see an Arab summit in Cairo; there was to be an African summit in July, and a non-aligned summit in October. The Russians let it be known that they were prepared to send a 'high-ranking delegation' for the High Dam ceremonies. The hint was taken. Would Khruschev himself be prepared to come? Within two days the answer came – yes, the chairman would be willing. The invitation was sent and accepted.

7

Grade A

THE SOVIET LEADERSHIP was anxious that the celebrations attending the completion of the first phase of the High Dam should be made a great occasion. All the leaders of Africa would be in Cairo in July, and the non-aligned leaders in October; all would want to go to see the High Dam. It would be seen as a victory for Egypt, and for all the under-developed countries of the Third World – a victory made possible by the skill and help of the Soviet Union.

I myself was to be closely connected with Khruschev's visit to Egypt. I had received an invitation to the May Day celebrations in Moscow, but had regarded this as a routine invitation to an occasion which I had by then already seen several times. So the last days of April found me in Sanaa, the capital of Yemen, taking another look at the war for my newspaper, and it was there that I received a telephone call from Alexei Adzhubei, Khruschev's son-in-law and editor of *Izvestia*. 'Why aren't you here?' he demanded. I explained that I had seen the May Day parade before. 'That's not the point,' he said. 'The idea is that you should come to Moscow, attend the celebrations, wait here till the big man (as he always called Khruschev) starts his journey to Egypt, and go with him to the Crimea and by sea to Alexandria. The big man has a lot of questions about Egypt he wants to ask, and he wants to be able to talk to someone who knows about Egypt and the Arab world and who isn't an official. So we thought of inviting you.' That was something completely different, and I said so.

It was obviously too late for me to be in Moscow in time for the parades, but there was a plane leaving Sanaa for Cairo in half an hour's time, and I was on it. Very early next morning I was in Cairo, where I found Nasser's secretary waiting for me at the airport with instructions that I was to go straight to the president's house. I saw Nasser, who told me he thought I should go on to Moscow at once. At a second meeting he gave me a summary of the topics which he wanted me to take up with Khruschev.

So it was late on the evening of May Day that I arrived in Moscow, only to find that I had left my yellow-fever certificate behind. The airport authorities provided me with a visa, but there was no way of getting round the health requirements. I was handed over to a stocky woman doctor who took me to the Sovietskaya Hotel, warned me not to leave my room for 36 hours, but said that I might receive visitors. My first visitor was Alexei Adzhubei who came to assure me of the great importance the leadership attached to Khruschev's visit. It was, after all, his first visit to an Arab country, and the Soviet Union had done so much for the Arabs. It would also be the first time he had set foot on African soil. 'There's nothing specific he wants to talk about,' said Alexei. 'He just wants someone who can answer any question that comes into his mind. So be prepared!'

One of those who had been invited to Moscow for the May Day celebrations was Ahmed Ben Bella, the charismatic leader of the Algerian revolution, and I could not help finding a certain irony in the reception being given him. It was not so long since we had been begging the Russians to make some reference to the Algerian revolutionary struggle in the joint communiques issued after our discussions with them, but they had always refused. Two considerations dictated this refusal. They had accepted the theory that the liberation of Algeria lay through the liberation of France – in other words, they accepted the settler argument that Algeria was a part of France – and that there must be a simultaneous revolution on both shores of the Mediterranean. They also had a very great respect for de Gaulle, and always treated him with considerable circumspection. They felt he was necessary for them in Europe as the only man who could stand up to the Americans. Yet now here was Ben Bella an official visitor in Moscow, just invested with the Order of Lenin and made a Hero of the Soviet Union.

I had breakfast with Ben Bella in the Kremlin. He was staying in the apartment which Nasser used to occupy. He told me that he had concentrated on two points in his discussions with Khruschev – Israel and Arab unity. 'I've tried a new argument on Khruschev,' he said, 'and one that I think he should understand. I've told him that Israel is incapable of being anything but reactionary because of its special links with imperialism and the US. At first he had thought Israel could be a progressive force in the Middle East, but I explained that that's against its nature. It is tied by an umbilical cord to the US. On the other hand Arab unity can never be anything but a progressive force because it's not the rulers who want it but ordinary people. The rulers have a privileged position thanks to the artificial frontiers in the Arab world, but the ordinary people don't see things in the same light. It is only through the masses that unity can be achieved.'

While we were talking Khruschev came in. 'So you arrived late!' he said. 'You've missed the celebrations!' I told him this was true, but that I had seen the popular celebrations in Gorki Street and other parts of Moscow. 'Well,' he said, 'we won't talk now. I'm taking our friend to the Crimea for a holiday, and we'll meet there. We'll have plenty of time for talking.'

★ ★ ★

Two days later Alexei Adzhubei picked me up early at my hotel. We went to the airport where we found all the people who were to come with us on the boat – Nina Petrovna, Khruschev's wife, and Rada, his daughter and Alexei's wife, Khruschev's son Sergei and his wife Galina, Alikhanov, the Prime Minister of Azerbaijan, Gromyko, Marshal Gretchko, Niporozhny, Minister for Electricity, Skatchkov, Minister of Economic Foreign Relations, Satyukov, the editor of *Pravda*, and his daughter Tanya, who was studying Arabic at Moscow University. Arrived at Yalta we went in a procession of cars through the mountains to a large house – almost a palace – by the sea, surrounded by attractive gardens. Khruschev was waiting to greet us, dressed in slacks, an open shirt and a broad brimmed hat. The atmosphere was relaxed and friendly – a family party.

Khruschev noticed that I was looking at a rock on the shore nearby which was surmounted by an enormous glass construction. 'Come along,' he said, 'I'll show you what that is.' He took me inside, and I found it was a vast swimming-pool, entiredly enclosed in glass and air-conditioned, so that it was possible to swim in it at any time of the year, even if outside it was snowing or the waves were breaking on the glass. It was a wonderful construction, completely equipped with bedrooms, a gymnasium, a room for massage and so on.

Lunch was on a balcony of the house, Khruschev showing true peasant hospitality, ready to do anything to ensure that his guests were enjoying themselves. I sat beside him throughout lunch, with an interpreter between us. 'Come, are you ready?' he asked. 'I'm going to be the journalist this time. I'll ask the questions, not you.' 'Mr Chairman,' I said, 'you must leave me some time for my questions.' 'No, no,' he insisted. 'No questions.'

Among those at this lunch was Petr Shelest, First Secretary of the Ukrainian Communist Party. What struck me particularly was the way in which Khruschev treated his colleagues – a sort of half serious banter, which could at times be embarrassing. For example, Shelest began an enthusiastic harrangue: 'Nicolai Sergeivich! Go on your trip, and don't worry about anything! Everything in the Ukraine is in splendid order! The grain harvest ...' and here he gave a lot of figures. Khruschev looked at him closely: 'Comrade,' he said, 'it seems to me you think I'm not going to come back from this trip, so you are very generous with your figures. But I am going to come back, and when I do you will have to give me a full account for all these figures.' Everybody laughed, but it wasn't entirely easy laughter.

The next day we all went on board the *Armenia*, the luxury passenger ship which was to take us to Alexandria. We sailed in the afternoon, and I went into the main saloon, where I found Khruschev. 'I didn't mean to come in here,' he said, 'there are too many cakes' (there were, indeed, a lot of large sweet cakes set out on a table). 'I shouldn't take any,' he went on, 'because I'm on a diet. When we get to Cairo you must tell them that I don't eat.' All the same he sat down, and took a cake. Then, though Rada tried to stop him, he took another. By the time he got up he had eaten six.

There was some talk about how we should spend the evening, and Khruschev asked Adzhubei to bring him a list of the films there were on board. None of them appealed to him, but he finally chose one called 'The Naked Diplomat'. He called to his Foreign Secretary: 'Gromyko, we're going to see this film just for your sake.' Then, turning to Gretchko, he added, 'You must count yourself lucky there isn't a film called "The Naked Marshal", otherwise we'd have seen that.'

At dinner a great deal of Armenian brandy was consumed. I sat beside Khruschev and noticed for the first time his curious way of drinking soup. First he poured a bit of soup from the cup into his plate, and then drank it from the side of the plate, without using a spoon. After dinner he again offered me a cigar.

The next morning Khruschev appeared on deck, in an open shirt and carrying a pair of binoculars. He called us to join him on the bridge. By then we were approaching the Bosphorus, and I saw that we had an escort of Turkish naval vessels, one ahead and one astern. Khruschev called Gretchko and gave him the binoculars. 'Look at these stupid people,' he said, 'they have got gun emplacements in those hills. But these are just children's toys and ought to be in a museum. Tell us what our new bombs can do, marshal!' Gretchko said, 'Even the experts can't imagine what the new bombs are capable of.' Khruschev turned to me. 'We now have warheads,' he said, 'which have so powerful a yield that we couldn't deliver them on Germany, because the fallout would contaminate the Soviet Union. When President Nasser was our guest we showed him a film of an atomic explosion. But that was in 1958. We were proud of it then, but now I feel ashamed. It was just a tiny thing, the size of a pea compared with the giants we've got now.' All this was said with a typical peasant's enthusiasm.

The ship stopped to allow a boat to come up with a senior Turkish naval officer on board who brought a message of greeting from the Turkish government. Khruschev would not allow himself to be interrupted. 'The imperialists don't understand', he said, 'that war has become impossible. It took Eisenhower a long time before he realized what nuclear weapons mean. A typical military man, he thought they were just bigger and better artillery shells. It wasn't until very late in the day that he understood that they represented a completely different race of weapons. I think the first one who grasped the nature of nuclear weapons was Kennedy. I think it was McNamara who made him aware.'

Later, when we were sitting on the bridge having a drink before lunch, Khruschev returned to the same theme. 'By now,' he said, 'the Americans do understand that war is impossible. Suez taught them that the days of gambling with atomic weapons were done. That is something that would lead to unthinkable catastrophes. Dulles used to boast about his brinkmanship – he would get all the world shivering with fear, seize what he wanted and then draw back from the brink. But it was the Egyptian people who turned the tables and put Dulles himself on the brink, and then, when we dispatched an ultimatum to London and Paris, Dulles was the one whose nerve broke. It was all his friends could do to escape with their skins.

'But now I think the Americans appreciate the realities of the situation. Kennedy and McNamara understood the real meaning of the Cuba crisis. They saw that there is no part of the world safe from nuclear weapons. The USA has always liked to fight its wars in other people's lands, but now things have changed. Every part of the globe is exposed.

'Some people didn't understand what we did in Cuba. They didn't

The author and 'the Red Tsar'. Moscow 1957.

A first sight of Egypt and of Africa. Nasser and Khruschev, Alexandria,
May 1964.

'Antiquities are best.' Nasser shows Khruschev and his wife the Egyptian
Museum in Cairo.

'The Egyptian people had
come to look on him as a
friend and ally.' Khruschev
between Gromyko and
Nasser.

'He is an excellent story-
teller.' Mikoyan addresses
the author and Sadat, while
Marshal Malinovsky listens.

Heikal the journalist and
Gromyko the hunter.

'A much better fisherman than I ever
expected.' The author and Podgorny,
August 1965.

The Puzzled Giant. Kosygin
and Sadat.

'The two sides were arguing
from completely different
premises.' Algeria's
Boumédienne and Kosygin in
Moscow, June 1967.

The Syrian Connection. As Minister of Defence, Hafez al-Assad is received in Moscow by Marshal Gretchko, August 1967

Plain clothes adviser. Marshal Zakharov and General Fawzi rebuilding Egypt's armed forces after the 1967 war.

'I know you think Ali Sabri is your man.' Ali Sabri, Brezhnev and Nasser.

Which category? Nasser and Brezhnev.

Warm friends in a cold climate. Podgorny and Brezhnev are hosts to Nasser, Mahmoud Riad, and the author.

The Soviet-Egyptian Treaty signed by Podgorny and Sadat, May 1970.

understand that we got everything we wanted. We made America realize that it was vulnerable. We obtained a guarantee for the integrity of Cuba and the Cuban revolution, and we forced them to take reciprocal action.' (Khruschev probably referred to the removal of some types of American missiles from Turkey.) 'War can never achieve its aims. But there is one thing you must always be very careful about – that is, the prestige of a big power. We had to give way to the Americans, because if the prestige of a big power is threatened it is capable of doing absolutely anything. The entire effectiveness of a big power is bound up in its prestige.

'The impossibility of war doesn't represent the sort of peace we would like, but it could create reasonable conditions in which we could build peace. What's the use of destroying each other? I once read something McNamara had said about the US having sufficient stocks of nuclear weapons to destroy the world four times over. In the Soviet Union we don't need all these weapons. Once is enough. There's no need to destroy the world four times; once is enough.'

Khruschev cut a lemon in half and began to suck it. 'Let's go in to lunch,' he said. Apparently he used to suck lemons to reduce his appetite. As we went down to the saloon he was still talking, and it dawned on me that so far I had not been asked a single question; Khruschev had talked all the time.

After he had sat down to table the monologue went on, and on the same subject. 'The last war', said Khruschev, 'was the last possible war. We weren't ready when it began, but by the end we had built up the necessary strength to bring us victory. After the war was over we made our first atomic bomb, and then our first hydrogen bomb. When I was appointed First Secretary of the Central Committee and learned all the facts about nuclear power I couldn't sleep for several days. Then I became convinced that we could never possibly use these weapons, and when I realized that I was able to sleep again. But all the same we must be prepared. Our understanding is not sufficient answer to the arrogance of the imperialists. We must never be taken by surprise again, as we were when Hitler invaded us. Do you know what happened to Stalin then? When he heard the news of Germany's invasion he went to his bedroom, and locked himself in. The next day he summoned us and said, "Comrades, the state which Lenin built is finished!" This hit us like a thunderbolt. Then the party and the people mobilized, and their strength more than made up for the collapse of the leadership.'

All this time Khruschev was addressing me mainly, but Gretchko and the others were all listening. Most of the rest of this lunch-time he talked about the war and particularly about his time as political commissar at Stalingrad. 'One day,' he said, 'we learned from some prisoners we had taken that the Germans were going to attack at three o'clock in the morning on a certain day. The Soviet marshal in that sector decided to mount an attack before the Germans began theirs. I went to him and said, "Comrade Marshal, when are you going to start your attack?" He told me at nine in the evening. "Do you want the advice of a peasant, Comrade Marshal?" I said. "If you really want to surprise them, you should start the attack at ten minutes to three. Then all their troops will be in their positions for the assault. They will be all keyed up, and every shell will find its target." The marshal looked at me, and said, "Comrade Commissar, this is a very shrewd idea. There may be something in it. Certainly it's worth trying." As I expected, the Germans were completely taken by surprise. Surprise is very important in war, but if it's to be effective you must have strong nerves.'

I did not see Khruschev that afternoon, but we met again at dinner. We were already seated, when Nina, his wife, came in. I stood up, but Khruschev looked at me crossly. 'Ach,' he said, 'sit down! Don't create protocol problems for me!' Then he went on talking about the war, as if there had been no interruption.

'The happiest moment in my life', he said, 'was when our troops crossed the Oder and found themselves on German soil. When I heard of the crossing I rushed there. I had nothing to do with that part of the battle but I went there because I felt that for me this planting of Russian feet on German soil was an act of revenge. I know that this is how a peasant feels, but we are still peasants. And those who underestimate Soviet peasants and workers had better beware, because our workers are peasants too in their origins.

'After dinner I'll show you something very interesting. It's a small model of the High Dam made by the workers of Tula. D'you know about Tula?' I told him that I did not. 'Don't you know the story of the Tsar, and the workers of Tula, and the flea? Well – once upon a time the Emperor of Germany wanted to send a gift to the Tsar of Russia. A mission arrived in St Petersburg bearing with them a very small box which they presented to the Tsar. He unpacked the box, but could find nothing in it. The box seemed to be empty. Then he got a magnifying glass and at last discovered a tiny flea, made out of silver. It had been sent him to demonstrate the unbeatable skill of German craftsmen. The Tsar was furious: "We must prepare an answer to this," he said. So his chamberlain suggested "Let's send this flea to the workers of Tula and see what they suggest." This they did. After a few days a box came back from Tula and was sent on to the Emperor of Germany. The Emperor opened the box, took a magnifying glass, saw the silver flea and turned to his courtiers. "Ah," he said "the Tsar has sent our flea back as an admission of our superiority." But one of the courtiers had brought a more powerful magnifying-glass and was looking at the flea. "Ah, those devils!" he cried. "What have they done?" asked the Emperor. "They have put a stirrup on the flea's legs," said the courtier.' Khruschev thoroughly enjoyed telling this story.

'In politics I'm still a peasant,' he went on. 'But some politicians nowadays like to make things sound very complicated, so that they can present themselves as specimens of some special sort of breed which can't be replaced. That's all nonsense. I never conceal my intentions from others – but the trouble is that other people refuse to believe me. In 1956 Bulganin and I visited Britain. Eden spoke to me about Middle East oil. He said "I want you to know that for us the oil of the Middle East is a matter of life and death. If the oil is cut off or interrupted, we shall fight." I said to him, "Mr Prime Minister, please remember that when you are talking about making war in the Middle East this is an area very close to the Soviet Union, and if war breaks out there we cau't sit idly by." Which makes it very odd that Eden should have been surprised when later that year we had to send him an ultimatum. On one occasion during that visit Bulganin was in a car with Eden and I was following in a car with Selwyn Lloyd. Lloyd said to me "A little bird told me that you have made another arms deal with Egypt." I told him, "I've got two little birds. One told me you have made an arms deal with Iran, and the other told me you have made an arms deal with Turkey." Selwyn Lloyd saw that his story about little birds wasn't going to impress me, so he shut up for the rest of the journey.'

*   *   *

The next morning we went on deck, and at last Khruschev started to talk to me about Egypt. I though I had anticipated every question he might ask, but I confess that I was not prepared for the first one.

'What is the desert like in Egypt?' he asked. 'How much of it do you cultivate?' I told him that we cultivated four per cent of the desert. 'What method do you use?' he asked. I tried to explain Egyptian methods of agriculture, but Khruschev broke in: 'This is all nonsense. You're wasting your time. Do you know what you ought to do? Chemical agriculture is the answer! Have you studied that?' I said we had not, so he launched into a description of an experiment he had seen, whereby you have huge glass containers full of water, into which you put chemicals without needing to use any soil. The motion of the water facilitates the process of growth, and after a few weeks you can harvest your crop. Khruschev thought this technique was going to be the salvation of the world. I explained to him the difficulty of reclaiming the desert. 'You don't need to reclaim,' he said. 'Fill your deserts with containers of water! Do you think President Nasser knows about this?' 'I don't think he does,' I said. 'I've got a report about it all, and a film,' said Khruschev. 'I'll send them to him. This could be better for you than the High Dam. Fill the deserts around you with containers of water and chemicals!' I told Khruschev that we were interested in desalination. 'We've got Kirchanov, a member of the Academy of Sciences, who's studying desalination,' he said. 'But that's no good for you. It's much too expensive. Glass and plastic water containers will provide you with everything you need.' All that morning our discussion turned on agriculture.

When we were having our pre-lunch aperitif I asked Khruschev what he saw as the most important events in his career – not personal matters but events which had proved to be turning-points. He thought for a bit and then gave me five examples – World War II and its effects on Soviet society; the Soviet Union becoming a nuclear power; the impossibility of war; movements of national liberation; and the dawn of the space age in 1957 with the Sputnik and Gagarin.

'Stalin didn't understand the effect the war had had on the Russian people,' he said. 'After the war they wanted a different sort of life. They wanted consumer goods. The people who had fought the war needed some reward. Even the capitalists appreciated that. When Bevin was working with Churchill he realized that the workers and returning soldiers weren't going to follow people like Churchill and other capitalists after the war. They were going to insist on changes in the social order. So he insisted that Churchill back the Beveridge Plan. That was the consequence of the participation of millions of workers in the war effort. Bevin wasn't the only person who understood that.

'When we became a nuclear power we broke America's monopoly. If we hadn't done that we should have been faced with a *pax americana*. That wouldn't have been tolerable, because it would have meant the world being dominated by one power.'

Then Khruschev had some remarks about cultural matters. 'I don't like using literature as naked propaganda,' he said, 'but I don't want an intellectual just to imitate capitalist ideas. That stuff they call abstract art – I've got no time for it. Unfortunately some of our best intellectuals start by selling their souls to the imperialists and then sell themselves completely – as Pasternak has done.'

After dinner we went to our cabins, and when I had been in mine for a short time Khruschev's secretary came in and asked me to go to see him. I found him in the sitting-room which was part of his suite. 'By the way,' he said, 'I meant to ask you what Nasser wants from me on this visit.' I said that we wanted a new loan of 200 million roubles. 'What?' he exploded. 'Two hundred million roubles for our new industrial development plan,' I repeated. Khruschev said something to his secretary which the interpreter did not translate. I asked what had been said. 'Wait, wait,' said Khruschev. In a little while the captain of the ship came in and saluted. Khruschev said something to him, and again I asked the interpreter for an explanation. He told me, 'the comrade says that because your demands are quite impossible he has instructed the captain of the ship to turn round and go back to Yalta.' Khruschev looked hard at me. 'Now, seriously,' he said, 'what is your last word?' 'Mr Chairman,' I expostulated, 'I wasn't given any authority to negotiate. I'm simply repeating what I was told.' 'We've given you enough,' said Khruschev. 'The High Dam – first and second phases, and a big loan for industrialization. Too much, in fact. One hundred million roubles is quite enough.' 'Mr Chairman,' I said, 'will you call the captain again, please?' 'Why?' he asked. 'I shall need one of his small boats,' I explained, 'so that I can row myself back to Yalta, because if I come back without the 200 million roubles Nasser will refuse to have anything to do with me.' 'All right,' said Khruschev grudgingly, 'we'll see.'

Adzhubei came in and we went off to the bar. 'There is brandy and vodka,' he said, 'and whisky if you want it. Our friend here,' turning to one of the ship's officers, 'is the political commissar on board and is responsible for the ship's catering. We are prepared for all contingencies on board when we have such distinguished passengers.' Whereupon the officer pressed a button, the front slid away from a cupboard, to reveal every sort of drink imaginable. 'You must organize yourselves in Egypt,' said Adzhubei. 'The party should be everywhere and should be able to take charge of everything.''

*   *   *

The next day was the fourth of our voyage, and the *Armenia* was approaching the Egyptian coast. Khruschev and I had a long discussion in the morning in the course of which he started to talk about Arab unity. He insisted that the only real unity was the unity of the working classes throughout the world. Then I made the mistake of bringing up the forbidden subject. 'Mr Chairman,' I said, 'working class unity isn't enough. Look at you and China. The proletariat is ruling in both countries, yet you are quarelling, and I think that a part of the quarrel is because of feelings of nationalism.' 'Ach,' said Khruschev. 'It's much more complicated than that.' 'All right, Mr Chairman, but you talk about "the great patriotic war", and you've told me yourself how at the beginning of it the party failed and it was the people who took the initial shock and gave the party a chance to consolidate itself.' 'You've got it wrong,' said Khruschev. 'The people can't do anything without being organized.'

Then Khruschev began to ask why we had been arresting communists and how he should bring the matter up with Nasser. 'All communists are out of prison now,' I told him. He went on to ask me questions about a great variety of subjects – Islam; the role of the mullahs; the size and population of Cairo, Egypt and other Arab countries; did we all speak the same language; what did the Arab League do; what had gone wrong with Qasim, and so on.

We were due to land the next morning, and that afternoon I was on the bridge trying to listen to news from Cairo radio on a small transistor set I had with me. Every bulletin was full of news about preparations for the Khruschev visit, and while I was listening he came up and asked me what I could hear. So I gave him a summary. Then he said: 'There is something – but I don't know whether I should tell it to you or not. However, I'm a frank man – I've got a report that your government is doing all it can to prevent people from coming out into the streets to greet me.' 'Mr Chairman,' I said, 'nothing could possibly be further from the truth than that.' 'Well, it seems they don't want me to have a big reception,' he complained. 'Can I tell you something?' I said. 'In the East, if you are someone's guest, the way people receive your guest reflects on you, as host. If the guest is received coldly, it's an insult to the host, not to the guest. The people who gave you that report don't know anything about the way things are done in the East.' 'Well,' said Khruschev, 'we'll see.'

At our last dinner on board Khruschev began the meal by gulping down first one large brandy and then another. Rada expostulated: 'Papushka! That's enough!' 'Nyet, nyet,' said Khruschev. 'That's my last brandy. Tomorrow I'll be a Moslem, like Nasser.'

We all went to bed early. While I was dressing the next morning Khruschev sent his interpreter to fetch me and I hurried over to his cabin. He glared at me. 'I told you yesterday that your government was playing down the reception for me,' he said. 'Now I've got proof. The person who's to meet me in Alexandria is Amer – Nasser isn't going to be there. You're sticking to protocol, because Nasser's head of state and I'm only Prime Minister.' 'That's impossible,' I said, 'there must be some mistake.' Khruschev insisted that that was what he had been told.

After a little time a boat came up to meet us at the limit of Egyptian territorial waters, with Marshal Amer in it. Nasser was awaiting us on the quayside. The misunderstanding was resolved, and Khruschev cheered up. He asked everyone how they had enjoyed the trip, particularly enquiring for the three journalists, Adzhubei, Satyakov and myself, whom he called 'the long-nosed intruders'.

The reception when we landed was quite indescribable. Many elements combined to make it a unique occasion – Nasser's prestige was at its height, and Khruschev had become a legendary figure, not just in Egypt. We all went by train to Cairo and then in a cavalcade of cars to the Kubba Palace where Khruschev was to stay. 'Well,' I asked him after we arrived there, 'what do you think of it?' I saw there were tears in his eyes. Never anywhere had he been received as the Egyptian crowds had received him that day.

★   ★   ★

A very full programme of celebrations and discussions had been prepared, and a number of other prominent guests had been invited for the ceremonies at Aswan, among them President Aref of Iraq and Ben Bella of Algeria, representing the two countries which then, together with Egypt, formed what was sometimes seen as the triangle of Arab unity.

The ceremony at Aswan was obviously a moving experience for Khruschev, but it was very exhausting for him because of the great heat. This was May, and Khruschev was not prepared for the temperatures you meet at Aswan at this time of the year. Nasser made a short speech, and so did Ben Bella. Aref, when it was his turn, interlarded his speech with long quotations from the Koran, which the crowd received with rapture. Khruschev, who followed, had a number of important things to say in his speech, including the announcement that the Politburo had bestowed the Order of Lenin and the title of Hero of the Soviet Union on Nasser and Amer (which made Egypt clearly Grade A) but he had to read it paragraph by paragraph so that it could be translated into Arabic by the interpreter. The applause was consequently rather perfunctory.

When we were all back in the hotel Khruschev asked me to come and see him – thanks to the time I had spent with him on the *Armenia* I had become the liasion man between him and Nasser. I found him sitting in his hotel room with nothing on but his underwear; the room was very cool because of the air-conditioning, but Khruschev was still perspiring heavily. He asked me, through his interpreter: 'When next does President Nasser intend to impose the company of this goat on me?' 'Which goat?' I asked. 'Aref,' said Khruschev, 'Aref – Aref – Aref. Look!' He had a copy of an Egyptian newspaper with him which he thrust into my hands. It contained a photograph of Aref, which Khruschev thought made him look like a goat.

Next day was to have been a rest day, but it was then that the row between Khruschev and Aref flared up, which I have already described in Chapter 1.

Khruschev's visit ended with some days in Alexandria. He and his party were installed in Ras el-Tin Palace, one of King Farouk's summer residences, while Nasser was miles away at the Maamurah rest-house. One evening Nasser offered to escort Khruschev back to Ras el-Tin but Khruschev told him not to bother. 'All right,' said Nasser, 'I'll send my deputy with you, and have a bit of a rest.' 'Which one?' asked Khruschev, 'Zakaria Mohieddin,' said Nasser. 'Ah!' said Khruschev, 'that's the man who's been arresting communists. You send him with me by all means, so that I can break all his ribs.'

At lunch that day at Maamurah Khruschev had been on his best form, but had shown rather a pathetic side too. With the coffee and desert the general conversation had ceased, and people were chatting to each other about future arrangements and so forth. Khruschev suddenly broke in: 'Nobody's talking! This is a dull party! Isn't there any music? You people don't know how to enjoy yourselves.' He turned to Gromyko. 'You make music!' he said, handing him a plate and rapping it like a tambourine. Then he turned to Gretchko: 'And marshal, you dance!' Gromyko took the plate with a watery smile, and Gretchko looked embarrassed. 'Let's all have coffee outside,' said Nasser.

So, on May 25, Khruschev left Egypt. The day before he left Nasser was able to announce that the Soviet Union had given Egypt a long-term loan of 250 million roubles for industrial projects. This, and the medals bestowed on Nasser and Amer, were proof that we were back in Grade A, so we had good reason to be content.

Khruschev was to leave by plane from Cairo airport, and shortly before his departure Adzhubei told me that his father-in-law was angry with me, because of something I had written. I was very surprised, because Khruschev had always been extremely generous in his treatment of me. 'What's the matter?' I asked. 'What I wrote about him was very friendly.' 'He'll tell you,' said Adzhubei. So I went to Khruschev's room in Kubba Palace to say goodbye. 'This visit has been a great pleasure for me,' I told him. 'It has been an historic occasion, and I could write a whole book about it. It was a privilege for me to be treated as a member of your family. But Alexei tells me you're angry with me about something.' 'Yes,' said Khruschev. 'It's something you wrote – about me being a peasant.' 'But, Mr Chairman, you've always spoken with such pride of being a peasant!' 'But you wrote I was like a peasant from a story by Dostoevsky – why didn't you say a peasant from Tolstoy?'

8

Pigeonholing and New Leadership

THEN, JUST AT THE MOMENT when Egyptian relations with the Soviet Union seemed to be on an even keel, and when it looked as if Egypt had achieved a satisfactory grading, came the news on October 15, 1964 of the dismissal of Khruschev. In few countries can the news of the Russian leader's fall have been received with greater shock than in Egypt. For Egyptians in every walk of life he occupied a special position. He was the man who had personally threatened the West at the time of Suez; only recently he had spent two weeks in their country, and they had seen his face every day over and over again on their television screens and in their newspapers. They had come to look on him as a friend and ally, and the terse communique from Moscow announcing his departure filled them with anxiety.

There was one immediate problem. Field-Marshal Abdel Hakim Amer had been invited as an official guest for the annual Moscow parade on November 7, which was now only three weeks ahead. There was much debate as to whether his trip should be cancelled, but in the end it was agreed that the most important thing was to make an on the spot assessment of the new situation. Amer therefore should go to Moscow, and again Nasser decided that I should go with him.

On arriving in Moscow I found great difficulty in gaining any evidence that would help me to an understanding of what had happened. I went to visit my old friend Pavel Satyukov, the editor of *Pravda*, but found he wasn't there – a new editor, Alexei Rumyantsev, now occupied his chair. I tried to talk to the liaison officers and interpreters attached to us, but without any success. For example, I asked one of the army liaison officers, 'what do you think about this Khruschev business?' 'I read the news in *Pravda*,' was his reply. 'If the party says his dismissal was necessary, that is good enough for me.' And he would say no more.

*   *   *

The new leadership consisted of Brezhnev, Kosygin, and Podgorny, with the eternal Mikoyan hovering only a little way behind them. There were real grounds for concern about their intentions towards Egypt, for amid all the speculation over the reasons for Khruschev's downfall, his Middle East policy was often mentioned. It was said that some east European countries had protested that the level of Soviet aid to Egypt was much too generous, and that no attempt had been made to exact better treatment for local communist parties in exchange for it. The high decorations bestowed on Nasser and Amer were also said to be the subject of criticism. No doubt Egyptian anxieties on this score were known in the Kremlin, for at the first meeting with Brezhnev he set out to allay them. 'What happened,' he said, 'has absolutely nothing to do with you or with our policy towards the Arab world. The party is not a matter of individuals but represents a collective will. Our relations with you are based on long-term decisions taken by the party, not by Khruschev.' This was an echo of the line taken by Khruschev himself after the removal of Shepilov.

But these assurances were not altogether convincing. Khruschev was known; the new leaders were still unknown. Moreover, the Egyptian delegation had, as usual, gone to Moscow in November with a number of points which it wanted to raise and requests which it hoped to see met, but it went back without receiving any answer to them. There had been a group from China, led by Chou En-Lai, in Moscow at the same time as the Egyptians, like them trying to size up the new situation, and the two delegations had compared notes. Naturally the Chinese had been pleased to see Khruschev disappear, but whereas the Egyptians thought the new Soviet leadership might make some policy changes, the Chinese believed it more likely that the former policies would be continued.

Sensing Egypt's continued unease the Kremlin decided to send Alexandr Shelepin to attend the victory-day celebrations on December 23, 1964. These were not normally a major occasion and were confined to Port Said, but Shelepin was no doubt sent because he had been particularly close to Khruschev. On arrival he explained that the new leaders had been so busy during the November celebrations – meeting a great number of people for the first time; confronting fresh problems – that they had not had time to deal with all the demands made upon them. He did, in fact, bring with him answers to some of the Egyptian requests which proved more or less satisfactory. He also spent a great deal of his time insisting that we should find nothing had changed.

★   ★   ★

Solicitous as Moscow had from time to time shown itself for the well-being of local communist parties, it could hardly have been prepared for the fate that was to befall the Egyptian party. For on April 25, 1965 the Egyptian Communist Party dissolved itself. The declaration in which this decision was made known deserves to be quoted in full:

DECISION BY THE ENLARGED CENTRAL COMMITTEE OF THE EGYPTIAN COMMUNIST PARTY

Following discussions which have been conducted in the party over the past two months concerning the problem of the unity of Egyptian socialists, and following the unanimous decision which was promulgated by the Central Committee, accepted by a majority of the Central Conference held to discuss the report of the Central Committee on this subject, and following local conferences, collective and individual discussions which arose from the decision of the Central Conference in which all members of the party expressed their points of view, it became clear that a majority of members of the party adopted the direction which had been accepted by the Central Committee.

The Central Committee accordingly demanded the convening of an enlarged meeting to include all responsible members from the districts and the central secretariat as well as those responsible for activities among the masses. Following this enlarged meeting, and after reviewing the results of intellectual work at all levels, the party has unanimously agreed to issue the following two decisions:

1. The independent status of the Egyptian Communist Party is terminated, and all its members are directed to apply individually for membership of the Arab Socialist Union and to struggle for the formation of a unified socialist party embracing all revolutionary forces in the country.

2. The report submitted by the Central Committee has been unanimously approved, and the enlarged meeting has agreed that

these decisions should be made known at all responsible levels of the Communist Party.

Signed, Central Committee of the Egyptian Communist Party.

This typically turgid report was given an equally wordy title: 'For a unified, enlarged, organized, popular movement for a progressive, revolutionary, unified party for all socialist forces under the leadership of Gamal Abdel Nasser.'

What had led to this remarkable – indeed, almost unprecedented – decision? Clearly the Egyptian communists had been greatly influenced by the regime's sweeping socialist legislation, by Khruschev's lengthy and successful visit to Egypt, by the creation of the Arab Socialist Union and by the formation inside it of the elite central cadre, the Vanguard. They had, of course, noted too Moscow's support for the creation of national fronts to include all progressive forces. But they were also conscious that, as a party, they had been singularly unsuccessful. They had nothing much to look back on except a history of internal quarrels, splits and wrong decisions. Burdened by their reputation as a party largely composed of Jews and foreigners, their problems must have seemed insurmountable, and the only way to escape from them would be to draw a line under what had gone before and start afresh. They were now acutely conscious of Nasser's massive popularity. No doubt they hoped that, if they could find a place inside the Vanguard, they would secure for themselves a dominating position in the ASU.

I had myself done what I could to provide them with a legitimate forum in which to express their point of view. *Al Ahram* used to have an 'Opinion' page in which contributors were free to express their own views. A great many of those contributing to this page happened to be communists, and this naturally provoked a good deal of criticism. I thought this showed that there was room for a forum where the Marxist point of view could be aired, and accordingly the review *Al-Talia* was founded. It seemed to me that, if we were to have elections under the new constitution, the far left had as much right as any other political group to make its views known and gain what support for them it could.

However, the party's recommendation that all its members should apply for membership of the ASU created problems. Nobody was keen to see them admitted en masse; and consequently they found their applications subjected to delays. Some had lost their jobs, and so we witnessed the somewhat ironical sight of the party leaders submitting a list of names of former party members to a special committee of the ASU which was supposed to find jobs for them. A good many of the applicants were looking for work in the press and in the theatre and films. Others asked for work on the shop floor of large factories, where they no doubt hoped their revolutionary impact would be greatest. The ASU preferred, not unnaturally, to direct them to small factories, or to upgrade them to clerical positions. The whole operation was a very peculiar one, but it was successfully completed.

★   ★   ★

The decision taken by the Egyptian Communist Party to dissolve itself created consternation and anger among the other communist parties in the Arab world. They did not believe that any party was entitled to take such a step, and not being within the immediate range of Nasser's influence were unable to understand the pressures to which their Egyptian comrades had been subjected. They viewed with suspicion the concept of 'nationalizing the class struggle' which had been adopted by Nasser, who felt that, though the class struggle was a reality which could not be ignored, the ferment it was bound to create would be considerably lessened if it was left to take its course within the framework of national unity. This the other communist parties thought an unhistorical approach. Moreover, they were uneasy over the charismatic influence exercised by Nasser over the Arab masses outside Egypt. With the memory of what had happened in Syria in mind (where one immediate result of the creation of the UAR had been the dissolution of all political parties, including the communist party) they feared that any country which joined Egypt, or came within the Egyptian orbit, would find its communist party treated in the same way. Nor could they forget the fate of the communists in Iraq.

So it was that, at a time when Egyptian–Soviet relations were in general improving, Egypt's relations with Arab communists were getting worse, and their attacks on Nasser and his policies were increasing in violence. At the other extreme the reactionary forces in the Arab world made full propaganda use of the decision, claiming that it proved there was no real distinction between Nasserism and communism, and that it was not Nasser who had absorbed the communists but the communists who had absorbed Nasser.

★　　★　　★

The same year saw a fresh crisis in Egypt's relations with the Soviet Union over arrangements for a new Afro-Asian solidarity conference. This 'second Bandung' was due to be held in March 1965 in Algiers. The Russians insisted that they were an Asian country and should therefore attend. The Chinese totally rejected the Russian claim, and the Afro-Asian movement accordingly found itself split in two, some governments supporting the Russians and some the Chinese. Neither Russia nor China would yield, and the Afro-Asian movement was only saved from complete breakdown by the coup d'état in Algiers on June 19, whereby Houari Boumedienne ousted Ben Bella. When the coup took place Chou En-Lai happened to be in Egypt, and after consultation with him and Nehru, Nasser proposed that the conference should be postponed. This was agreed to, and everybody's face was saved.

But the incident left a legacy of ill-feeling. Egypt had found itself unable to back the Soviet point of view. While accepting that the Soviets had a role to play in Afro-Asian affairs, it was felt that a summit conference attended by Podgorny, Brezhnev and Kosygin would hardly deserve the name of Afro-Asian. It would have the appearance of being held under the sponsorship of a superpower. The Russians were conscious of Egyptian reservations on this score, and interpreted it as further evidence of a lack of confidence in the new leadership.

★　　★　　★

So once again it seemed that a meeting at the highest level was necessary, and the proposal was made that Nasser should pay an official visit to Moscow which would be a return for Khruschev's visit to Egypt. The proposal was accepted. This would be Nasser's first sight of post-Khruschev Russia, and the new leaders were determined to make it a great success. All the leadership was at the airport on August 27 to meet the Egyptians, and the party had been mobilized to fill the streets with cheering crowds.

The triumvirate was very conscious of the importance of the Middle East in the international scene and were anxious to prove to Nasser that Soviet policy there was a party concern and had never been Khruschev's personal prerogative. So, after two formal meetings, Brezhnev said to Nasser: 'You have seen the Soviet Union before; what we need in this visit is time to talk. I suggest we should spend the weekend outside Moscow, getting to know each other better, as human beings, and not with a green baize table between us.'

The place chosen for this weekend meeting was a hunting lodge called Zagidova, a short drive from Moscow, its walls covered with the heads of elk and other game. All the leaders were there when we arrived – Brezhnev, Podgorny, Kosygin, Shelepin, Mikoyan, Gromyko Polyanski – and as it was early afternoon Brezhnev proposed that we should either go shooting or fishing. There was a large lake, formed by a dam, where duck could be shot, and a smaller lake for the fishers. All except Dr Fawzi, the Foreign Minister, and myself opted for shooting. He and I were each provided with a small boat and a man to row it, and a rod and line. I quickly became aware that I was a much better fisherman than I had ever suspected. For more than two hours I pulled fish out of the lake at the rate of about one a minute. The sun began to set, and I shouted to Dr Fawzi, who was at the other side of the lake, 'I've had a tremendous catch; I've got 110!' But Dr Fawzi, who had never before had a rod in his hands, had done almost as well – his total was 60. 'It seems to me,' he said, 'that this is either a party lake or a public relations one. The fish come to you voluntarily!'

A little later the shooters returned. Brezhnev had got 18 duck, Nasser twelve, Kosygin ten, Sadat, Zakaria Mohieddin and Mikoyan three each, and Gromyko two. Marshal Malinovsky seemed reluctant to disclose his bag, but Brezhnev pressed him – it transpired he had shot nothing. 'Next time,' he said ruefully, 'I'm going to ask our people to invent a ground-to-duck missile for me.'

Dinner followed. The mood was slightly strained. Nobody mentioned Khruschev, but everyone was trying to recreate the atmosphere as it had been at similar gatherings when he was still in power. His was the absent genius presiding at the feast.

After dinner most of our hosts and their guests went to bed early, but I stayed up talking to Mikoyan – or rather, listening to him talk. He speaks excellent English and is a very good story-teller, and I found his reminiscences fascinating. It was well after midnight before we finally broke up and I made my way up to my bedroom. All the bedrooms in the hunting lodge had numbers, and I found mine, as I thought, but when I opened the door I could locate neither the light switch nor my bag. I went back into the corridor, but there was nobody about; everyone else was asleep, and all the guards were on the ground floor. No matter, I thought, I'll sleep in my shirt. So I climbed into bed, only to find to my great surprise that there was somebody in it already. Was the accommodation so limited that we were expected to double up? I had no means of knowing, and in any case there was nothing that I could do about it. So I turned over and tried to sleep. But my companion was restless; he snored, and pulled the blankets off me and over him, so that I got little rest. Dawn came at last, and I looked up to see my companion of the night peering over me with a puzzled expression on his face. It was Nikolai Podgorny, President of the Soviet Union.

I made what apologies I could, put on my clothes, and went downstairs in search of breakfast, but found nobody stirring except Mikoyan and Dr Fawzi. However, we had nothing to complain of, since Mikoyan treated us over breakfast to another instalment of his reminiscences.

★   ★   ★

Lenin, said Mikoyan, had never liked Stalin; he had a high opinion of his ability, but disliked the brutal and terrorist side of his character, which had already been manifested. 'In his will,' said Mikoyan, 'Lenin asked all of us to choose as his successor a man with Stalin's good qualities but without his defects. We looked and looked, but we could find no alternative to Stalin. Even Nadia Krupskaya, Lenin's widow and his closest companion during the last days of his life, agreed with us that it would have to be Stalin – and this in spite of the continuous quarrels she had with him. Stalin knew nothing about Lenin's will, even after he had been confirmed as Lenin's successor, until some of the comrades mentioned it by chance. Then Stalin asked for a meeting of the Central Committee and offered us his resignation. We refused it, and asked him to carry on, but to try to overcome the tendencies which Lenin had feared and criticized.

'For the next ten years,' Mikoyan went on, 'Stalin behaved correctly. But then he started to change. The ruthless side of his nature asserted itself, and remained in the ascendant till the Hitler war. In the first days after the German armies invaded Russia he had a complete nervous breakdown. He stayed in his room, drinking heavily. But then he pulled himself together and took over direction of the war. He did a wonderful job. Unfortunately, when the war ended Stalin became the man of blood again.'

Mikoyan had something to say about Trotsky too. He described him as a highly intelligent man, but so vain and full of himself that he was ready to burst. 'He was an actor by nature,' said Mikoyan.

★　★　★

At lunch that day Brezhnev turned to Nasser and said: 'I raise my glass to you, President Nasser, as a Hero of the Soviet Union!' It was clear that the new leadership was trying to convey, in a tactful manner, that there was no truth in the rumours that Khruschev's downfall was partly due to the favourable treatment he had shown towards Egypt. Marshal Malinovsky backed him up: 'When you arrived at Moscow airport,' he said to Nasser, 'some of my officers asked me why they couldn't see the gold star of the Order of Lenin on your chest.'

Then, as if at a prearranged signal, Brezhnev turned to Malinovsky and said, 'Marshal, are there any good stories circulating among the military?' 'Well,' said Malinovsky, 'there's the story about the husband who comes home to find his wife in bed with another man. The Russian husband pulls out his revolver to shoot his wife's lover, but Natasha dashes in between them crying "shoot me, but spare him!" The German husband glares furiously at his wife, but she says, "But Karl, why did you change your regular time for coming home?" The Chinese husband, his eyes blazing with anger, shouts at his wife, "Han, I give you ultimatum number 365!"' This was just at the time when the Chinese were in the habit of giving the Americans 'ultimatum number 365', or whatever it was, over the shelling of the offshore islands of Quemoy and Matsu, and everybody round the table appreciated the reference. There may also have been in this story, with its mockery of the Chinese leadership, an oblique rebuke for the support which most Arabs were giving at this time to the Chinese point of view about the forthcoming Afro-Asian conference.

Nasser determined to put the pleasant and relaxed atmosphere at Zagidova, and the Soviet's obvious determination to persuade us that nothing had changed, to the test. By now Egypt had run up a considerable debt with the Soviet Union over arms purchases, largely because of the continuing fighting in Yemen, where civil war had been raging since 1962. Nasser pointed out that this too should be seen as a national liberation movement – an anti-imperialist war – and he said he thought it would be appropriate if some of the debt we had incurred were to be cancelled. Our hosts took his point, and agreed to cancel $500m of the debt.

9

Trouble for Everybody

1964 DREW TO A CLOSE and 1965 opened. It was to prove a year of trouble for everybody – for Egypt, for the Soviet Union, for the US, and for the Arab world as a whole.

In Egypt the first five-year plan had been brought to a successful conclusion, but a great deal had been spent on capital investment, including the High Dam, without there being much to show for it to the public. Wages were good, but there was not a lot available in the markets to spend them on. It had been known, when the decision to go ahead with the High Dam was made, that it would have an inflationary effect, but when this actually happened everyone became alarmed.

Looking back, I think this situation should have been met by increasing the rate of development, but there were other influences at work which made for caution. In the first place there was the war in Yemen, which was costing the huge amount – for Egypt – of £E40–60 million a year. And it was proving a very difficult war for the Egyptian army to fight – a guerrilla war against tribesmen for which it had not been trained and which seemed to offer no prospect of ending. So there was a tendency to indulge the officers in Yemen, even at the expense of discipline. Corruption was winked at. The free port of Aden provided a tempting opportunity for the purchase of exactly those consumer goods which were in short supply at home. Moreover Egypt was at odds with the backers of the other side in the Yemen war. Saudi Arabia's oil revenues were increasing, and they were able to give increasing support in cash and arms to the royalist forces. An attempt was made to reconcile Egypt's differences with Saudi Arabia at the meeting between Nasser and King Feisal in Jidda in August, but this achieved nothing.

Then there were repercussions from the socialist laws. These had come in two waves – in 1961 and 1962 – and had resulted in a greatly enlarged public sector. The owners of the concerns which had been nationalized held aloof, and while many of the new managers were excellent, some were not so good or were too scared to take the initiative.

So progress in the public sector was slow. Because of this, and because of the complications arising from the Yemen war, it was decided to follow a policy which, in my view, was contrary to the regime's true revolutionary drive. It had originally been agreed that the first five-year plan should be concerned with light and medium industries, and the second with heavy industry, and especially machinery. But now the scope of the second plan was severely restricted, and Zakaria Mohieddin was appointed Prime Minister on October 2, charged with the task of carrying out classic deflationary measures.

There were also difficulties with the Americans. President Johnson was annoyed by Egypt's efforts to produce its own rockets, with the aid of German scientists. It was also rumoured, incorrectly, that Egypt was hoping to manufacture atomic weapons. So President Johnson suggested that America should be enabled to inspect the Middle East for rockets and atomic weapons. The reason given was to prevent further atomic proliferation, but the American aim was at least as much to gain some measure of control over Egypt's arms programme. In any case, Egypt rejected the American suggestion, as did the Israelis (with more reason, because their atomic research had reached a very advanced stage of development). This upset President Johnson, who in January 1965 cut American deliveries of grain to Egypt by half, and later reduced them to practically nothing, without informing Nasser of his intentions.

★   ★   ★

For the Arab world as a whole 1965 was a year of fresh complications. On January 1 Fateh, the Palestinian national liberation movement, appeared on the scene with the publication of a communique No 1 announcing an attack with explosives on the Israeli water pipeline at Ain-Bone. The Palestinians had hitherto left the initiative to others. They had hoped that the formation of the UAR would be the beginning of a new chapter of unity from which they, with the rest of the Arab world, would benefit, but they were disappointed. They had high hopes from Qasim's revolution in Iraq, but this too only brought disappointment. So now they determined to act for themselves. They operated mainly from Syria, where the left wing of the Baath Party, led by Salah Jedid, had taken over and begun to pursue a fanatical and irresponsible policy. Syria was at odds with Iraq, where Abdel Salam Aref, continued to pay lip service to the idea of Arab unity, while doing nothing about it. He felt, with some reason, that Nasser trusted Ben Bella more than him – Egypt and Algeria had taken the same line over preparations for the abortive 'second Bandung'. The Arab countries were, in fact, in an extremely fluid state, one characteristic of which was that, thanks to Saudi Arabia's increasing oil revenues, the conservative regimes were becoming richer and more active. A strange new amalgam of political, intelligence, and oil interests emerged. The CIA was deeply involved with the Yemen's royalists, and the Israeli air force made some drops of arms and provisions to beleaguered royalist pockets.

★   ★   ★

The beginning of 1965 saw the triumvirate of Podgorny, Brezhnev, and Kosygin safely in the saddle in the Soviet Union but confronting a daunting array of problems. The quarrel with China had seriously damaged Russia's relations with Third World countries and with the countries of eastern Europe. Nasser had raised the subject with the new leadership when we were in Moscow, pointing out the harm it was doing to national liberation movements everywhere. 'We've tried with you, and we've tried with the Chinese,' he said, 'but it's no use. Both of you are asking us to take sides, and that puts the whole Afro-Asian movement in a terrible dilemma.'

The answer given by his hosts was that they had done their best to reach an understanding with the Chinese but found it quite impossible. 'The Chinese oppose the idea of coexistence,' said Brezhnev. 'We don't see any conflict between coexistence and the continuation of the revolutionary liberation movements. Coexistence isn't something static. But anyone who opposes coexistence is speaking in favour of war – of total war – and the avoidance of war isn't just one option, but a necessity, in view of modern weapons. We would even claim that by eliminating the possibility of war we are giving greater flexibility to the revolution.'

At this same meeting Kosygin made a significant contribution. 'The real problem,' he said, 'is the Chinese claim that because they subscribe to the same doctrines as ourselves we must share everything with them. That is quite impossible. If we began to share out the resources of the Soviet Union between the members of the socialist camp we should all be weak. Communist countries should accept the fact that the Soviet

Union has primacy. They should recognize that there are two essential requirements for the Soviet Union – it must be strong, and it must be a model for the principles and practice of communism.'

'We have helped China a great deal,' Kosygin went on. 'England built an industrial base in eighty years. The Soviet Union built its industrial base in twenty-five years. China has built up a base in ten years, but that is because they had our assistance. They still need our experience and our resources.'

This was all very well, but Egypt had found that practically all the communist parties and communist governments with which it had dealings, and especially the North Vietnamese, were complaining of the bleak choice with which the Russians insisted on confronting them – 'either us or the Chinese'. In December 1964 the Russians sent out an invitation for an international conference of communist parties to be held in Moscow the following March. This was accepted by all except the parties of China, Albania, Rumania, North Korea, North Vietnam, Indonesia and Japan, but other parties, including those of Britain, Cuba, Italy and Poland, expressed reservations. Ceausescu, the Rumanian leader, sent a letter to Nasser in which he said: 'We have explained our position over the Sino-Soviet dispute clearly. We do not accept that the Soviet Union should monopolize either the facts or their interpretation.' Even Castro refused the Russian request to give them open support in the dispute.

The Chinese were a little later to be responsible for one small and, in a way, rather ridiculous source of friction between Egypt and the Soviets. It became known on October 27, 1966, that they had successfully tested their own guided nuclear missiles, and that the man in charge of the Chinese missile programme was the German, Dr Wolfgang Pilz. Previously, Dr Pilz had been working in Egypt on our missile programme, but after the deflationary measures taken in 1965–6 our programme had been cut back. There was no more work for Dr Pilz, who left Egypt and was next heard of in China. The Soviets thought that, because of Dr Pilz, Egypt was, perhaps, in some way coordinating missile production with China. They actually made official enquiries about this.

★　★　★

Then there were the European communist parties. Most of them were angry, and some of them, particularly the Italians, were almost in a state of revolt over the affair of the 'Togliatti will'. Egypt had had especially close relations with the Italian Communist Party for quite a long time. Although originally, at the time of the 1919 revolt in Egypt, it was the French Communist Party which assisted at the foundation of the first Egyptian Communist Party, somehow during the 1930s supervision over its activities passed to the Italians. This was continued after the war, and in 1959 it was representatives from the Italian party who presided over the discussions aimed at unifying the various splinter groups into which the Egyptian communists had divided. Nor was it only with the small Egyptian Communist Party that its Italian counterpart, the largest communist party in western Europe, had close links. The government-sponsored Arab Socialist Union maintained a cordial relationship with it too, and in fact at this period hardly a month passed without a delegation from Italy coming to Egypt for some reason or another.

As has been seen, the Soviet Union was trying to diversify its interests in the Arab world, to avoid concentrating all its attentions on a single country – Egypt. In the same way Nasser thought it would be a good idea to diversify Egyptian interests in the communist world, as a possible way of putting moral pressure on the Soviet Union. The Italian was one of the most independent and active communist parties anywhere in the world at this time, and it was reasonable for Nasser to suppose that it might be able to give him some useful insights into the new leadership in Moscow. He hoped that, just as Egypt had at the time of the Czech arms deal been able to use China as a form of leverage on the Soviet Union, so now it might be possible to use some of the European communist parties in a similar role.

What had happened over the 'Togliatti will' was that Khruschev, just before he fell, had been toying with the idea of a conference on the China issue, and Togliatti, secretary-general of the Italian Communist Party, had been invited to Russia with the promise that he would be able to meet Khruschev to discuss the conference idea. But when he arrived he was told that Khruschev was touring the 'virgin lands' project with Lord Thomson, the Canadian newspaper owner. He was advised to go to Sochi in the Crimea and have a rest until Khruschev was ready to receive him. This he did, and while he was in a sanatorium at Yalta he tried to organize his ideas in the form of a written report which he intended to be the basis for his discussions with Khruschev. He had almost finished this report, and was adding the final touches, when he had a stroke. He was rushed to hospital but died almost immediately (August 21, 1964).

The first thing that his wife, who was with him when he died, did was to go to the table by his bed where his papers were, extract the report and put it in the bosom of her dress. She was extremely bitter about what had happened, and communists everywhere were shocked that Togliatti had been left for several weeks unvisited because Khruschev was gallivanting around the country with a capitalist press baron. Brezhnev tried to make amends by accompanying Togliatti's body back to Rome.

The Soviets wanted to get hold of the 'Togliatti will' but were unable to do so, until its contents were made public by the Italian Communist Party on September 4, 1964. The main point Togliatti had been trying to make was that the communist movement ought not to be monolithic but should aim at unity through diversity. He felt that the communist movement was harassed by the *diktats* of one party over the others – that contemporary Marxist thought showed no originality and was facing new problems with old answers. He spoke too of the revival of nationalism. 'The differences between one country and another are very great,' he wrote. 'Every party therefore must learn to act in an autonomous manner. . . . Even in the socialist camp it is necessary to be on one's guard against uniformity imposed from without.'

These ideas were, of course, heresy in the Kremlin, and the whole business of Togliatti's death and will was a contributing factor to the downfall of Khruschev. And there was another factor which at this time played a considerable part in the debates affecting the Soviet leadership and which had its bearing on Soviet policy towards the Middle East. This concerned the role of nuclear weapons.

I think Khruschev calculated that since nuclear weapons could not be used militarily, they could only be used politically, and this required a special technique. At the time of Hungary and Suez he threatened the use of nuclear weapons, leaving it to others to escalate the conflicts if they wanted to, but knowing very well that they would not. On the other hand, during the Cuba crisis Khruschev was operating in an area where the Americans enjoyed military superiority, and so his political use of nuclear weapons proved ineffective and he had to back down. After Cuba a great many of the top Soviet military, including Marshal Gretchko, accused Khruschev of failing to appreciate that nuclear weapons could not be used as a political weapon unless there were conventional forces to back them up. So it was that the post-Cuba period saw the emergence of Admiral Sergei Gorshikov, who turned the Soviet navy into a world-wide force. I recall one occasion when Egypt was asking Brezhnev for a fighter-bomber to match the Phantoms which America was supplying to the Israelis. His answer was that they had nothing to match the Phantoms. 'We made the mistake under the previous leadership,' he said, 'of relying on nuclear weapons. This meant we were left far behind in the development of our traditional capabilities. So now we have no fighter-bomber that can match the Americans. We shall catch them up, but at present there's a gap.' Over Cuba the Soviets had been faced with the alternative of a conflict which would be fought out with traditional weapons, in which they were inferior, and of escalating to the nuclear level, which was something they were not prepared to do. That was Suez in reverse.

So the Russians were trying to build up sufficient conventional forces to be able to treat with the Americans on a basis of equality, believing that only on such a basis could they discuss detente. But immediately they came up against a formidable obstacle – Vietnam. I remember Kosygin, when he was in Alexandria, saying what a pity it was that just when the Soviet Union was ready to talk seriously about detente the war in Vietnam intruded to complicate everything.

This was a time when the Americans seemed prepared to take risks everywhere, not just in Vietnam. It was the heyday of the CIA, which was actively recruiting mercenaries for Yemen, and very active in Latin America. The Johnson administration's policy of operating from local pivots, by which one power in an area was given the capacity for non-nuclear intervention in local situations, meant that Israel was invested with new importance.

So, what with the debates which had preceded Khruschev's downfall, with the fundamental issues now being posed by the 'Togliatti will', and with the conflict between the need for detente and the need to meet increasingly brash American policies, the Soviets were under considerable pressure. International events, such as the seventeen-day war between India and Pakistan in August 1965, the growing strength of the military in Indonesia and mounting attacks on the Indonesian Communist Party (PKI) in the winter of 1965–6, and the disappearance of Nkrumah in February 1966 were additional sources of worry.

Nasser was still there, but the general trend of national liberation movements favourably inclined to the Soviet Union seemed to be on the wane. Something had clearly gone wrong, but the Soviet leaders were unable to analyse exactly what. Cairo repeatedly told them that the Sino-Soviet conflict must be held largely responsible for disarray in the Third World's ranks. On their side, the Soviets did their best to demonstrate their solidarity with the Arabs by intensifying their propaganda against Zionism, and this in its turn was to confront them with some unexpected consequences.

One of the failures of Soviet communism is that it has never succeeded in solving the Jewish problem. The Soviet leaders have either tried to pretend that the problem does not exist, or, with more justification, that it is only kept alive by malign outside forces. But now it was the Soviet Union's own policies which were aggravating the problem. The more Zionism was attacked in the Soviet press, the more Soviet Jews became conscious of their identity. Demands to emigrate to Israel grew. The Soviets complained that the CIA was recruiting Soviet Jews, which was undoubtedly the case, and that Israeli institutions were acting as intermediaries. They also asserted that some of the clandestine leaflets circulating among Jewish dissidents had been printed inside the Israeli embassy in Moscow, and that Israeli consuls were helping in their circulation during the visits which they paid to Jewish communities throughout the Soviet Union. Evidence confirming this reached Cairo and was passed on to Moscow. The Soviets hinted broadly that it was because of the stand which they had taken on Egypt's behalf that they were running into this fresh domestic difficulty.

* * *

The new Soviet regime certainly had much to think about, and echoes of its attempts at re-evaluation reached Cairo. Its members still insisted that the change of leadership was in no way connected with policy towards Egypt and the Arabs, but there can be no doubt that one of the criticisms levelled at Khruschev was that his dealings with Egypt had in fact been dealings with one man only – which was true enough, because the Egyptian regime was synonymous with Nasser. There was a fundamental split over policy in the Kremlin, and the Middle East played a big part in it, some of Khruschev's critics, notably Suslov, making use of the same arguments that local Arab communist parties had been using. By concentrating all their efforts on supporting

Nasser, the argument went, local communists were putting themselves in an equivocal position: the stronger Nasser became, the weaker they became, and if he tried to achieve unity they would find themselves dissolved.

The other communist parties in the Arab world were angry at the decision of the Egyptian Communist Party to dissolve itself, and Khaled Bakdash was the most forcible critic of this decision. He was able to speak from a position of unique authority. The Syrian Communist Party was cooperating with the left wing of the Baath Party, under Salah Jedid, which was now in power. Bakdash, a veteran communist of proved ability, had achieved something which the Soviet Union had always been demanding from local communist parties – his party was actively participating in a national front government, and had even got a minister in the cabinet. This, to other communists, was a comprehensible achievement, whereas the concept of Arab unity was something they had never understood. They were against it, both because it conflicted with the doctrine of working-class unity, and, more particularly, because of the way in which Nasser's supremacy was reducing them to ciphers. Consequently the advice the Arab communists were giving to the Soviets was that it was a mistake for them to put all their eggs in one basket; they should disperse their energies throughout the Arab world and not concentrate them all on one country, which was the same thing as concentrating them all on one man.

Before and after the Twenty-third Congress of the CPSU, which met in Moscow between March 29 and April 8, 1966, there was a wide-ranging discussion on what the relationship between the Soviet Union and the Arab world, and between communist parties and the national liberation movement as a whole, should be. Not for the first, and not for the last time the Soviet leadership found itself in a dilemma, torn by the rival claims on it as a superpower and as the motherland of the revolution. On occasions the leadership has been able to produce suitable ideological clothing in which to dress the necessities of superpowerdom, and at other times it has been possible to present action in the interest of the state as the natural outcome of ideology; but now there was no easy way of reconciling the twin obligations.

Almost all the Arab communist leaders were in Moscow for a month before the congress began, and stayed on in Moscow for several weeks afterwards. There were lengthy debates inside each Arab party, and between the various parties, supplemented naturally by discussions with experts from the Central Committee. But they were dealing with a jigsaw puzzle into which not all the pieces could be properly fitted.

No final agreement was reached, but, as often happens in the communist world, the debate was continued in the pages of party journals, the protagonists on this occasion being Khaled Bakdash, speaking on behalf of the Arab communist parties, and that doughty theoretician, Ulianovsky, expounding the Politburo line. At the heart of the argument was a question which, in one form or another, has cropped up repeatedly in policy debates – how far should communists go in co-operating with progressive but non-communist movements, and even in accepting their (temporary, of course) leadership. This was something that exercised Lenin in his struggle with the Mensheviks, and which had been given a new interpretation by Stalin when he ordered communists to meet the threat of fascism and war by the creation of popular fronts. Now, with the tide in the Third World running strongly along the lines of national liberation under the leadership of a charismatic leader, the old argument was revived in a new setting.

* * *

Khaled Bakdash opened the printed debate with an article in the December 1965 issue of the Cominform monthly, *Problems of Peace and Socialism*, called 'The National Liberation Movement and the Communists'. In this many familiar arguments were emphatically restated. Bakdash started by insisting that even though the Soviet Union and other socialist countries pursued a policy of alliance with some of the newly free countries in Asia and Africa 'this does not mean that the communist parties and the democratic forces generally in the latter must under all circumstances support their governments and renounce the fight for democratic freedoms'. No other social group, no class, and no individual, he said, could take over the historic mission of the working class. He admitted that situations might arise in which another social group or individual leader was 'carried to the fore on the tide of the struggle against fascism, imperialism, feudalism and, in some cases, also against the big bourgeoisie'. They should be supported; 'But we must be on our guard against attempts to justify such alliances by spurious theories repudiating the role of the working class.'

Bakdash insisted that the proletariat must be the leaders of socialist transformation and that 'the future depends on the struggle between the classes and on the outcome of this struggle'. He cast doubts on the argument that those who have come to accept Marxism partially can be induced to accept it completely at some future stage – 'There are those who say that the supporters of the so-called "Arab", "African", or "Islamic" socialism will, eventually, discover that the only real socialism is scientific socialism. . . . Experience shows that this is not the case.' He rejected the idea that the superstructure in a country always reflected changes at the base: 'On the contrary, international and domestic factors can cause sudden changes in the superstructure capable of influencing the base:' Referring to land reform in countries like Algeria, the UAR, and Syria, he said that the machinery of state alone, with army and police, was not sufficient to deal with the problems involved: 'What is needed is an influential authoritative revolutionary mass party enjoying the confidence of the people.' He charged with sectarianism those who argued that measures against the big bourgeoisie carried out by non-communist groups do not deserve the name of socialism: 'At the same time there are no grounds for saying that the given country has taken the socialist way. To take this view would be tantamount to saying that the leading role in establishing socialism no longer belongs to the working class but has passed over to the nationalist groupings and the small bourgeoisie.'

In an obvious reference to the Egyptian Communist Party Bakdash denied the right of any communist party to dissolve itself, and quoted the decision of the Seventh Congress of the Comintern in March 1918 as evidence that the call to communist parties to preserve their identities and carry on independent activities was addressed as much to parties in the colonies and semi-colonies as to parties in the West. He added that experience had shown that sudden changes of government can overnight alter the general trend of development and jeopardize changes that have already taken place.

The official answer to Bakdash came in an article by R. Ulianovsky entitled 'Some Problems of the Non-Capitalist Development of Liberated Countries' which appeared in the Soviet monthly magazine *Kommunist* for January 1966.

'Life,' wrote Ulianovsky, 'demands the creation of a left-wing bloc in which the more conscious and better equipped Marxist-Leninist elements would play the role of friend and helper of the national democrats – the role of the ideological beacon of socialism and advanced fighter. The adherents of scientific socialism in such a bloc are capable of giving a correct orientation to it. . . . If the Marxist-Leninists undertake this mission in a left-wing bloc they will help the progressives to avoid making mistakes and will thus exert a beneficial influence at critical moments of development.'

Ulianovsky criticized communists in underdeveloped countries with no working class, who wanted to set up a dictatorship of the proletariat before introducing socialism. This would mean that capitalism would first have to be developed in order to create a working class based on industrialization – an idea already proposed elsewhere and rejected.

He said that the ideology of the national democracies had its objective reasons. A long time would pass before national revolutionary parties would move towards Marxism–Leninism. Marxists should be flexible so as not to irritate the masses and should not forget that those who accepted Marxism partially now could accept it completely tomorrow.

Ulianovsky criticized communists who, while claiming Marxist purity, isolated themselves from the masses. His advice to communists was:

1. At the stage transitional to setting up the new society, the machinery of the state should work in conjunction with the aims of non-capitalist development.

2. Special attention should be paid to the armed forces, and those elements which do not believe in the non-capitalist way to development should be removed.

3. The machinery of the state should be purged and reorganized.

4. The labouring masses should be mobilized to fight for the creation of the new society, and their role in administering the country should be increased.

5. It is important to strengthen, and where necessary set up, an avant-garde political party able increasingly to adopt the theory and practice of scientific socialism and on that basis to manage and control the state.

Ulianovsky showed himself aware of some of the problems even in the advice he was giving to communists. These included the following points:

'By no means all national democratic leaders are capable of achieving iron discipline or organization, nor are all citizens used to the hard work essential for building the new society. It is typical for some representatives of national democracy to manifest undue haste, verbal radicalism and insufficient persistence in achieving their goal.

'Conservative elements among national democrats are trying to prevent the spread of scientific socialism, and the most extreme right wing is openly spreading an anti-communist ideology.' This must be prevented.

Communists must fight against religion, but must do so tactfully.

Some national democrats and even communists, he went on, try to adapt scientific socialism to local conditions in accordance with geographical, historical, cultural, national and racial factors. These people maintain that within the context of revolutionary values, 'national and racial unity is more valuable than class unity'. This is wrong and must be combated.

The conclusion which was drawn in Cairo from all this was that a big debate on policy was continuing in the Soviet Union, and that it was probably influenced as much by events in Africa and Asia as by the furore caused among European parties by the 'Togliatti will' and all that. It looked as though there was probably agreement between the Soviets and Arab communist parties that the communist movement must remain united, though the various elements in it would be allowed to retain a degree of freedom of action. But there was a considerable contrast between the views of Khaled Bakdash and Ulianovsky – Khaled Bakdash wanting each local party to be an individual entity raising high the banner of Marxism–Leninism in an almost Stalinist fashion, whereas Ulianovsky was trying to keep them inside the national organizations. Information was coming in that the Soviet Union was trying to work out an alternative policy. Ties between it and local communist parties had been weakened in the 1960s, when increased reliance was being placed on the national liberation movements, but the sudden disappearance of people like Ben Bella and Nkrumah had made the Soviets realize that the existence of a progressive leader was no guarantee that progressive policies would be maintained. They had allowed local communist parties to be swept away only to see the progressive leaders follow them into oblivion. But we suspected there was still a division of opinion in the Politburo – Podgorny, Suslov and Ponomarev backing greater dependence on local communist parties, with Brezhnev, Kosygin and Shelepin opposing them. The final conclusion was that, since the debate was not yet finalized, the Soviet Union would pursue a flexible policy, while local communists would probably try to infiltrate or consolidate their positions inside the left wing of national organizations.

*   *   *

The hardening of American policies towards the Middle East, and the fundamental review of Russian policies, had one unexpected consequence in Arab countries – the emergence of what came to be considered American and Russian 'lobbies'. Just as it was known that there were individuals in the Soviet Union whose interests had become tied up with Egypt's, and who could be regarded as our friends, so there were individual Egyptians who gained the reputation of being particularly friendly with the Soviet Union or America. But this was largely due to a misunderstanding. Field-Marshal Amer was often placed in the Soviet lobby, but this was only because it was his duty to keep in close contact with the Soviets for everything connected with the armed forces; the same was true of Ali Sabri from the point of view of general coordination, Aziz Sidqi ('the Tsar of Egyptian industry') from the point of view of industrialization, and Sidqi Suleiman, Minister of the High Dam. All these had to be continuously dealing with the Soviet Union and were naturally encouraged to be on as good terms as possible with those with whom they had to deal. In the same way most of the contacts of people like Zakaria Mohieddin, Abdel Moneim Kaisouny and Said Marei were with the West, so they had the label 'American lobby' stuck on them. But these labels were essentially meaningless.

The alarm which both the Egyptian and the Soviet governments felt over the apparent recklessness of American policy led to an increasing exchange of information between them. This was useful at the time, but was to cause a great deal of trouble a year later. Meanwhile the need for fresh high-level contacts was felt, and so it was arranged that Kosygin should come to Cairo in May 1966. Before this visit took place there was, reported the Egyptian embassy in Moscow, an attempt by the ruling circles in the Soviet Union to make a thorough investigation of the exact state of affairs in Egypt. They wanted to know, for example, how much backing Nasser had from the army and from the people, how strong the Socialist Union was, how able it was to defend itself and Egypt's social revolution, how far rightist or religious elements had infiltrated the army, and whether there was any political organization inside the army, what was the strength of the reactionary forces inside the country, and so on. All these questions, which could have been interpreted as interference in Egypt's internal affairs, were not directly raised but came up in several meetings which the Egyptian ambassador in Moscow had with Semyonov, the assistant to the Minister of Foreign Affairs.

★   ★   ★

Shortly before this, in April 1966, a Syrian delegation, headed by Yusuf Zuayin, then Prime Minister, had paid a visit to Moscow, and it was clear that the Soviets were busily trying to improve relations with a number of Arab countries, including Syria and Algeria, where Boumedienne was now firmly in the saddle. They were, in fact, adopting a much more flexible attitude to the Arab world as a whole. But, while in pursuit of diversification their contacts with other Arab governments increased, they continued to accord Egypt and Nasser a special relationship which was denied to the rest. Force of circumstances, and pressure from communist parties in the area, had obliged them to abandon their original promise that policy to the rest of the Arab world would be coordinated through Egypt, but to make this abandonment more palatable they made a point of informing Cairo about their talks with other Arab leaders. Thus, when Kosygin arrived in Cairo he told Nasser that the Politburo had asked him to report on the results of the Zuayin visit. He spoke of the Soviet agreement to help the Syrians in the construction of a dam and hydro-electric station on the Euphrates, and asked Nasser whether he approved. Nasser was astonished – 'Anything,' he replied, 'that can be done for any Arab country must be welcome to us.' In a lighter vein Kosygin asked Nasser if there was any special significance in the fact that the three chief men in Syria – the President, the Prime Minister and the Foreign Minister – were all doctors. Nasser's answer was: 'Can you tell me if there is any special significance in the fact that Brezhnev, Podgorny and you are all engineers?'

Kosygin no doubt realized that Egypt's increasing demands on the Soviet Union in so many fields – arms, industrialization, credits, wheat, and so on – were bound to create friction and would require understanding on both sides. So, though he was searching in the questions he asked, he was tactful in the way he asked them. He was particularly interested in Egypt's relations with the new regime in Syria. The Soviets gave the impression of wanting Egypt to demonstrate its backing for the left-wing Baathist government there, which included the communists, and of being fearful that a quarrel might blow up between Egypt and Syria comparable to the one between Egypt and Qasim's Iraq. Kosygin also asked a lot of questions about political organizations in Egypt – how cadre groups inside the ASU were developing, and so on.

Then the discussion ran into trouble. Because of the deteriorating situation in the Middle East – the growing tension between Syria and Israel, the increasing bellicosity of the Syrian regime which was accusing Egypt of doing nothing to help the common struggle, and the heightened activity of Fateh, Nasser had felt obliged to put in a request for more arms and, at the same time, for postponement of interest payments on some of Egypt's debts to the Soviets. Kosygin explained that, unfortunately, these requests, which had been forwarded by Egypt's ambassador in Moscow to Semyonov in the Ministry of Foreign Affairs, had been received too late for consideration by the Politburo before he left. He was anxious to explain how the new leadership functioned, emphasizing that any requests should be forwarded to Moscow at the earliest possible moment, so that they could be properly processed. Each request had to be considered by the appropriate agencies – economics, industry, armed forces etc – in the light of a general directive from the Politburo, and then the recommendations of these agencies had to be considered and approved by the Politburo. All he could say was that when he returned he would see that Egypt's requests for arms were dealt with through the proper channels.

As to Egypt's request for postponement of interest payments, Kosygin explained that the problem was a very difficult one. Such a request did not involve Egypt alone; it raised a matter of principle which other countries would inevitably take note of. He said that the indebtedness of Third World countries to the Soviet Union amounted to 24 million roubles, and if there was a general slowing down in the repayment of these debts it would upset the whole overall planning of the

Soviet Union. The Soviet Union was a planned economy, he said, and they had to know exactly what was going to be needed year by year in each field of expenditure. He referred to the exceptional problem with which the Soviet Union was faced by the war in Vietnam. 'The Chinese,' he said, 'talk a lot, but it is we who have to do the giving.' He complained that the North Vietnamese had large quantities of Russian arms of excellent quality which they were not using; they wanted to stockpile for a strategic reserve. Even so, the Soviet Union had given the North Vietnamese everything they asked for, and had even offered them weapons about which they knew nothing, and had sent them technicians to teach the use of these. He revealed that the Soviet Union had even offered to send military contingents to North Vietnam, but said that the North Vietnamese had rejected the offer, and the Chinese had let it be known that they would not accept the presence of Russian troops in North Vietnam. When Kosygin mentioned that the North Vietnamese wished to build up a strategic reserve of arms Nasser could not resist the temptation to put in a reminder – 'We too,' he said, 'want to accumulate a stock of arms.'

Kosygin told Nasser that when he had spoken to Ho Chi-minh about the expansion of the war in Vietnam, saying that if there was no settlement the Americans would put in more troops, or the war would go on for ever, Ho had astonished him by saying 'I want them to send more troops.' Ho had told Nasser that the Soviets had nothing to do with the policies of those fighting in Vietnam: 'Those who think that China is encouraging us to fight in order to strengthen their point of view must be mad. Even if someone came to us and asked us to mediate we would say Hanoi was nothing to do with us – he would have to talk to the National Liberation Front in South Vietnam.'

In one of his messages to Nasser, Ho recalled meeting Lenin in the company of MN Roy, the Indian communist, when both of them had told Lenin that the real centre for world revolution could not be in Europe; it would have to be in Asia, because it was there that lay the massive new proletarian forces.

Another request which we had to make to Kosygin while he was in Cairo concerned wheat. Nasser explained to him the difficulties which we were encountering with the Americans; we had been taking 1.5 million tons a year from them, but now they were threatening to cut this down, or to stop supplying us altogether. He wanted to know whether, if this happened, he could count on the Soviet Union to come to Egypt's rescue. Kosygin was quite frank in admitting that grain supplies were the Soviet Union's weak point. He asked why Egypt didn't grow more wheat. Nasser explained that what Egypt grew was a matter of the most profitable use that could be made of the limited amount of fertile land available. One feddan could produce £37 worth of wheat a year, or £120 worth of sugar cane, or £250 worth of fruit and vegetables. Kosygin appreciated this argument. 'We'll see,' he said. 'It all depends on the harvest. I can't promise anything. You'll have to wait for two things – nature and the Politburo.'

It was two months after this that the answer to Nasser's request came in a typically indirect way. At the reception being given in Moscow by the Egyptian ambassador to celebrate the anniversary of the July revolution a senior official came up to him and said: 'Don't quote me, but I think that now would be a suitable time to put in a request for wheat.' In such small but significant ways did the Russians who had regular dealings with Egypt help to consolidate their positions.

Kosygin has always been a man who revels in facts and figures. This came out particularly when, at one stage of his visit, the subject came up of the possibility of building an underground railway system as a means of relieving Cairo's chronic traffic problem. Would the Soviet Union be able to help? Immediately Kosygin was firing off technical questions – it was as though a dam had burst in this normally rather reserved character. What sort of soil would the engineers encounter? Was it rock or clay? What proportion? Detailed figures for construction costs in every possible circumstance flowed from him. He showed the same absolute mastery of technical detail when, later, he discussed electrification of the High Dam.

*   *   *

On the whole I think the new Soviet leaders were now beginning to feel they knew more or less where they were with Nasser, but the rest of the Arab world produced almost nothing but headaches for them. They were particularly frustrated by the bitter polemics exchanged between the rival Baathist regimes in Damascus and Baghdad. Delegations from each of these regimes visited Moscow in the summer of 1966, and Kosygin took the opportunity to ask Dr Ibrahim Makhous, the Syrian Foreign Minister, why his government didn't coordinate policy with the government of Iraq. 'I'm only the Foreign Minister,' said Makhous, 'the party determines policy. But don't forget – there is blood between us and the government of Iraq.' 'Blood?' exclaimed Kosygin. 'What d'you mean?' 'It's a vendetta!' said Makhous. Makhous also complained to Gromyko that Khaled Bakdash had told the merchants of Damascus' great Hamidiyeh bazaar that they were very important to the Syrian economy and that it was only the wicked Baathists who were trying to crush them. Not surprisingly, the Soviets found all these parochial feuds incomprehensible.

When, a little later, the Iraqi Prime Minister, Abdel Rahman Bazzaz, started talking about 'those irresponsible people in Damascus', Kosygin, with pardonable exasperation, said: 'It would be better if you spent less time hitting each other over the head and more time hitting Israel on the head.'

It was around this time that a considerable increase in KGB activities in the Arab world became noticeable. Before that there had been little need for the Soviets to make special efforts to acquire information – the arms traffic they had with Egypt and other countries provided more or less all the opportunities they needed for acquiring it. But now they felt there were many puzzling questions to which they required an answer, particularly in regard to Egypt's relations with America, of which they were perennially suspicious. A visit like that which George Woods, President of the World Bank, paid to Cairo was certain to provoke their lively alarm. Two attachés at the Egyptian embassy in Moscow, who had each been caught trying to smuggle in one hundred gold coins, were arrested and told that they would be released if they agreed to work for the KGB.

It was no doubt as part of the same campaign that some of the Egyptian army officers on courses in the Soviet Union were astonished one day to find that the Russian text book assigned for their sociology studies was called *Scientific Fundamentals of Communism*. They also found communist literature deposited in their bedrooms. As there was a written agreement with the Soviets that Egyptian officers studying with them should not be subjected to any political indoctrination, Amer wrote to Gretchko to complain.

★   ★   ★

There can be no doubt that by the summer and autumn of 1966 the Soviets had become extremely worried about the general world situation. They felt that President Johnson was capable of almost anything – 'He's more dangerous than Dulles', as Brezhnev told U Thant – and they found it incongruous that at this period of tension those Arabs whom they counted as friendly seemed unable to compose their differences with each other. Surely at least the progressive regimes – Egypt, Iraq, Syria, Algeria – should be able to present a united front and not indulge in talk about blood and vendetta? They remembered Abyssinia, Spain, the Saar and Austria, and feared that once again local quarrels might lead to big power involvement and wider wars.

In a despatch dated October 7, 1966, the Egyptian ambassador in Moscow, Mourad Ghaleb, provided a detailed analysis of the situation seen through Soviet eyes, of the dangers which they saw threatening Egypt and of the precautions which they felt should be taken. The Soviets, he wrote, believe that a new American policy towards the area is in process of formulation. Owing to de Gaulle's action in withdrawing from the NATO command the US has lost its base in France. Italy offers no alternative. At the other end of the Mediterranean Turkey is still in American hands but public opinion there increasingly resents American influence. The southern shore of the Mediterranean offers a possible alternative strategic area, and this would explain the enormous pressure currently being put by America on Tunisia, Morocco, Libya, and even Algeria. The only country which does not fit in with this strategy is Egypt, so the American aim must be to destroy Egypt and the dominant position which it occupies in the Arab world.

Mourad Ghaleb went on to say that the Soviets had assured him they had received information that the Americans were reinforcing their North African bases (which in effect meant Wheelus Field, over which the Libyan government had no control) with missiles, and that these could be used against Egypt or Syria in the event of war. This would mean that American missiles might be fired from one Arab territory at targets in other Arab territories, and that in this case it would be very difficult for the Soviet Union to make an appropriate reply. This, perhaps, was what the Americans wanted. The Soviets feared that the CIA might be used to create conditions which would lead to the outbreak of armed conflict in the area. Should this happen, Egypt would be branded the aggressor, and American intervention would follow, to be presented as an effort to safeguard peace.

In the light of this analysis the Soviets urged the institution of a continuous and intensified campaign against the existence of foreign bases in the Arab world and North Africa. They also urged efforts to reconcile inter-Arab differences and to avoid any steps which might escalate Arab–Israeli tensions into open war. The final Soviet warning was that the new American policy might be inaugurated by the offer of massive aid to Egypt. It would be tempting for Egypt to accept this, but in fact it should be seen as bait designed for the ultimate destruction of Egypt, and should be resisted. Clearly the Politburo had been doing a great deal of thinking on the subject. They appreciated the key role which Egypt still played, and described their relations with Egypt as 'warm'. Egypt was still the most important Arab country in their eyes, but its Grade A status was slipping slightly.

A month later, in November 1966, Amer was in Moscow, and Kosygin raised with him the Arab–Israeli question. It seemed that, for the first time, the Soviet Union had begun to try to think seriously about possible solutions for the problem. Might there not, asked Kosygin, be some means of diminishing the level of arms in the area? This was the sort of question Egypt was more accustomed to hear from the Americans than from the Russians.

★   ★   ★

For some time Nasser had felt that it would be a good plan to invite Brezhnev to Egypt. The suggestion had been informally made, and at first Brezhnev reacted with enthusiasm. What, he wanted to know, would be the occasion for such a visit? He was told that the power station operated by the High Dam was to be opened, and this he accepted as suitable. But then Moscow began to have second thoughts. It was feared that such a visit for such an occasion would remind people too forcibly of Khruschev's visit; comparisons would inevitably be made. So they sent a letter of apology, postponing the visit. 1967, they pointed out, marked the fiftieth anniversary of the Russian Revolution and they wanted to put on the best show possible. Moscow was being cleaned up, the people mobilized, extra consumer goods were being provided, and all members of the Politburo were scattered round the country preparing for the celebrations. In fact, there had been some criticism of the amount of time Brezhnev had spent recently on visits abroad, mainly to the countries of eastern Europe, and it was obviously felt that this was a time when the leaders' attention should be concentrated on the home front.

But because there was so much to discuss, and because the Soviets were undoubtedly aware of the suspicions rife among the Arabs and in the Third World generally about the implications of detente (there was much talk at the time about 'a new Yalta'), they decided to send Gromyko on a three-day visit to Cairo in March 1967. Gromyko was naturally not a substitute for Brezhnev, but as soon as he arrived he was careful to explain that he came, not in his capacity as Minister of Foreign Affairs, but as candidate member of the Politburo; he pointed this out, he said, to stress the fact that the Soviet's relations with Egypt were regarded as so important that they remained the concern of the Politburo. Gromyko assured Nasser that the Soviet Union had no secret agreement with the US. 'This hasn't happened, and will not happen,' he said. 'The Americans are trying to cause trouble. They like to give the impression that their relations with us are continually improving, and that we and they consult together on everything. But this simply isn't true. For example, the American chargé d'affaires tried to get in touch with our ambassador in Cairo shortly before I was due to arrive here. Our ambassador thought that perhaps the Americans wanted to raise matters connected with my visit and asked for instructions from Moscow. We told him to go ahead and meet the American chargé. But when the American came he had nothing to say about my visit, which leads us to conclude that his only purpose was to give you people the impression that the US and ourselves coordinate our policies.'

Nasser raised with Gromyko the question of Soviet arms sales to Iran by an agreement made in February 1967. Why did they sell arms to the Shah's reactionary regime when their friends, such as Egypt, were having continual difficulty in obtaining the arms they needed? 'You think, Mr President,' said Gromyko, 'that this arms sale has been arranged in coordination with the Americans. But this isn't exactly true. It was we who took the initiative with the Shah. The American aim is to isolate the Soviet Union from its friends and create an atmosphere of Soviet–American collusion, in the hope that this will damage the world communist movement and national liberation movements everywhere, and deepen the Sino-Soviet conflict by appearing to justify the Chinese claim that detente is simply another word for collusion, and weaken the fighting spirit of the Vietnamese. But in fact I can assure you that relations between us and the Americans are extremely tense.'

★   ★   ★

But in spite of Gromyko's assurances there was widespread suspicion of what was going on between the Russians and Americans, and this was not confined to Arab governments. The Indians were known to share it, and the Algerians went as far as to suggest calling a meeting of all governments which had close dealings with the Soviet Union to compare notes.

There was in fact a good deal of comparing of notes by Arab governments in Cairo and other capitals such as London, Washington and Moscow, where Arab ambassadors had adopted the habit of holding regular informal meetings. The general impression was that the Soviets were so preoccupied with the dangers of an escalating war in Vietnam, and so frustrated by the difficulties which they encountered in their dealings with the Arabs, that they were almost prepared to wash their hands of them. 'The Arabs can go to hell,' was the consensus view of Soviet feelings.

The Syrians, for example, reported that the Soviets were taking an extremely tough line over the question of debt repayments (they as well as Egypt had problems in meeting their obligations); in fact they said that the Soviets had not only refused to allow any discount on the purchase price of new arms, but had actually increased the price. The Syrians, who had a large surplus in their tobacco crop which they wished to export, had asked the Russians to buy it, but for the first time the Russians refused to take any tobacco. When the Syrians complained, the answer they got from the Soviet Ministry of Foreign Affairs was that they were the architects of their own policies and should be prepared to pay the price for them; if they couldn't afford them, that was just too bad.

The Algerians said that when they had suggested paying for wheat, due to be shipped to them by the Soviet Union as a result of a trade agreement, by sending iron ore in exchange, the Soviets refused – though later they had accepted. The Algerians had complained to Moscow of what amounted to Soviet dumping tactics by the supply of natural gas to Italy in competition with Algerian gas, but the only answer they had had was that every country was free to do what it liked.

By the beginning of May 1967 the impression was growing that something was going to happen in the Middle East, though nobody could tell what would happen, or where, or how. Cairo was receiving warnings from Moscow about Israeli troop movements, which heightened the feeling of tension. These warnings were, of course, well intentioned and based on fact, and may perhaps be seen as one of the ways in which a superpower hopes to maintain its influence over a local power – when scared, the local power is bound to consult the super-power. In the case of Israel and America, of course, the roles were reversed. It was Israel which fed Washington with alarmist stories as part of the process of keeping the Americans involved in its fate. America's relations with Israel were, so to speak, conducted from the inside, whereas Russia's relations with the Arabs were conducted from the outside. The Arabs were always insisting to the Soviet Union on their independence, while the Israelis preferred to emphasize to the Americans their close mutual dependence. This difference was to have important consequences both during and after the 1967 war.

10
The Trap

IT IS NOT MY INTENTION to tell again the story of the 1967 war, either militarily or diplomatically, or to try to apportion blame for the disaster. I would rather confine myself to considering the effects which the war – including the events leading up to it, and its immediate aftermath – had on Arab–Soviet relations.

The mood of the Soviet Union in the summer of 1967, as I hope I have been able to make clear, was hesitant and uncertain. There were new men in the Kremlin, and they were men of a new type. Khruschev was the last of the revolutionary generation who had been agitators first and only later become party bureaucrats; Brezhnev and his colleagues represented the new generation of managers and ideologists. When these men looked beyond the borders of the Soviet Union they cannot have got much comfort from what they saw. Heavy expenditure abroad had put a severe burden on the Soviet economy and brought few returns. Countries like Indonesia and Ghana had turned hostile and were defaulting on their debts; even countries like Egypt and Syria, which remained friendly, were petitioning to default. Communist governments and parties in Europe were asking awkward, and perhaps heretical questions. China was openly hostile. Inside the Soviet Union itself, a dissident movement, linked with the Jewish problem and so affecting relations with the US and the Arabs, had raised its head. And on neither of these flanks were relations easy. The US, under President Johnson, seemed to be going through a period of reckless adventurism, yet some detente with the US was essential if the crippling burden of expenditure on arms was to be moderated; the Arabs, especially those in the progressive camp, were at loggerheads with the West and so were stepping up their demands on the Soviet Union. Hence the paradox that it was the nominally revolutionary Soviet regime which was advocating caution and was intent on preserving the status quo, while it was the conservative American regime which, by its actions, was stirring up violent change.

I do not believe that the Russians had ever evolved an overall strategy for the Arab world. They had been sucked into the complexities of the Middle East scene before they realized what was happening. Only when they had become deeply involved did they begin to ask themselves whether the Arabs wanted them there for their own sakes, or simply because the Arabs had become disenchanted with the West. This was an uncomfortable question to ask, implying as it did that the Soviet Union was, in a sense, a second choice. I remember a discussion I had with a member of the Soviet Central Committee: 'We give you all this aid,' he said, 'but what do we get out of it? You still talk, and sometimes even write, like Westerners. Why, for example, are there no Soviet films on show in Cairo, but only American ones?' 'If we showed Soviet films,' I said, 'nobody would go to them. They are mostly to do with the war, and very crude.' 'But if you used the right propaganda, and educated people,' he insisted, 'they would be persuaded to go to them. In any case, even granting that people don't want to see our films, why should you let them see American films? These are poison. The result of showing them is that whenever the West chooses to beckon, you'll go running to them.'

He need not have worried; America was not beckoning. Over the past year or two there had been a noticeable change of attitude by big business in America towards the Middle East. Americans may not like a regime, but if they think it is stable enough to be a good risk they will do business with it. In the 1950s and early 1960s Americans, while loathing much of what Nasser stood for, had looked on him as almost the only stable element in an unstable area and, indeed, as the only Arab capable of standing up to the Soviet Union and to communist infiltration. But by 1965, given Egypt's more radical legislation and closer ties with Moscow, they began to turn against him. Moreover, after the coup inside the Saudi ruling family in November 1964 which overthrew King Saud, Washington felt it imperative to secure the position of his brother and successor, King Feisal, whose kingdom thus became closely linked with American interests. American planes were stationed in Saudi Arabia; American oil companies became active in the recruitment of mercenaries for the Yemen war, and in 1961 a man with an oil background, John McCone, was appointed the new head of the CIA.

Unfortunately the progressive camp, in which Egypt was the leading member, was itself disunited. Iraq under Abdel Salam Aref's brother,

President Abdel Rahman Aref (President Abdel Salam had been killed in a helicopter crash on April 13, 1966) was still isolated; in Algeria Boumedienne, deeply suspicious of the cost of foreign involvement, kept his own counsel. The Syrians were indulging in what Lenin described as the 'infantile disorder' of left-wing deviation. The Palestinians of Fateh continued their lonely and not particularly effective programme of sabotage.

★   ★   ★

About the beginning of May 1967 Anwar Sadat, then chairman of the National Assembly, was on his way to North Korea for an official visit, and stopped in Moscow en route, where he met Kosygin. The usual question of arms supplies was discussed, and he too raised the matter of the sale of Soviet arms to Iran, which Nasser had already brought up with Gromyko. Kosygin was even more vigorous in his defence of the Soviet action than Gromyko had been. 'You must understand that Iran is our neighbour,' he said. 'The Americans, the British, and even the Japanese are there. We can't tell the Shah "go to hell, you are a Shah and we are communists!" We must have a presence in Iran. There is a plan for a large-scale arms programme for Iran, in which all the western countries including West Germany are involved. We must have our plan to neutralize the Shah. If he makes an approach to us, we can't say "No. Go and get what you want from the Americans and British." We can't limit our commercial exchanges with Iran to the buying and selling of water-melons and apricots. Tell me,' Kosygin went on, 'should we leave Iran alone, or try to take care of it? Which is better for you – Soviet arms in Iran or American arms?' Sadat tried to argue, but without much success.

On his way back from North Korea Sadat met Podgorny and Vladimir Semyonov, Deputy Minister for Foreign Affairs, who gave him a confidential warning that the situation in the Middle East was in their view extremely critical. They had learned that the Israelis were massing their forces on the Syrian frontier and that an attack was planned for some time between May 18 and 22. The Syrians had already passed on similar information to Cairo, their estimate being that eleven Israeli brigades were confronting them. Not a great deal of credence had been attached to the Syrian reports, but now that they were confirmed by the Russians Sadat naturally felt they must be taken extremely seriously. He was not due back in Cairo until May 14, so he tele-graphed a summary of his Moscow conversations through the Egyptian embassy in a secure cipher, and immediately on his return went to Nasser's house and described in fuller detail the warnings which he had received.

It was on the basis of these warnings that on May 16 Nasser pro-claimed a state of emergency and decided to send troops into Sinai. This was done with a good deal of publicity, because he was worried lest the Israelis and others might think the Egyptian army was too involved in Yemen to be able to come to the assistance of Syria. Para-doxically the people most perturbed by Egypt's troop movements were the Russians themselves. True Egypt was acting on information supplied by them, but they had intended their warning more to prepare the Egyptian government psychologically for a crisis and to encourage closer consultations than to spur it into independent action. Once again a superpower had failed to understand the nature of its relationship with a local power.

Amer asked the Soviet ambassador in Cairo if his government could, through its satellite observations, give him any clearer picture of the disposition of Israeli forces on the Syrian borders. The ambassador said he would try to obtain this. Moscow came back with the reply that they were unable to determine whether the Israeli concentrations were a deliberate provocation or whether they were precautionary measures to guard against any attempt by the Syrians to take advantage of Israeli's national day (May 15) to launch an attack. Coming from Moscow, the idea that the Israeli troop movements might be defensive rather than offensive was something quite new. Moscow was now, in fact, speaking two languages at the same time – the language of alarm and the language of restraint.

The Israeli Minister of Labour, Yigal Allon, happened to be in Moscow at about this time on a visit which was described as 'touristic'. The Israeli ambassador gave a reception in his honour at which a number of Soviet officials were present, including Semyonov, who gave him a warning that any attack by Israel against Syria, or any other Arab country, would have the effect of making the Soviet Union Israel's enemy. Allon said that no attack against Syria was being prepared – as far as the Israelis were concerned Arab countries could choose any political or social system they liked. The Israelis, he said, were 'not toys in the hands of others' (meaning the Americans). But he complained of Fateh infiltrations, and said that Israel had the right to arm its people for the defence of its territory.

The Soviets passed a report of this conversation on to Cairo too. But such reassurance as it gave was couched in vague language, nor did Semyonov's comments to the effect that, remembering what had happened in 1956, 'we should all be on our toes' help much. Meanwhile on the ground the crisis was escalating. Egyptian troops moved into Sinai on May 18, and to make their presence there credible, Nasser asked the UN the same day to remove its forces between Rafah and Taba – he did not ask for the total removal of UN forces, only for them to be taken away from the Egyptian frontier. But U Thant, prompted by Ralph Bunche, insisted that the peace-keeping mission of the UN forces in Sinai was an integral matter. There could not be hostilities in one sector, from which UN forces had been removed, and a continuing UN presence in the other sectors. If any of the UN forces went, they would all have to go.

★　　★　　★

The Soviets were in touch with the Americans, and both agreed that U Thant should go to the area; he left New York for Cairo on May 22. President Johnson and Kosygin sent Nasser letters urging him to co-operate with the Secretary-General. Meanwhile Egyptian troops had occupied the UN positions which meant that, since a state of war between Israel and Egypt persisted, a blockade of the Gulf of Akaba could become effective. U Thant, in Cairo, where he arrived on May 23, suggested there should be a moratorium for fifteen days, starting from the date of his return to New York, and that he would advise the Israelis not to try to send ships carrying the Israeli flag into the Gulf of Akaba, or to try to bring in strategic materials in non-Israeli ships. He recommended that Egypt, in turn, should not attempt to exercise its rights in the Gulf as a belligerent.

Nasser accepted U Thant's proposal for a moratorium, understanding that Israelis had accepted it too, and that it had been made with the backing of the two superpowers.

But the really critical contribution by U Thant came in a message which was cabled to Nasser on May 30. This proved, in fact, to be the real turning point in the crisis, since Nasser assumed that its contents had been agreed by the American and Russian governments, and that it meant that no offensive action was going to be taken by Israel during the next two weeks – that is, before June 14. The first assumption was correct; the second was to prove disastrously wrong. I do not believe that U Thant realized the use that was being made of him, but the standing which he enjoyed with Egypt, combined with the fact that Zakaria Mohieddin, the Egyptian Vice-President, was at the same time invited to Washington to continue negotiations, effectively ensured the restraint in Cairo for which U Thant pleaded and from which Israel was to be the beneficiary. For some reason U Thant's message has never been published, so it is worth giving in full:

Mr President,

I know from my recent talks with you and Foreign Minister Riad that you fully understand my motives in making this direct, personal, and most urgent appeal to you. You will note that what I am asking you to do springs solely from my desire to do everything that I possibly can to avert the catastrophe of a new war in the Middle East.

During my visit to Cairo your position and policy with regard to the Straits of Tiran was made clear to me. I wish to emphasize that a favourable response by you to my appeal would be without prejudice to that position and policy. I am seeking time, even a short period, in order to provide a reasonable opportunity for consultations and other international efforts to find a way out of the existing critical situation. I wish to call your attention specially to what I said in my report to the Security Council on May 26. In my view a peaceful outcome of the present crisis depends on a breathing spell which will allow tension to subside from its present explosive level.

I therefore urge all the parties concerned to exercise special restraint, to forego belligerence, and to avoid all other actions which could increase tension, in order to allow the Security Council to deal with the underlying causes of the present crisis and seek solutions.

I now appeal to you, Mr President, as I am appealing to Prime Minister Eshkol and to all concerned, to exercise the utmost restraint at this critical juncture. In particular, without asking any commitment from you, or indeed any reply, may I express the hope that for the next two weeks from your receipt of this message there will be no interference with non-Israeli shipping seeking passage through the Straits of Tiran. In this regard, I should advise you that in any case it is my understanding that in the normal course of events no Israeli ship is expected to seek passage through the Straits of Tiran in the next fortnight. Indeed, according to the best information available to me no ship flying the flag of Israel has in fact sought passage through the Straits in the last two and a half years. I can assure Your Excellency that I personally, and the international community in general, would greatly appreciate such a gesture by you.

Please be assured of my best wishes and personal regards,

U Thant

★   ★   ★

This letter was not, of course, intended to deceive, though by creating a false sense of reassurance in Cairo this was the effect it had. Nasser himself had doubts about how much should be read into it, all the more since the atmosphere of crisis continued to mount. It was learned that Israeli troops were being moved from their positions in the north against Syria to the south. Nasser called in the Soviet ambassador and spoke to him very frankly. 'I want you to understand', he said, 'that everything that is happening now follows from the information and advice which we have received from your government. You are responsible to me for all this. Your people in Moscow must understand that politically, and on the military plane, I want this to be translated into material aid as quickly as possible. We need an airlift. I propose sending our Defence Minister, Shamseddin Badran, to Moscow to discuss deliveries.'

Shamseddin Badran's visit turned out most unfortunately. On May 23, the day before he arrived, the Soviet government had put out a strong statement which, while stressing the importance of preserving the peace, branded Israel as a disturbing force in the area. Badran met Kosygin on the day of his arrival, who said: 'I think you must be very pleased with the declaration we put out yesterday. It doesn't leave any room for doubt about our intentions. The UAR has achieved its objectives – and by peaceful means [he was referring to the thinning out of Israeli troops on the Syrian frontier, the withdrawal of UN troops in Sinai and Egyptian control of the Gulf of Akaba]. So now the most important thing is to cool things down and not give Israel or the imperialist forces any cause for triggering off an armed conflict. Now you've got what you want we can look sympathetically at your requests. Marshal Gretchko will discuss them with you.'

So next Badran saw the Soviet Defence Minister, Marshal Gretchko, his first deputy, Marshal Yakobovski, and Marshal Zakharov, the Chief of Staff. Gretchko also urged the need to prevent matters developing to the point of armed conflict, but said he was sure the imperialists would still find ways of exploiting the situation. He thought it likely they might create trouble in the Gulf of Akaba by trying to send an Israeli tanker into it, guarded by American naval units, which would provoke a clash with Egypt and provide a pretext for Israeli intervention.

Gromyko, whom Shamseddin Badran then saw, said he thought that the overall situation had improved because of the greatly enhanced Soviet naval strength in the Mediterranean. The development of events, he said, had brought considerable political gains for the UAR, but now was a time for restraint. He said that the Soviet ambassador in Tel Aviv had reported that Abba Eban, Israel's Foreign Minister, was extremely worried and had emphasized Israel's wish to avoid a conflict. Kosygin had received a message from President Johnson, and they were keeping in touch with each other. Kosygin was preparing a reply in which the actions of the US and of its agent, Israel, would both be condemned. Gromyko said his government rejected the idea of a four-power conference on the Middle East (this had been suggested by de Gaulle, and was opposed by the Egyptian government also, because it was felt it would amount to no more than a revival of the old western tripartite idea, with the Soviet Union, Egypt's friend, in a permanent minority of one). Gromyko reported that the British Foreign Secretary, George Brown, had been in Moscow in May, but unfortunately the ideas on the Middle East he expressed had been identical with those of the American government, showing just as much hostility towards Egypt.

It was when Badran and his party were leaving that the real misunderstanding took place. Marshal Gretchko had come to the airport to see them off, and he was chatting to Badran at the foot of the aircraft steps. He said: 'Stand firm. Whatever you have to face, you will find us with you. Don't let yourselves be blackmailed by the Americans or anyone else.' After the plane had taken off the Egyptian ambassador in Moscow, Murad Ghaleb, who had heard Gretchko's remarks, said to him, 'That was very reassuring, Marshal.' Gretchko laughed, and said to him (in Russian), 'I just wanted to give him one for the road.'

So the Badran mission produced three conflicting views on what the Soviet attitude was at this critical moment. Ahmed Hassan Fikki, the Egyptian Assistant Foreign Minister, who had been a member of the mission, reported his clear impression that the Russians wanted Nasser to de-escalate. Shamseddin Badran, on the other hand, as a result of Gretchko's parting words, was telling a different story. Finally, the Egyptian ambassador felt himself obliged to advise Nasser, in a confidential letter, that Gretchko's expressions of support should not be taken at face value. Unfortunately, owing to a series of administrative delays, the ambassador's letter did not reach Nasser until after the battle had started. If it had arrived in time it might possibly have made a considerable difference. The Syrian Prime Minister, Nureddin Atassi, who arrived in Moscow on May 29 shortly after Shamseddin Badran left, was also sending Cairo messages from various Soviet sources assuring Nasser that everything would turn out all right.

One message from the Egyptian ambassador, Murad Ghaleb, which did reach Nasser at about this time he found hard to interpret. Apparently the counsellor at the Egyptian embassy had been at a dinner at which the American ambassador, Llewellyn Thompson, was also a guest. Thompson had told the counsellor that he had received an invitation to the Egyptian embassy for the following Monday for a farewell reception which Murad Ghaleb (who was doyen of the Diplomatic Corps) was giving to the departing Finnish ambassador. 'I want your ambassador to tell me in complete confidence,' said Thompson, 'whether over these next few days my presence in his embassy would cause him any embarrassment.' 'But you have always been a frequent visitor to our embassy,' said the Egyptian counsellor. 'But', Thompson said, 'things might happen in the next few days which could make my presence embarrassing.' Nasser showed me the telegram in which the ambassador reported this exchange, and asked me what I made of it.

★   ★   ★

Then came June 5. At first the Israelis were successful in producing a good deal of confusion in people's minds as to who had started the war. Indira Gandhi, the Indian Prime Minister, fired off an extremely concerned telegram to Kosygin as soon as she heard that hostilities had started. Kosygin told her in reply that the Soviet government knew from its own sources that Israel was the aggressor and that Israel had the backing of some of the big powers, with which it had had close contact over the past few days, and that it had not made the attack alone. He said that the Soviet Union stood firmly at the side of the UAR, and that it had always been the policy of the Soviet Union to give support for the independence and security of struggling nations.

For any of us in Cairo at that time to be told that the Soviet Union was standing firmly by our side would have seemed very remote from reality. Amer, as the news from Sinai came in, was in a state of almost complete collapse. On the afternoon of June 6 he summoned the Soviet ambassador, and poured out a flood of accusations at him. He said the Americans had taken part in the destruction of the Egyptian air force (this was generally believed at that time to be the case), and the Soviet Union had given no help of any sort, not even an accurate picture of the disposition of Israeli troops. Was this the meaning of the word detente, he demanded? Was it detente or collusion? Once again, as in 1956, everyone was talking about collusion, only this time there were fears of a double collusion – between America and Israel, and, in the name of detente, between America and Russia.

There was a widespread impression that the Americans had been actively involved in the Israeli attack, probably through the supply of arms, coordination of intelligence and so on, and evidence has subsequently come to light of the extent to which Johnson gave the Israelis the green light to go ahead. Nasser hinted at America's involvement in his resignation speech on June 9, and this was not propaganda but what he genuinely believed.

In fact the Americans played their cards with considerable skill. On June 8, two planes with American markings, apparently coming from bases in Saudi Arabia, flew over the Suez Canal. Only half an hour after they had been observed Nasser received a message from Kosygin, relaying one from President Johnson, saying that the overflying of Egyptian territory by American planes was in no way meant as a hostile action against Egypt but was explained by the fact that an American ship in the Mediterranean had been hit and they were rushing to its assistance. The American 'spy ship' *Liberty* had, as was quickly known, been attacked by Israeli planes with considerable loss of life. But the whole incident, including the use by Washington of Moscow as a channel for communication with Cairo, was somewhat bizarre, and encouraged the widespread conviction in the Arab world that the Soviet Union's policy of detente had let it into what amounted to collusion with the Americans. But opinions differed over whether the Russians were dupes of the Americans or were too frightened to be able to come to the help of their friends.

There was some other evidence to support the charge of collusion. On May 25, Eban and the Israeli Director of Military Intelligence had been in Washington. The Egyptian ambassador went that evening to see Eugene Rostow, Under-Secretary for Political Affairs in the State Department, who said: 'I'm talking to you in the name of the President. Eban came here without an appointment and asked to see the Secretary of State, and was immediately received by him. He said he had information from Israel that Egypt was going to attack that night. I must warn you that if this is correct the US will be in opposition to Egypt.'

The Egyptian ambassador reported these remarks in an urgent telegram to Cairo. At 3 a.m. the following morning the Soviet ambassador in Cairo went to the office of Sami Sharaf, secretary to the President, and asked to see Nasser because he had an important message for him from Moscow which he was instructed to hand over without delay. Nasser was woken; he put on shirt and trousers and went to the reception room downstairs, where the ambassador greeted him with many apologies. He had, he said, a message from Kosygin to the effect that the Americans had contacted him with the report that according to Israeli sources Egypt was going to attack at dawn, and they implored Egypt to desist. Nasser said that Egypt had no such plan.

Amer quoted this incident too among the charges he levelled at the Soviet ambassador. 'It is you who prevented us from making the first strike,' he said. 'You deprived us of the initiative. That is collusion!'

★   ★   ★

The Soviet leaders were naturally extremely upset at the charge of collusion, and responded favourably to the proposal made by President Tito that representatives of all the Warsaw Pact countries and Yugoslavia should meet in Moscow on June 9 to discuss 'the situation created in the Middle East by Israel's aggression'. Tito had urged that a disastrous impression would be created if the socialist camp appeared to be doing nothing while one of the leading non-aligned countries of the Third

World was subjected to an all-out military attack. All those who attended the Moscow meeting, with the exception of Rumania, promised aid to the Arabs and agreed to break off diplomatic relations with Israel. President Tito felt this was not enough. He proposed a meeting of leaders of East European communist parties and heads of state to discuss ways of assisting the Arabs. These, with only Rumania absent, met in Budapest on July 11 and 12 and agreed to coordinate political, economic and military aid 'including steps which may promote the development of industry and agriculture for friendly Arab states'.

There had already been an incident involving the Yugoslavs which had helped to complicate Egypt's relations with the Russians. At the height of the battle Cairo had asked Moscow for an immediate airlift of arms and had been almost immediately told that this was on its way. But nothing arrived. Two days passed, and then Amer demanded to know from the Soviet ambassador what had happened. The ambassador said the Yugoslavs had not given the planes involved in the airlift overflying rights. Nasser sent a personal message to Tito asking if this was so. Tito replied that, on the contrary, they had from the first hours of the fighting given the Russians overflying rights for any aid they wanted to send to Egypt. The explanation for all this was probably a bureaucratic muddle somewhere along the line, but it created a bad impression.

★   ★   ★

The Security Council had of course been in almost continuous session since the fighting started, and on June 13 the Soviet Union submitted a resolution along the usual lines, calling for condemnation of Israel's 'aggressive activities' and for the 'immediate and unconditional' withdrawal of Israeli forces behind the armistice lines. This was defeated. Already evidence was beginning to be revealed of an understanding which had been worked out between the American and Israeli governments, and which was to remain effective for many years to come – and which, indeed, in essentials is still operative today. This covered three points: first, America would give Israel full backing at the UN and in no circumstances would allow her to be branded an aggressor; second, America would not press Israel to withdraw from the territory she had occupied except in exchange for a complete peace; third, America would see that the balance of arms remained weighted in Israel's favour.

So, with American policy and the threat of an American veto effectively blocking progress in the Security Council, the Russians reverted to the idea of a special emergency session of the General Assembly, as in 1956. Sufficient support for the proposal was forthcoming for this to meet in New York on June 19. But after two weeks of heated debate none of the four resolutions submitted to the Assembly received enough votes to be adopted.

In the atmosphere of tragedy and disillusion which marked the immediate aftermath of the war everybody was inevitably trying to blame everybody else for what had happened. Egyptian soldiers and airmen muttered against the Soviet experts, and the latter proved quite capable of giving as good as they got. One of the experts, who had been attached to the air force, wrote a report in which he claimed that its officers, especially those in the Cairo West base, were lazy and incompetent. The Russian claimed that, after the first Israeli strike, he had noticed that there were three Sukhoys still intact on the runway, so he told some of the pilots to fly them to safety. They said they had no orders, and after a quarter of an hour the Israelis came back and destroyed these planes too. This report reached General Fawzi, the new Minister of War, and helped to exacerbate feelings. Some of the resentment felt against the Russians found its way into the press.

On May 12 the Egyptian ambassador in Moscow sent a telegram saying that the Soviets felt very deeply about the criticisms of them being aired publicly and privately in Egypt. They strongly resented the insinuations that they had somehow been involved in a conspiracy against the Arab states. The ambassador pointed out that the real struggle facing the Arabs was still essentially against the imperialists, and that for this massive assistance would be required, which could only come from the Soviet Union. 'While I fully appreciate that there are bound to be strong feelings at a time like this,' he wrote, 'I would urge the need for an objective look at the situation. It is most necessary that in these days of crisis we find a way of coordinating our policies with those of the Soviet Union. They have assured me that they are serious in their determination to do anything in their power to liquidate the consequences of aggression.'

*   *   *

Perhaps the mood of this period can best be illustrated by a consideration of the ill-fated Boumedienne/Aref visit to Moscow. Boumedienne had tried to send some Algerian contingents to take part in the battle, but everything was over before they could arrive. In Algeria, as in all other Arab countries, the war had created much bitterness. There was a general feeling that during it the Soviet Union had stood idly by while its friends and allies were sacrificed. Boumedienne summoned the Soviet ambassador and told him that he intended to go to Moscow, with or without an invitation, to explain to the Soviet leaders the strength of feeling in the Arab world. This he did, on June 12, but achieved nothing. However, following the meeting of the 'confrontation states' (Egypt, Syria, Iraq, Jordan and Algeria) in Cairo between July 10 and 13, it was agreed that Boumedienne and President Aref of Iraq should go to Moscow as official delegates for the other Arab governments. They arrived in Moscow on July 17, and had meetings with the Soviet leadership the same day and on the following day. They were accompanied by Ismail Khairallah, the acting Iraqi Minister of Foreign Affairs, and Colonel Taher Zubeiri, the Algerian Chief of Staff. On the other side were Brezhnev, Kosygin, Ponomarev, Marshal Gretchko, Kuznetsov, the first deputy Minister of Foreign Affairs, and Zhiporin, the head of the Middle East department in the ministry.

Aref, as a head of state, opened the proceedings. He thanked the Soviet Union, on behalf of all Arab governments, for the help it had already given, but expressed the hope that the Soviets would increase both economic and military aid, since nobody could suppose that current diplomatic negotiations were going to do more than buy time in which the Arabs could regroup their forces.

This gave Brezhnev his cue. 'Let us look at things as they really are,' he said. It was now plain that Israel had been planning its aggression for a long time; it had a population of only two and a half million but an army of 350,000 soldiers – in other words a quarter of its population was under arms. Egypt had a population of thirty million, but only one per cent of its people were under arms. The percentage was the same in Syria. The Israelis had also prepared the home front for war; the Arabs had not. 'Can any country make war in these conditions?' asked Brezhnev.

Brezhnev pointed out that in the brief period which had elapsed since the fighting started the socialist countries had had two meetings to consider what steps should be taken. Such meetings were not easily arranged or lightly undertaken; their purpose was serious, not propaganda. He went on to describe what he considered to be 'the roots of the problem'. Israel, by itself, he said, was nothing. It depended for its existence on American aid, and the reason why the Americans kept Israel alive was because they wanted the oil of the Middle East, which represented sixty per cent of the world's known reserves. To get at this oil, they had tried to keep the Arab world under their control, but after the appearance of progressive regimes there this had proved impossible; the Americans could not themselves attack the Arab nation, but they could attack through Israel.

'Now,' said Brezhnev, 'we want to criticize you a little, because without criticism there is no love. We are confronted with a dilemma. You feel yourselves unable to recognize Israel, even indirectly, but we all want to see the Israeli forces withdraw. Is there not possibly a contradiction here?' He said it was the imperialists who wanted the status quo to continue, without any resolution in the UN condemning Israel or ordering its troops to withdraw, because without such a resolution the Israelis would stay in the territories they had occupied indefinitely. The people who would suffer as a result would be the Arabs, and friendly countries like India which were harmed by the closure of the Suez Canal. Brezhnev made it clear that he wanted Arab support for the resoutions they were preparing to put forward at the UN, either in the Security Council or in the regular session of the General Assembly, even if this involved the Arab governments in some form of recognition of Israel. He said he understood the enmity which existed between the Arabs and Israel, but this need not necessarily lead to the liquidation of Israel. He recalled Russian history, and again reverted to the Treaty of Brest-Litovsk, when Lenin had made the realistic but temporary sacrifices which circumstances demanded.

The Russian arms which had been captured by the Israelis were obviously a very sore subject. 'I am sad', said Brezhnev, 'because our reputation was bound up with your reputation. I am sad because the most modern arms we supplied you with have now been sent to America or West Germany. We gave you our planes, but you had no pilots; we gave you our tanks, but you had no crews.' Soviet experts attached to the Arab armies had reported that the drivers of some tanks had been sent into action with less than six hours' training. How could such a thing be permitted? Again he went back to the Arabs' need for time to build up their armed forces and their economies and to prepare their people politically for the battle. This meant there would have to be negotiations, aimed at securing a resolution which would command the support of a two-thirds majority in the General Assembly and so leave Israel isolated.

Kosygin joined in, reinforcing his colleague's arguments. 'You maintain that the Arab countries can't agree to ending the state of war with Israel,' he said. 'But where does this leave you? If the state of war continues, Israel will not withdraw. America, Germany and other governments will support Israel. But are you ready for war? We have made our assessment, and would have been happy to be able to tell you – "all right, go ahead". But the assessment made by our experts is different. They say that for you a resumption of the war is out of the question. I want to tell you that you are following a completely inflexible policy.

'Revolutionary slogans can work against the interests of the Arabs. Look at China. They are taking a very hard revolutionary line, and say that if you go to war they will help you. But what can they help you with? Ten articles? A hundred meetings? Revolutionary ideas expressed in words don't mean anything unless they are backed by real power.'

Once again Kosygin insisted on the need for the Arabs to consolidate the home front and to get rid of all those opposed to the progressive path. It would, he thought, take at least two years for the Arabs to complete the first stage of their preparations, and in that period 'they should not pursue a dogmatic policy in their dealings with the imperialists' – they should be flexible. He concluded by saying that ending the state of war was not important. What was important was gaining time to consolidate the Arabs' military forces and the progressive regimes.

Aref protested that ending the state of war would mean opening the Suez Canal and negotiating a peace settlement directly with the Israelis. Kosygin said that was not necessarily the case. It could be done through the UN, and if the Israelis tried to get out of a commitment to withdraw the state of war would have to continue.

Boumedienne tried to explain that the Arab–Israeli conflict should be seen as just one link in the long chain of the conflicts being waged by imperialism against the people. He begged the Russians not to think in terms of a solution through the UN. Voting at the UN wasn't going to do anything about the difficult and dangerous problems of the Middle East. As he saw it, the Americans knew that they held all the trump cards in their hands and were not going to agree to any resolution which did not reflect their point of view one hundred per cent. The real target of the Americans, Boumedienne insisted, was the destruction of all progressive regimes.

Boumedienne said the Middle East conflict fell into two parts – what was called the Palestinian problem, which was a legacy of the 1948 fighting, and the problem of aggression, which was the outcome of the recent war. America wanted to liquidate both problems at a stroke, for the benefit of Israel and at the expense of progressive regimes in the area.

Brezhnev asked Boumedienne what, granting the correctness of his analysis, he thought should be the solution. Boumedienne said they had two choices – either to accept the *fait accompli* and negotiate, and so destroy the progressive regimes, and perhaps be rewarded with the return of some territory, or to adopt a position based on principle. The Arab states could give some concessions, said Boumedienne (though he did not specify what), but there was a limit beyond which they could not go, or they would face collapse.

The two sides were, in fact, arguing from completely different premises and with completely different ends in view. This two-day debate in Moscow can stand as a classic example of the difficulties and misunderstanding which inevitably arise in relations between a superpower and those local powers with which its interests have become bound up.

Brezhnev, Kosygin and the others were obviously deeply hurt. It seemed that everything they and their predecessors had tried to do in the Arab world had been destroyed. Their concern had now little or nothing to do with ideology, but was to preserve as much as they could of their position as a superpower in an area where they had great political and economic investments.

★   ★   ★

The decision was taken in Moscow that Kosygin should attend the special emergency session of the General Assembly, and the question was naturally asked whether he would meet President Johnson while he was in America. The Politburo was split on this and many other matters arising out of the June war, with the military and ideologists accusing the politicians of having lost control over events. So, when the Burmese ambassador in Moscow asked Suslov if such a meeting was likely he was told there was no chance of it – no good could come of talking to the Americans. But in fact we know that Brezhnev had defended his Middle East policy against his critics in a three-hour speech to the Politburo, at the end of which the decision to send Podgorny to Egypt was taken. Podgorny went straight from the Politburo meeting to the airport on June 21 and Brezhnev went with him to see him off. This was intended as an almost unparalleled gesture of solidarity.

Kosygin stopped at Paris on his way to New York on June 16, where he dined with de Gaulle, and while in America he had two meetings with President Johnson at Glassborough, New Jersey.

11

One Gap in the Circle

It would be difficult to overstate the traumatic effect which the June war had on Egypt and the whole Arab world. For a time everyone was in a state of shock, unable to appreciate the magnitude of the disaster or to face its implications. There was a tendency to see things in terms of the past – a tendency which, to begin with, even Nasser shared. Thus, when Podgorny was in Cairo at the end of June 1967, and a question was asked about the Gulf of Aqaba, Nasser answered that whatever it was could be decided 'after the withdrawal'. He was assuming that the aftermath of 1967 would follow the pattern of Suez.

But fairly soon a more realistic attitude began to assert itself. It was obvious that events in the outside world were not going to stand still, and that if the Arabs were to exert any influence over them they would have to understand the changes in the international balance of forces which the war had brought about. As the weeks went by a good deal of evidence accumulated to throw light on Russian and American attitudes. There was the unsatisfactory visit that Podgorny made to Cairo at the end of June, which I have described elsewhere;[1] there were the reports which President Aref and Boumedienne brought back of their discussions in Moscow; there was the total failure of the emergency UN session to achieve anything, and the fruitless talks which, during the session, Kosygin had with President Johnson at Glassborough.

All this led Nasser to certain conclusions. He realized that the June war, like any other war, would be followed by political negotiations aimed not so much at peace as at patching up some sort of equilibrium. He felt that, with all the military and political cards in Israel's hands, it would be impossible for him to engage in such negotiations himself; if he did, he would simply be asked to sign the terms of a diktat, like the Germans at Versailles in 1919, and in spite of all the Russians'

---

[1] *Road to Ramadan* (Quadrangle, 1975), p. 46 ff.

encouraging talk about Brest-Litovsk this was something he was determined not to do.

So Nasser came to the conclusion that the only course was to leave the negotiating process to the Russians. They could at least talk to the Americans as one superpower to another, and if it was detente which, as many Arabs believed, lost them the war, it might be detente which could salvage something for the Arabs from the peace.

Nasser told the Russians that he reserved his position on only two points – nobody could ask him to give up a square foot of Egyptian territory, nor could he surrender any of the rights of the Palestinians. Apart from these two points the Russians could discuss anything, and when they did so, Nasser was convinced, they would realize the impossibility of a settlement on any acceptable terms. Only when they had themselves achieved this realization would they be willing to produce the arms which the Arabs must have for the inevitable next round.

Needless to say, the Arabs themselves needed less convincing of the uselessness of the negotiating process than did the Russians. They had only to watch the arrogant behaviour of the Israelis in victory to appreciate this. So it was that at Khartoum summit in August 1967 a clear-cut and uncompromising line was worked out to restore harmony in the Arab ranks.

But it was not going to be easy for the Russians to act on the Arabs' behalf. Inevitably the war left a legacy of mutual distrust and suspicion. The Arabs accused the Russians of coming to their aid during the fighting with too little and too late, both in respect of arms and diplomatic support. The Russians indignantly denied the charge; it was the Arabs, they said, who had failed to fight, either through some innate defect of character or because of their effete class structure and incompetent leadership. So Nasser's policy was to get the Russians more involved in the Middle East than ever before. He wanted to ensure that they felt Egypt's defeat was their defeat; that their prestige was bound up with that of Egypt.

A start with the new policy was made almost at once. Marshal Matvei Zakharov, Chief of the Soviet General Staff, came to Egypt with Podgorny and stayed on to advise on the reorganization and re-equipment of the Egyptian army. Nasser explained to him what he saw as a three-stage strategy – to begin with, Egypt and the other front-line Arab countries would have to remain on the defensive; then they could move on to active deterrence; and finally would come the liberation of lost territories. The Soviets agreed with this outline, and a meeting of the Central Committee in Moscow, at which of course the leading military were present, calculated that it would be at least two years before the Arabs were ready for any full-scale military activity.

Since it fitted in with his plans for greater Russian involvement in the area, Nasser welcomed a suggestion Podgorny made when he was in Cairo, that the Soviet Mediterranean fleet should come to Egypt for rest and recreation. He would have liked even better to see Soviet warships in Port Said – if one was hit during an Israeli raid, this would have really brought matters to a head. All the same, he had to be firm in refusing further demands the Soviets made which would have created what would have been in effect an autonomous Soviet base in Alexandria.

★   ★   ★

Nasser was not the only one to have worked out a clear diplomatic strategy following the June war. As far as could be made out in Cairo the Americans knew exactly what they wanted and how to get it. Their main aim was to preserve the existing stalemate in the Middle East, which was based on Israel's military superiority and occupation of Arab territory, and was supported by America's tacit alliance with conservative regimes in the Arab world. The weakness and ineffectiveness of the progressive Arab regimes, and any friction which some of them, notably Egypt, might experience in their relations with the Soviet Union, of course fitted in with this strategy. For however much assistance the Soviet Union might be prepared to give to the progressive regimes by way of economic aid or arms, it would never be able to compete with the resources of the US and its friends in the Middle East. So the Americans were in effect leaving only one door open to Arab leaders, like Nasser, who might want to break out from the position of stalemate, and this would lead to direct negotiations with Washington. In effect what the Americans were saying was – 'If you want anything you must come to us, and you must talk on our terms.'

However, experience had taught Nasser that there was no point in talking to the Americans except from a position of strength. So it was essential to keep the front line active, and to persuade the Russians that they must be prepared to take a calculated military and diplomatic risk in the area. In the end they were persuaded to do this, though the process of persuasion took a long time.

The Russians fairly quickly discovered that it was impossible to talk to the Americans about the Middle East in isolation. With the Nixon era a great deal began to be heard about 'linkage', and the problems of the Middle East had to be discussed in conjunction with other matters, such as Vietnam, European security and arms limitation. In fact, it sometimes seemed to us as though the rate at which arms reached Egypt from the Soviet Union depended directly on the state of Russia's relations with the Americans – when these were good the delivery of arms ground to a halt; when they deteriorated, the flow started up again.

To begin with, I think, the Soviets had high hopes of Nixon – just as they had, after President Johnson announced on March 31, 1968, that he would not be a candidate for re-election in November, begun to modify the extreme mistrust they had come to feel for him. They had told Cairo then that they thought Johnson, in these new circumstances, would be prepared to take unpopular initiatives, and that some of these might be connected with the Middle East. In this they were disappointed, but disappointment did not prevent them, after Nixon's victory, from passing on to Cairo their belief that Egypt would probably find the new President reasonable to deal with.

In fact, the Soviet attitude towards the Americans during the whole of this period was capable of undergoing sudden and sometimes dramatic fluctuations. For example, in May 1969 they begged Nasser to use every effort to halt the 'war of attrition' across the Suez Canal – a war which they had earlier agreed to be militarily and politically necessary. They accompanied this plea with alarming forecasts of the risk Egypt ran of seeing all its industrial centres destroyed, and they suggested a whole series of ingenious formulas, worked out by them, which they thought might succeed in stopping the fighting. It was in line with this shift of attitude that in his 1969 May Day speech Brezhnev referred only to 'imperialist aggression' in Vietnam, without mentioning the US by name. And for the first time for many years there was nothing in the May Day slogans about Israel.

Some of these fluctuations in policy can be attributed to the fact that, as usual, the top Soviet leadership did not always speak with the same voice. Not for the first time, the soldiers tended to use more bellicose language than the politicians. After the Israeli raid on the military post at Ras Zafarana in the Red Sea on September 9, 1969, Marshal Gretchko complained to members of the Egyptian mission in Moscow: 'You should be more daring. You should have stopped them. What has happened to the meetings of what you call the confrontation states? Where is your unified command? Why are you afraid? The Soviet navy in the Mediterranean is following the American Sixth Fleet like a shadow. They can't do anything. If the Americans put their marines into Israel we are ready to land our troops in your territories. And then I should like to see who would win!'

Even Kosygin, who usually took the lead in calling for restraint, was capable of doing a bit of needling. At about the same time a Syrian delegation was visiting Moscow, headed by the head of state, Nureddin Atassi, and including the Minister of Defence, General Mustafa Tlas. Kosygin accosted him: 'I don't seem to hear anything about you, General,' he said. 'I hear about battles on the Egyptian front, and on the Jordanian front, but you Syrians are doing nothing.' General Tlas said, 'No, I work in silence.' 'There is no harm in people sometimes talking out loud about their good deeds,' said Kosygin.

Nasser had gone to Moscow in July 1968, and had been due to go there in June 1969, but the visit had to be postponed. He sent a verbal message to Kosygin (not to Brezhnev, since this was a governmental not a party matter) saying he hoped that the supply of arms to Egypt was not going to fluctuate according to the state of Soviet–American relations. Kosygin, in reply, said that so far they had not achieved anything positive in their negotiations with the Americans. All they had heard were pious hopes that the provisions of Security Council resolution 242 would be implemented and assurances that there would be no rewards for aggression. He insisted that there was no link between Soviet arms for Egypt and their negotiations with the US. Their impression was that the Americans wanted a solution of the Middle East problem but that they were capable of trickery and double-dealing. 'Please don't forget,' said Kosygin, 'that the Americans hate us, and will go on hating us and opposing us. But there are many issues, such as the arms race, European security and of course the Middle East, which make a dialogue between them and us necessary.'

Kosygin pursued the same theme when he met a visiting Egyptian delegation in Moscow at about the same time. 'You must try to cool the situation,' he said. 'I can understand that it is impossible for you to allow enemy planes to overfly your territory, or enemy tanks and guns to find targets in your territory, without replying in kind. But don't let the situation get out of hand. You must preserve your troops, your weapons and your ammunition. You must use this breathing-space for training your forces. You must not do anything that can be taken advantage of by the Israeli warmongers. You must consolidate the home front, and build up as much support as possible in world public opinion.'

* * *

In June 1969 there was a conference in Moscow of world communist parties, which was attended by all available communist parties from the Arab world. By then Gromyko had produced yet another proposal for a Middle East settlement which bore remarkable similarities to the American proposal for a settlement which had been leaked to the Jordanian and some other Arab governments. They both seemed to commit the Arabs to such things as direct negotiations with Israel, joint Arab–Israeli patrolling of the frontier areas and so on, all of which were quite unacceptable at that time. During the Moscow conference the Arab communist parties tried, but failed, to persuade the other delegates to support a resolution asserting the rights of the Palestinians. This difference of opinion only became known when Ali Jaafar, the Secretary General of the Moroccan Communist Party, stated at the closing session that he was only able to sign the resolution of the conference with reservations, because of its failure to make any reference to the rights of the Palestinians.

Nasser hoped to be able to use Arab communist parties, as well as other well disposed intermediaries like President Tito, Indira Gandhi, and some of the east European governments, to add their influence towards persuading the Soviets that the Egyptian attitude to a nego-tiated settlement was the correct one. With this end in view the Gromyko proposals were shown to the Syrian communist leader, Khaled Bakdash, both in the original Russian (he could read Russian) and in an English translation. After reading both versions he was shown the American proposals. He could not help noticing the similarities, and admitted that there was no Arab communist who could defend the Gromyko plan – and no Arab nationalist who could defend it either. Bakdash's explanation of what had happened was that the Americans were always accusing the Russians of encouraging the Arabs in their rejection of a peaceful settlement, so the Russians wanted to demonstrate to the Americans that it was the Arabs who were being negative. They had therefore drafted a proposal close to American thinking, and when Egypt and the other Arabs urged them not to put the Gromyko proposals forward they were able to claim that it was the fault of the Arabs that nothing came of them.

Khaled Bakdash confessed that he was disappointed at the attitude of other communist parties over Palestine. 'We have to admit', he said, 'that there is quite a bit of Jewish influence in European communist parties, and that if it had not been for Soviet influence the resolution on the Middle East at the Moscow conference would have been weaker. Over Zionism the Rumanians showed themselves more royalist than the king – the Israeli communists were prepared to recognize the rights of the Palestinian people, but the Rumanians refused.' Khaled Bakdash added that nobody should ever forget that the confrontation in the Middle East was part of the world struggle between imperialism and liberation and between reactionary and progressive forces. 'World Jewry', he said, 'is ranged against the Soviet Union, and that is something which the Soviets have to take serious note of.'

The Secretary-General of the Jordanian Communist Party, Fuad Nassar, was also shown the Gromyko proposals. His explanation was that the Russians were very conscious of the problem posed by their own Jewish minority. Someone had told him that there were more than a million Jews in Moscow alone.

★   ★   ★

Although Nasser wanted the main burden of negotiating with the Americans to be left to the Russians, it was never his intention to avoid all direct contact with the US himself. So when, in March 1969, the death of Eisenhower (always remembered with affection in Egypt for the part he had played in enforcing an Israeli withdrawal from Sinai in 1956–7) provided an opportunity, Dr Mahmoud Fawzi, assistant to the President for foreign affairs, was sent to Washington as special envoy for the funeral. But when he got back to Cairo he reported no change in the American position. He had been told that there could be no new developments until diplomatic relations between the two countries, broken off at the time of the June war, were restored. This unhelpful message was passed on to Moscow, with the suggestion that the

Soviets would be wrong to pin too many hopes on Nixon. They replied with an assurance that they fully realized how obstinate the Americans were proving.

By now, in fact, the Russians were beginning to appreciate, as Nasser had always known they would, the unrewarding nature of negotiating for a Middle East settlement with the Americans. The first phase of Russia's post-1967 involvement in the Middle East could thus be considered completed; now it was time to move on to the next phase. Since Nasser believed that American policy was aimed at leaving only one gap in the negotiating process for the Arabs – a gap which led them inevitably to Washington – he was determined that when Egypt entered this gap it would do so in the company of the Russians. So he encouraged their military involvement to a deliberately exaggerated extent – for example, by his request for the presence of Soviet military advisers down to battalion level.

The real turning-point, which conclusively raised the Middle East conflict from a local to a superpower level, was the secret visit Nasser paid to Moscow at the end of January 1970. On this occasion Nasser explained to Brezhnev and his colleagues that Egypt was naked in the face of Israel's deep penetration raids. It had become impossible either to protect the civilian population in the interior or to start work on the military preparations which were essential for any eventual attack across the Suez Canal to regain Egypt's lost lands. He asked the Russians to install an effective missile wall against Israeli attacks, and when the Russians pointed out that it would take several months to train Egyptian crews in the use of the SAM-3 missiles, Nasser suggested that the Russians should send their own crews for them. He said he was not asking the Russians to man the front line, which would remain the responsibility of the Egyptian forces, but he was asking them to look after the defence of the rear.

Such a step would, of course, have far-reaching international implications. An adequate defence system would require aircraft as well as missiles; there would have to be Russian operational planes stationed in Egypt in addition to Russian crews manning the missiles. But after a full meeting of the Politburo had been summoned agreement was reached. By the beginning of April 1970 the new missiles and planes with their Russian crews had begun to arrive in Egypt.[1]

---

[1] I have given a fuller account of the Moscow visit in *Road to Ramadan*, p. 83 ff.

This dramatic initiative in the military field was paralleled by fresh developments in the diplomatic field. On December 9, 1969, the Secretary of State, William Rogers, made a speech in which he suggested that Israel should withdraw from occupied Arab territory in exchange for 'a permanent peace based on binding agreement', and that details of a peace settlement should be worked out between the two sides with the help of the UN mediator, Gunnar Jarring, on the analogy of the Rhodes armistice agreements of 1949. Neither Israel nor the Arabs responded to the Rogers Plan with much enthusiasm, but Washington followed it up by sending Joseph Sisco, the Assistant Secretary of State in charge of Middle East affairs, on a tour of the area in April 1970. Though hostile demonstrations prevented his arrival in Amman he was courteously received in Cairo, where he had a long if not particularly productive talk with Nasser. Then, in his May Day speech, Nasser maintained the momentum by appealing to the US to reconsider its support for Israel. Either the US should compel Israel to withdraw from the Arab lands it had occupied, he said, or it should stop supplying Israel with arms; otherwise the Americans were in effect participating in the illegal occupation of the Arab lands. Nasser sent Nixon a letter containing extracts from his May Day speech, and on June 25 Rogers announced a fresh initiative – the American government was taking steps to reactivate Dr Jarring's mission and called on Israel and the Arabs to 'stop shooting and start talking'. He also proposed a ninety-day ceasefire and a reaffirmation by both sides of support for Security Council resolution 242.

On July 23 Nasser, to the surprise and consternation of many Arabs, told the Congress of the ASU that he was prepared to accept the Rogers initiative. A number of considerations had led him to this unexpected decision. He felt that the period of the 'war of attrition 'was over. It had served its purpose by giving Egyptian forces along the Suez Canal their baptism of blood and fire, and it had in its later stages effected what Abba Eban called 'the erosion of the Israeli airforce'. To have continued this limited battle would have been pointless; something new was required, and preferably a policy which would enable him to complete Egypt's defensive missile network.

*   *   *

Further light on Egyptian thinking around this time is shed by a 'thinking aloud memorandum' prepared for Nasser by a small committee on which senior officials from the army, intelligence and Ministry of Foreign Affairs were represented. It was intended as background material for the visit which Nasser was due to pay to Moscow, starting on June 29, 1970 – the last visit, as it was to prove – and he studied it before leaving. The paper covered three areas – the military situation; Egyptian–Soviet–American relations; the internal situation in Egypt and the other Arab countries. The following is a summary of its main conclusions:

The Military Situation

1. Militarily Israel is now concentrating on ensuring control over a strip of the west bank of the Suez Canal 25 kilometres wide. Israel aims at keeping the skies over our forward troops open to its aircraft as compensation for its inability to raid in depth due to the Soviet presence.

2. Israel regards this as the surest guarantee for its continued occupation of Sinai and the best method of facing the war of attrition.

3. The installation of Russian SAM-3s and the completion of missile cover for our armed forces means that the military situation is changing qualitatively in our favour. It places the Israeli forces in Sinai in a difficult position since it makes possible for us a crossing of the Canal.

4. What conclusions may be expected from this qualitative change? Has the possibility of an Israeli–Soviet collision, particularly in the air, to be reckoned with? Would this in turn lead to an American–Soviet confrontation? What steps are the Soviets likely to take to guard against such an eventuality?

5. The previous paragraph highlights the contradiction between our own interests and those of the Soviet Union. For us, air cover for our forces is so important that there must be no delay in its completion. But the Soviets, while understanding the importance of air cover, also see its dangers. It is therefore in their interest to delay until they have made a careful appreciation of the situation.

6. The most important subject for discussion in Moscow is how to coordinate Egypt's interests and the Soviet Union's calculations.

Egyptian–Soviet–American Relations

1. The Soviet presence in the UAR, the real prospect of its increase and the consequent increase of Soviet influence in the Middle East, has become a fresh source of anxiety for the West, and faces the Americans

with a situation which may oblige them to initiate a direct dialogue with us.

2. The increasing Soviet presence gives us a favourable bargaining position *vis-à-vis* the US, which could lead to some pressure being exerted by the US on Israel with the aim of securing a settlement before the Soviet presence has reached irreversible proportions.

3. In this case the effect of Soviet aid to Egypt would have been solely to act as a means of exerting pressure on the US.

4. What would then be the situation, should a settlement be reached? The US would emerge as the power which, by its pressure on Israel, had achieved a settlement. This it would have done without spending a dollar, while the other superpower, which had initiated the process, and in doing so spent its treasure and even its blood, would be left on the sidelines.

5. This consideration can account for the harder line being taken by the Soviet Union at the four-power talks in New York.

6. It also accounts for the hostility shown by the Soviet Union to the idea of direct talks between Egypt and the Americans.

7. The Soviet Union aims at being itself the instrument for achieving a settlement, since it is the party which has paid the price for one. The Soviets are undecided whether it is better for them to deal with the Americans themselves or to leave the negotiations to us.

8. Hence the contradiction between Soviet and Egyptian interests. A genuine balance between the two must be sought.

The Internal Situation in Egypt and the Arab Countries
1. Cautious moves by the Soviets in the military field, combined with the precautions being taken to prepare for all political contingencies, give the Soviet Union an opportunity to achieve some of its aims in Egypt and other Arab countries.

2. There can be no doubt that the Soviet Union hopes to make use of us for securing entry to some Arab countries which have been closed to it, such as Libya, and for consolidating its position in others, such as the Sudan.

3. The Soviet Union hopes to persuade us to alter the structure of some of our institutions so that it can rely on Egypt's continuing to pursue an anti-imperialist, pro-Soviet policy, and at the same time

isolating and weakening those forces which the Soviets designate as nationalist but, by their background and inclinations, basically anti-Soviet.

4. The Soviet Union aims at solving the problem of anti-Soviet feeling in the armed forces by liquidating the elements opposed to them, especially those among the senior officers.

*   *   *

While he was in Moscow on this last visit Nasser told Brezhnev of his intention to give his public support to the Rogers initiative. Brezhnev was not a little surprised; how could Nasser accept something which, as Brezhnev put it, 'had an American flag on it'? Nasser explained that it was just because of the American flag on it that he thought it could be useful. He felt that a new stage was opening up for Egypt. The war of attrition along the Suez Canal had been going on now for nearly a year. It had proved costly for Egypt, particularly as a result of Israeli air raids against civilian targets in the Delta and through very heavy casualties to the workforce engaged in building fortifications along the Canal's west bank. But it had been relatively more costly for Israel, where there was a great deal of gloom at the almost daily lists of killed and wounded along the Canal. It was known that Israel would welcome a ceasefire, and a ceasefire had advantages for Nasser also. It would enable him to complete his missile wall and to concentrate on preparing for the operation to recover lost Egyptian territory, plans for which were then known by the code name 'Granite One'.

Brezhnev understood Nasser's arguments for responding favourably to Rogers, but may not have been wholly convinced. It was during this Moscow visit that he told Nasser he had come round completely to the Egyptian point of view, and that he now thought the Israelis would never give up anything except if forced to do so, and that in this they had the support of the Americans.

Yet though the Russians had begun to adopt a more realistic estimate of American intentions, they remained inhibited by their conviction that the whole Middle East area was of such importance to the Americans that it would be highly dangerous to put too much pressure on them there. So in effect the Soviet Union was prepared to give limited support to the Arabs when they attacked Israel, and so, by implication, attacked American interests in the Middle East, while the Americans were prepared to give unlimited support to the Israelis when they attacked the Arabs and so, by implication, the interests of the Soviet Union.

Nor, I think, were the Russians ever really at ease over Egypt's direct contacts with the Americans, once these had started. They were suspicious over what was going on and wanted to be told everything. For example, when Joseph Sisco came to Cairo the Russians asked to be shown the minutes of the meeting which he had had with Nasser. Nasser said he would give the Soviet ambassador a full briefing – which he did – but he refused to hand over the minutes. The Russians must have realised as well as we did that the Americans had left just one gap in the circle round Egypt, and that if Nasser could be lured into it, and concede that a Middle East settlement could only be reached with American assistance and on American terms, one consequence would be that the Soviet Union would be left completely out in the cold.

12

The Puzzled Giant

DURING THE THREE YEARS which elapsed between the June war and the death of Nasser Arab efforts to recover from the catastrophe were conducted simultaneously on several different levels. First, there was the continuing military struggle, involving the war of attrition on the Suez Canal front, and the retraining and re-equipping of the Egyptian and Syrian armies. Second, there was the level of international diplomacy, in which Washington, Moscow and the UN, as well as the governments of the Arab states and Israel, were involved, and which has been touched on in the previous chapter. Third, there was the process of adjustment going on inside the Arab world. Fourth, there was the attempt to find a new and more successful basis for cooperation between the Soviet Union and the Arabs.

I think there can be no doubt that the Russians were absolutely sincere in their wish to evolve such a working relationship with their puzzling new friends and allies, the Arabs. And in the same way those Arab governments, led by Egypt, which had come to rely to a greater or lesser extent on the Russians, were trying with no less sincerity to take the measure of the enigmatic giant who still seemed to offer the only hope of rescue from their oppressive difficulties.

For neither side was the process of enquiry and adjustment an easy one. Extraneous events, which were often not strictly speaking of direct relevance to Arab–Soviet relations, were constantly intervening to pose new problems and arouse old suspicions. There was, for example the question of Czechoslovakia. It was while Nasser was in Moscow in July 1968 that Dubcek's attempts to give communism 'a human face' brought his government to the brink of a direct collision with the Soviets. By the time Nasser arrived the Soviet leadership had probably already decided that the dangerous Dubcek experiment would have to be ended by force, but it was extremely worried about the effect such an action might have on a country like Egypt. Egypt and the Soviet Union were now intimately linked, and there were large numbers of Soviet experts in Egypt. Might the Egyptians take Soviet military intervention in Czechoslovakia as a warning of the fate awaiting them if they stepped out of line, and so back away from the Russian connection while there was still time? And even if the Russians succeeded in allaying Egyptian fears on this score, might not Nasser voice disapproval of this apparent breach of the *pancha sheela*, which expressly forbade intervention by one country in the internal affairs of another? The Russians' main anxiety was to prevent any condemnation of themselves by the non-aligned governments as a body, and obviously Nasser was the key figure in determining these governments' reactions. They were even more anxious about the possible reaction of Tito, who had tried to mediate between them and Dubcek, and they asked Nasser, while he was in Moscow, if he would use his influence with Tito.

I found myself playing a minor but unexpected part in the manœuvring which went on during the days immediately preceding the Russian invasion of Czechoslovakia on August 20, 1968. I had interviewed President Tito on my way back from Moscow, where I had gone with Nasser, on July 12, and when I got back to Egypt I decided that what he had to say was so important that I ought to give it as much publicity as possible. The best way to do this would be make it the basis of my regular Friday article in *Al Ahram*, but this would mean holding it up for a week, until July 19. Then on July 15, I got a cable from the Villa Brionca in Brioni saying that the President wanted his interview to be released immediately, and that the Yugoslav news agency, Tanjug, was proposing to release the text that same evening. I sent an urgent telegram to Tito explaining what I was planning to do, and received the answer that the part of the interview he was really interested in was the beginning, where I had asked him questions about Czechoslovakia. He would agree that Tanjug should confine itself to the release of this part only. That was an arrangement that I found quite acceptable.

The question I had asked Tito was what he thought of current events in Czechoslovakia and whether he saw any resemblance in them to what had happened in Yugoslavia in 1948, when he had had his quarrel with Stalin. His answer had been: 'The nature of what is happening in Czechoslovakia is different. In my view we should not exaggerate it or dramatize it. I cannot believe that there are people in the Soviet Union who are so short-sighted that they would resort to military force to resolve political problems which are purely the domestic concern of Czechoslovakia. Some steps have admittedly already been taken which almost amounted to forcible intervention, but fortunately we heard today that most Soviet forces inside Czechoslovakia are withdrawing.[1] There can be no doubt that interference by a state or group of states in the internal affair of another state is a great mistake. Moreover, I did not believe that there is anything about the present situation in Czechoslovakia which constitutes a threat to socialism. If the West did intervene, or threatened intervention, Czechoslovakia has the means with which to defend itself – it has an army, a communist party, a strong working class. In Yugoslavia we too have an army, a communist party, and a strong working class. This means that nobody can save our socialism for us, because we have strength enough to save our own socialism ourselves.'

Tito's warnings were of no avail. The Russian chargé d'affaires was instructed to contact Nasser at midnight on August 20 and to request an audience. Nasser, who was in Alexandria, was woken up, and the chargé arrived. Having apologised for disturbing the President in this way, the Russian explained that the important message which he brought had to be delivered before 4 am. Nasser looked at his watch and said 'It's half past three.' Then came the message. It read: 'The situation in Czechoslovakia has reached a critical stage. Certain elements are aiming at the destruction of socialism in Czechoslovakia and at altering the balance of power in Europe to the benefit of the imperialists. This could affect the whole world. We have information which shows that what is happening in Czechoslovakia is linked with events elsewhere, for example in Vietnam, and in the Middle East, in the same way that last year imperialism prompted Israel to liquidate the resistance of liberated regimes in that area. For these reasons the Czechoslovak republic has sent an urgent request to the Soviet Union and other friendly nations, asking them to provide assistance with their armed forces. These forces will be withdrawn from Czechoslovakia the moment the danger is past, and when the legitimate forces in the country conclude that there is no longer any need for allied forces to remain on their territory. We would like Your Excellency to know that our considered moves in this matter resulted from an appeal by the government of Czechoslovakia, which is concerned for the interests of liberated countries.' The message went on to

---

[1] Soviet forces were in Czechoslovakia for Warsaw Pact manœuvres.

elaborate on the dangers threatening liberated countries and to ask the Egyptian government to appreciate the reason for the action being taken and on whose behalf it was being taken.

Nasser's answer was: 'I fully appreciate the message which you have given me, but we had thought that other methods would have been found for dealing with imperialist conspiracies.' The chargé said: 'I am glad, Mr President, that you appreciate the dangers. The situation concerned us so closely that we were obliged to take action. It had become a matter of days, and even of hours.' Nasser: 'The problem is that the imperialists will use what you are doing against you. When I was in Moscow I felt that things were moving rapidly. I knew that there were to be meetings of the Supreme Soviet and the Central Committee. So I suspected that some action was about to be taken, though I hoped it would not be as drastic as this, and that you would maintain diplomatic contacts with the Czechoslovak authorities.' Chargé: 'We have done all we could, but . . .' Nasser: 'I would like to thank you for informing me about your action in advance, but it would be contrary to my feelings and my principles if I did not tell you that I have some reservations about it.' Chargé: 'Once the Czechoslovak problem has been solved a solution of the Middle East problem will become much easier, because the imperialists will realize that the forces of liberation are not to be treated lightly, and that any attempt to tamper with them will entail certain consequences.' Nasser: 'To speak to you frankly – I am not going to question what you say. I do not wish to start an argument, so I will make no comment. The Egyptian press will not attack your government's action. But I want you to be quite clear about my own point of view. What has happened is also important because of its effect on our relations, and your relations, with Yugoslavia. Czechoslovakia for me is a matter of principle, but for Yugoslavia it is a matter of vital national interest. I should certainly like to believe that this could lead to a new stage in the Middle East.' Chargé: 'I think that this new stage has already begun. I have served in my country's diplomatic service for twenty years, of which thirteen have been spent in the UAR. I was here during the tripartite aggression of 1956, and the June aggression of 1967. This is the first time that I have felt my government is taking a decision of fundamental significance. Such a decision covers more than the action with which it is immediately concerned; it is in itself a policy, the effects of which will be reflected everywhere in the world.' After a bit more conversation Nasser again thanked the Russian chargé, but ended by repeating that he wished Brezhnev to be left in no doubt about his point of view.

It was easy to see what the Russians were aiming at. They had chosen to give Nasser advance warning of their action in Czechoslovakia (he was the only Arab leader they did warn) in the hope that he could be persuaded into a favourable reaction which would set the tone for the rest of the Arab world. At the same time they were very conscious of his close links with Yugoslavia and hoped that he might be able to mediate there too to some extent. And the chargé's message was undoubtedly intended to give hints that through Russian contacts with the Americans some favourable developments in the Middle East situation might be looked for.

Nasser had promised the Russian chargé that the Egyptian press would not criticize the invasion of Czechoslovakia. This was a difficult attitude to maintain, and in fact, after some of the communists who were now inside the ASU had written articles in support of the invasion, I decided that I would have to write one article which would explain, for the record, the Egyptian point of view.

In the course of this article I wrote: 'We cannot tolerate the intervention by one state in the affairs of another state, especially if this intervention is carried out by armed force. No excuses can justify such a step. To say, in the case of Czechoslovakia, that the communist regime was in danger is not sufficient. The Czechoslovak leadership had a right to choose its own road to communism, all the more since it was clear that the road which it had chosen had enjoyed the backing of the Czechoslovak people. If communism was in any danger, this was because of shortcomings by the Czechoslovak leadership. If a certain set of social beliefs were incapable of being defended by Czechoslovakia's own leaders it is not possible that they can be better defended from outside. Military intervention is wrong. The personality of the person who commits a crime does not alter the gravity of the crime. We cannot change the rules because a crime is committed by a friend rather than by an enemy.'

The Russians protested about this article, but neither they nor we wanted to provoke a quarrel. What particularly worried Nasser was that what he had come to regard as the emergency route for arms and aid from the Soviet Union to Egypt via Yugoslavia might be imperilled. In fact this route did cease to function for two months, but then restarted. Tito too, though shocked by the Russian action, was anxious not to let it build up into an open dispute.

*   *   *

The complications which could lead to misunderstanding were by no means all on the Russian side. It was often those movements in the Arab world which claimed the revolutionary label which were to puzzle the Russians most. Thus, just before the conference of world communist parties met in Moscow there had been a coup d'état in the Sudan (May 25), which ousted Mohammed Ahmed Mahgoub and brought Jaafar el-Nimeiry to power. The small but active Sudanese Communist Party took part in the coup and some of its members were given posts in Nimeiry's first government. This naturally seemed to the Russians a very promising development.

Following the coup, Ahmed Suleiman, who had been First Secretary of the Central Committee of the Sudanese Communist Party, was sent as ambassador to Moscow. He and Khaled Hassan Abbas, a member of the Revolutionary Council, were charged with negotiating help for the new regime from the Soviet Union. They did not feel that this ought to present any real difficulty. So when they were received by Podgorny they explained that the Sudan's economy was in bad shape and asked for a loan of £50 million (sterling) in cash, for the purpose of bolstering the economy and buying arms. Podgorny exploded: 'Haven't you consulted your Egyptian friends?' he said. 'They will tell you that we never give cash loans – it's a matter of principle. And why do you want to buy arms? What is this craze for arms? What's come over all the liberated countries in Africa? What threat is the Sudan under that it needs our arms?'

Further negotiations with Podgorny and Nicholai Patolichev, the Soviet Minister of Foreign Trade, got nowhere, so Ahmed Suleiman sent a message to Nasser asking if he could help. He said Nimeiry had been shocked when they reported their lack of success – and so would Nasser please tell him how he should deal with the Soviets. Nasser obliged. 'It's agony dealing with them,' he told Nimeiry, 'but in the end you get most of what you want. And as they are the only source of arms you have to deal with them.' So Nasser found himself called on to act as interpreter between the communists of Moscow and the communists of Khartoum.

*   *   *

Then in January 1970, three months after the coup in the Sudan, came the revolution in Libya which overthrew the monarchy and brought to power a group of young officers, led by Muammar Ghadaffi, who considered themselves disciples of Nasser. At first this too appeared to the Russians a promising development, though they found all the talk about Islam difficult to comprehend. But before long the leader of the Libyan revolution seemed to spend more and more time attacking the Soviet Union and communism. Ghadaffi denounced 'foreign navies' in the Mediterranean indiscriminately, which struck the Russians as ridiculous since they were only there to balance the American Sixth Fleet. He also denounced 'imported ideologies', and appeared unaware of the universal validity of communism.

Moscow sent a delegation to Libya headed by Salikh Betaiev, First Secretary of the Communist Party in the Tartar Republic and a member of the Central Committee. Ghadaffi met the delegation but showed himself in no mood for compromise. He said his people were not communists and wanted no outside forces in the Mediterranean. Then, on another tack, 'How many minutes did it take your regime to recognize Israel?' he demanded. 'The Americans recognized after four minutes. You recognized after four hours. Where's the difference?'

Betaiev pointed out that, as there was no communist party in Libya there ought to be no problems between the two countries, but this made no impression. After he got back to Moscow and reported, an attempt was made to assess the nature and aims of the Libyan revolution but it cannot have been very profound since the only decision come to was that the chief mufti of the Soviet Union, Ziyautdin Babakhanov, should visit Libya and that a delegation of Libyan ulamas should tour the Moslem republics of the Soviet Union. It cannot be regarded as much of a setback to Arab–Soviet relations that neither journey materialized.

*　　*　　*

But probably there was no movement in the Arab world which was more of a puzzle to the Russians than that of the Palestinians. They found it impossible to fit the Palestinians into any acceptable category. As far as they could see the Palestinian resistance was a purely nationalist movement, without any social content. Such bodies as the Popular Front for the Liberation of Palestine, which did talk in recognizable social terms, appeared to them a bunch of fanatics and were in any case outside the main stream of the movement. In Soviet eyes a guerrilla movement, such as the Palestinians were trying to be, should direct itself at the urban and rural proletariat; the Palestinian bourgeoisie, the Soviets believed, was bound to be so concerned for its own interests that it would collaborate with the Israeli occupiers. Once again, the Russians failed to understand the strength of nationalism, which is capable at certain periods of history of transcending the class struggle. When a whole nation faces a common enemy it must be united; when one part of the nation is in confrontation with another part it will be divided. Both stages occur in the life of most nations and one may merge imperceptibly into the other, but it would be wrong to deny the validity of either.

At the time of which we are speaking it would have been ridiculous for the Palestinian leaders to commit themselves to a social programme of the sort which would have satisfied the Russians, even if they had wanted to, which they did not. The West Bank was still essentially a traditional society which would have found such a programme meaningless or alarming. It would also have alienated the West Bankers' main financial backers in Saudi Arabia and the Gulf. Even in these early days the Palestinian movement was spending about one million pounds a month, which it had to rely on these backers to supply. The Soviets were equally unable to understand the PLO's religious links, and Yasser Arafat's references to Jerusalem as a 'holy city'.

In Russian eyes the operations conducted by Fateh, the militant vanguard of the Palestinian resistance, were nothing but a source of trouble, doing little harm to the Israelis and giving them an excuse for stepping up repression, and it had only been at Nasser's insistence that the Russians made contact with the Palestinians. The Russians tend to judge resistance movements by the strictly practical standards which were applied to them during World War II – how much actual damage do they do to the enemy, militarily and economically? By these standards, of course, the Palestinians were of little or no account. But the Russians failed to appreciate that in certain circumstances, especially when the resources available to the resistance and those they are resisting are greatly disparate, even unproductive acts of resistance have a symbolic value. This was true of the Palestinians in the early days of Fateh. It was a time when Golda Meir and other Israelis were denying that any people such as Palestinians existed, so even the explosion of one bomb, though it might do little or no harm, was enough to show that after all they did exist and did not accept the alien occupation of their country.

But after the battle of Karameh in March 1968, in which Palestinian guerrillas fought off a large Israeli armoured force, the prestige of the Palestinian resistance inside and outside the Arab world greatly increased, and this was something the Russians could not ignore. Even so they moved slowly. In February 1970 they took the initiative of inviting the Palestinians to Moscow, though the invitation was only sent in the name of the Afro-Asian Solidarity Committee. It was, naturally accepted, but unfortunately the Palestinians were at that time far from being united. Almost all the divergent tendencies in the Arab world were reflected in the delegation which turned up in Moscow, its members bickering among themselves.

Yasser Arafat, representing Fateh, was naturally among the delegates, but the highest official he saw was Mazarov, the First Deputy Prime Minister, as well as Ponomarev, Ulianovsky, and Romantsev of the Central Committee. The Russians insisted that their meetings should be kept secret, but they gave the Palestinians a guarantee that they would be considered in the same category as those Arab countries which directly confronted Israel and would be eligible for aid as such. They asked a great many questions about the resistance – how it was organized, what its aims were, how it hoped to achieve them, and so on. But they also made it clear that they wanted the Palestinians to recognize UN resolution 242, whereas the Palestinians were thinking along very different lines since this resolution made no mention of them except as a 'refugee problem'. In Russian eyes the main usefulness of the Palestinian resistance was probably as a potential means of pressure on Israel and the US. The degree of importance which they attributed to it is probably accurately reflected in the space devoted to the arrival of the delegation in the Soviet press – three lines on the back pages of *Pravda* and *Izvestia*.

★   ★   ★

Although Egypt's relations with the Russians had been longer and closer than those of any other Arab country, occasions for friction and misunderstanding were not lacking. There was, for example, the question of Egypt's debts to the Soviet Union. These had grown to a considerable size, and the Russians cast around for possible ways of offsetting them. There had been a good deal of talk about Egypt's potential oil supplies, especially in the Siwa area of the western desert, and the Russians were resentful at the concessions which had been given to American companies. Semen Skachkov, and other Russian experts, suggested to Nasser that joint Soviet teams should be engaged to drill for oil. This was done, but whereas the American companies produced oil, and paid Egypt royalties, the Russians, who were unable to drill below 4,000 feet, compared with the 17–18,000 feet reached by the Americans, produced nothing. The Egyptian treasury had to bear the cost of their endeavours.

Then there was the question of the Soviet experts. There can be no doubt that the presence of so many Soviet experts and advisers caused friction. In addition to the considerable difficulties of language, customs, social distinctions and so on, the Russian experts had automatic access to the authorities in Egypt, and this caused a good deal of resentment in the higher levels of the Egyptian bureaucracy. The military were upset over delays in the delivery of weapons and equipment, and when news of these delays spread, as inevitably it did, a much wider circle began to feel let down. The Americans naturally did all they could to exacerbate these sentiments, saying that while Sinai was occupied by the Israelis the rest of Egypt was occupied by the Russians, and making similar remarks. Wholly unjustified though such accusations were, their constant repetition had some effect.

*   *   *

It was the presence of these Soviet military advisers which was at the root of a small but significant incident in which I found myself involved. The incident illustrated the flimsy grounds on which Russian suspicions of Egyptian motives could be aroused and the difficulty of dispelling them.

It was in the brief period in 1970 during which I agreed to act as Minister of Information that I accompanied Nasser to Moscow on his July visit of that year. One of the subjects which was discussed with the Soviet leadership was our request for still more military advisers – we wanted them to be available even down to battalion level. Brezhnev seemed reluctant to agree to this. 'We are afraid,' he said, 'that if there are too many of our experts in Egypt popular feeling may build up against them. People may start calling it "neo-imperialism".' Nasser assured him that this would not happen. 'I'm in charge,' he said, 'and if I ever felt that the Russian experts were interfering in our affairs I would collect them together, put them in a boat at Alexandria, and ship them to Odessa.' Brezhnev was not particularly pleased by this remark, and suddenly he turned to me. 'Gospodin Heikal may know about that,' he said. I asked him what he meant. 'Your Ministry,' he explained, 'has made a report saying that there is popular feeling against the Soviet experts.' 'My ministry?' I said, astonished. 'Never!' Nasser told me I had better check, and though I insisted that no such report existed Brezhnev repeated the charge. 'I'm sure there is a report in Gospodin Heikal's department which declares that the people feel strongly about the presence of Soviet experts,' he said.

The discussion moved on to other matters, but as soon as I got back to Cairo two days later I started making enquiries. What I found was rather grotesque. When I took over the ministry I had asked Tashin Beshir, who was later to become President Sadat's official spokesman, to head a committee looking into the effectiveness of the work carried out by the information department of the ministry. Part of this department's work was to conduct a daily survey of public opinion. This was done by collating reports from a number of subordinate information offices throughout the country. Tahsin Beshir and a colleague of his in the office, Osama el-Bass (now an under-secretary at the Ministry of Foreign Affairs), went to Mahalla al-Kubra, an industrial town in the Delta, and asked the local director of information how he compiled his daily report. They wanted to know whether there was any scientific basis for the report; did the local official suggest topics for investigation, and if so, how were they chosen? They were told there was nothing scientific about the reports; they were compiled from what people heard sitting in the cafés or from what they read in the newspapers. Tahsin Beshir and his colleague pressed their questions. How, they asked, can you really know what people think about things like the military situation or the economic situation or the possibility of an Arab summit? For example, in one of your reports you say that people 'are happy about the Russian presence'. How can you be sure? What is that judgement based on?

As far as I could make out, these enquiries at Mahalla al-Kubra were the only basis for Brezhnev's accusations. It may be that, because the town is one of the main industrial centres in Egypt, the Russians had some form of liaison there. What did astonish me was that within three weeks of the two officials from my ministry making their private enquiries a full, if inaccurate, report of the incident should be on the desk of the First Secretary of the Communist Party of the Soviet Union in Moscow.

I explained to Nasser what had happened, and he was satisfied. Whether he told Brezhnev, and whether Brezhnev too was satisfied, I don't know. It was enough for me to know that Nasser considered the incident closed. But I found it rather frightening to discover how easily the grand strategy of nations could become mixed up with gossip.

★   ★   ★

After his talks with the Soviet leaders, Nasser went to the Bervikha hospital for two weeks of treatment. He returned to Cairo on July 21. He had been urged by his Russian doctors to rest, but no sooner had he started a ten days' rest in Mersa Matruh (the doctors had insisted on at least a month) than the civil war between King Hussein's army and the Palestinian guerrilla forces in Jordan broke out. Nasser inevitably became involved in the efforts to end this conflict and September 21 saw the opening of a conference in Cairo of Arab heads of state which he had summoned. A week later the conference ended, but fate intervened. Nasser died.

13
Doubts, Plots, Hesitations

NASSER'S DEATH convulsed the Arab world. Outbursts of grief, as spontaneous as they were profound, were to be seen everywhere from Morocco to the Arabian peninsula. Deep sorrow was shown in the Third World as a whole. But, though on the surface the Soviet Union preserved its usual disciplined face, in no other country were the shockwaves from the death of this single Egyptian more acutely felt.

The Soviet leaders had, of course, known that Nasser was ill; it was their own doctors who had diagnosed the gravity of his condition and who had tried, in vain, to force on him a less exacting regimen. They had striven not to become too completely dependent on one man, and had consequently from time to time made an effort to cultivate leaders of other Arab countries. But in the end they had always been brought back to the realization that Egypt was the key country in the Middle East and Nasser without any rivals as an Arab leader.

The Soviets had continually had fresh evidence of the authority which Nasser exercised over other Arab governments and over the masses in every Arab country. They had seen revolutions break out in countries like the Sudan and Libya for which his ideas and person had been the inspiration. More recently, they had seen him defuse, almost single-handed, the critical situation which had arisen in Jordan when King Hussein's army cracked down on the Palestinian *fedayin* (guerrillas). It was Nasser who had brought pressure on King Hussein to attend the Cairo summit; it was Nasser who had brought pressure on the Syrians to halt their armoured advance into Jordan. This final achievement of Nasser's impressed the Russians all the more since the Jordan crisis had threatened to bring them into collision with the United States. At the height of the crisis the American Sixth Fleet had been carrying out special manoeuvres in the Mediterranean, using live ammunition, and President Nixon had flown in to attend them. Elliot Richardson, Secretary of the Department of Health Education and Welfare, had said that the guns of the Sixth Fleet were intended to be heard in Moscow as well as Cairo. Also it was known that Israel had been poised to intervene in Jordan, with American approval. Had this happened Moscow could hardly have done nothing about it. Here was another case where a local quarrel might have ineluctably escalated into superpower confrontation.

But Nasser had summoned all the Arab kings and presidents to Cairo; they had come, and had agreed on ways and means to end the fighting. Now Nasser was dead.

*   *   *

Kosygin came to the funeral, but he had much more to do than express the condolences of the Kremlin. He came to study, to consult and to warn. After the funeral he asked to be allowed to meet all the leading figures in Egypt. Three meetings were arranged; the first a closed session dealing mainly with military matters, and two more covering a wider political field.

Kosygin had two main grounds for anxiety – that Nasser's heirs might be divided, their rivalries giving reactionary elements a chance to regain power; and that, partly perhaps as a result of these rivalries, the new leaders of Egypt, whoever they were, might try to prove themselves by rushing into a new battle with Israel. So he repeatedly warned against 'divisions and adventurism'. As far as the first went, he could only give advice; but for the second he had the means of applying pressure, by slowing down the shipment of those arms due to Egypt under the January and July agreements which would be essential for any crossing of the Suez Canal, such as bridging equipment.

Kosygin showed himself almost desperately anxious that Nasser's death should cause as little dislocation as possible. 'Let me tell you how we used to deal with things when Nasser was alive,' he said at one of the meetings, almost as though he had forgotten that many of those present had been close associates of Nasser for many years and had accompanied him on his journeys to Moscow. 'We never had any secrets from him, and he never had any secrets from us. It is essential that each of us should tell the other everything. Each side must be able to understand what the other is thinking. We don't want to interfere in your plans, but don't forget that our troops are here in Egypt. We have a community of blood, as well as a community of interests. This is very important, and something that you must always take into consideration.'

Kosygin's message was one of caution. He had made it plain that the Russians wanted the ceasefire to be extended. He told the meetings that, while the Soviet Union in no way questioned Egypt's right to recover its lost territory, the measure of Egypt's readiness to do this through war would be when the Egyptian high command could say that the Soviet advisers and experts were no longer required. This was a point he particularly emphasized. 'We want to help you to reach that day as quickly as possible,' he said, and he urged the need for the intensified training of Egypt's armed forces, their political indoctrination, and the mobilization of the masses behind them. The Soviet Union, he insisted, would never let Egypt down, but ought not more attention be given to the possibility of a diplomatic solution?

★   ★   ★

The funeral guests departed; the days of mourning ended. The choice of Anwar Sadat as president to succeed Nasser was confirmed by plebiscite on October 15. He faced a complex and baffling situation at home and abroad. For anyone to step into Nasser's shoes was an almost impossible task. Nasser had been a world figure as well as a charismatic leader of the Egyptian people, and critics would be quick to make unfavourable comparisons with his successor in both capacities. In fact, as we now know, Anwar Sadat was to prove a much more resourceful and original president than anyone expected, and in nothing was his personal style to be more forcefully demonstrated than in his dealings with the Soviet Union.

Looking at Sadat's presidency over the six and a half years between his coming to power in September 1970 and the early months of 1977, which is where this narrative ends, his relations with the Soviet Union can be seen to fall into five phases. First, there was a period of uncertainty, in which Sadat was occupied in trying to establish himself at home and he and the Russians were taking each other's measure. It was not an easy period, and during it the seeds of later misunderstandings were sown. The next phase was one of growing tension, reaching a climax with the expulsion of the Soviet experts in July 1972.

The third phase was the watershed – the October war of 1973. During it for a brief period Egyptian–Soviet relations reached a pinnacle of cordiality which had not been known since the days of

Suez. But this interlude was quickly followed by phases four and five, in the first of which the Soviets were effectively excluded from the negotiations for a Middle East settlement, and in the second of which the attempt was made by Egypt and America, working in harmony, to exclude them from the Middle East altogether.

★   ★   ★

When Sadat took stock of the diplomatic and military problems which he had inherited he found that two distinct and largely contradictory initiatives were in train. On the one hand there were the moves towards a settlement of the Arab–Israel conflict, and on the other hand preparations for a new war.

The Rogers Plan had been launched by the Secretary of State on December 9, 1969, and he had followed this up on June 25, 1970, with specific proposals for a ceasefire along the Canal. These had been accepted by Nasser, and a ceasefire had come into effect on August 7. Both the American and Russian governments were keen to see the ceasefire extended, and in spite of Israel's rejection of his plan and Arab scepticism, the American Secretary of State was still actively engaged in his search for a peace formula.

But preparations for war were going ahead much more purposefully than negotiations for peace. In the three years before his death Nasser's attention had been concentrated, to the exclusion of almost everything else, on ways and means of recovering from the disaster of 1967 and reversing its consequences. He had set up a commission, headed by General Hassan el-Badri, to investigate the causes of the defeat, and had spent hour after hour studying its findings. With the help of the Soviet advisers, Marshal Zakharov and General Lashinkov, he had supervised the programme of training for the armed forces and had been assiduous in his attendance at manœuvres.

Nasser was keenly conscious that the war had undermined Egyptian leadership in the Arab world, and that King Hussein's repression of the Palestinians had put out of action the only genuinely revolutionary element to emerge in it. The two props of progressive Arabs had been knocked away. Nasser felt that, in the eyes of Arabs everywhere as well as of his fellow countrymen, the only justification for his remaining in office, and not disappearing from the scene as he had wished to do in the immediate aftermath of the war, would be if he could eventually lead his armies into a successful battle for the recovery of lost Arab territory and lost Arab honour.

By the time he died preparations for the next round of fighting had reached quite an advanced stage. The operation code-named 'Granite One', which laid down the basic strategy which the October war implemented, had been approved. The armed forces knew their destiny, and welcomed it. For them only the hour when they were to strike remained to be decided. Anyone who had attempted to divert them from their destiny would have been demanding the impossible, and would have invited the armies' obloquy, or worse.

While Sadat was still feeling his way forward he had really no alternative but to continue both initiatives – to let the military preparations go ahead, but to treat with all seriousness the search for a peaceful settlement. His first test was what to do about renewing the ceasefire along the Canal, which was due to expire on February 7. On February 4, in an address to the National Assembly, he made his decision known; he would agree to an extension for one month, and at the same time he suggested that, if Israel withdrew its troops from the east bank of the Canal, Egypt would start clearing the Canal so that it could be opened again to shipping. The proposal was quite a practical one; it happened to be in line with ideas which Moshe Dayan had been floating for some time, that Israel's position would be improved politically as well as militarily if it moved its troops away from this international waterway and back to the strategic passes in Sinai.

The Russians approved this gesture, but they were still puzzled to know what to make of the new president. They had viewed with misgiving his choice of Dr Mahmoud Fawzi as Prime Minister. Dr Fawzi was a moderate, well known and respected at home and abroad, but his appointment had been strongly opposed by Ali Sabri and others whom the Russians had come to look on as their special friends and allies inside the Egyptian government. They had noted, too, Sadat's increasing contacts with the Saudis, though it was in fact quite natural that these contacts should be made, since under Nasser he had had responsibility for affairs in the Arabian peninsula and the Gulf, including the Yemen war. Now Kamal Adham, who was among other things counsellor to the Saudi king and head of the Saudi intelligence machine, became a frequent caller at the presidential mansion. This was not something to reassure the Russians.

* * *

Sadat was very conscious of Soviet suspicions, and was anxious to allay them. At the same time he was acutely aware of the delays in deliveries of promised equipment for the armed forces. Two items in particular were a source of constant anxiety – one was the bridges necessary for a crossing of the Suez Canal, and the other the lack of a fighter-bomber capable of matching the Phantoms which Israel now possessed. Such an aircraft was essential both to give protection to the troops for the crossing and to mount retaliatory raids in answer to the depth raiding to which Israel had been subjecting Delta towns and villages. These raids had understandably provoked bitter anger and a growing clamour for revenge. In order both to calm Soviet fears and to explain Egyptian needs, Sadat decided to send Sharawy Gomaa on a secret visit to Moscow, taking with him a private letter from the President to Brezhnev. Sharawy Gomaa was chosen because he was Secretary General of the ASU and as such responsible for the Vanguard organization – a body which the Soviets looked on with a good deal of hope.

The letter was dated February 4, the day when extension of the ceasefire was announced. It began by introducing Sharawy Gomaa as 'my colleague and friend, whom I trust completely' – somewhat ironical in view of the fact the two months later he was to be behind bars on a charge of plotting Sadat's overthrow. The President spoke of the need to stand up to what he called 'the unholy alliance between the enemies of progress, liberty and peace'. It was, he said, in response to Soviet wishes that the ceasefire had been extended, but he described this as 'a very hard decision'.

'I have asked Sharawy Gomaa to give you full information of what the US is trying to do to us now,' the letter went on, 'and what we are up against. But we are not going to sell our liberty to the imperialists. We know what the developments are likely to be; we know our responsibilities. Our nation is going to fight to the end. We had hoped you would be with us for the completion of the High Dam. Our friend Podgorny was with us, and we hope that you will join us in happier times.' (A reference to the invitation to Brezhnev to visit Egypt, first accepted and then postponed.)

Sharawy Gomaa came back from Moscow without achieving anything concrete. So President Sadat decided that before the ceasefire finally ran out on March 7 he would go himself to the Soviet Union, taking General Mohammed Fawzi, the Minister of War, with him.

The visit, which was kept secret, began on March 1. His meeting with Brezhnev, Kosygin and the other Soviet leaders turned out to be a difficult one. All the doubts and hesitations about Egypt which had been building up in their minds while Nasser was still alive were accentuated now that he was dead. They knew that Egypt was planning some military operations, but not their nature, and they were content not to know because they did not want to be saddled with responsibility for the planning or conduct of the operations.

At his first meeting with Brezhnev, Sadat, after thanking his hosts for all they had done ('I still tell my people that if it was not for the Soviet Union and its support we should be in real trouble'), recalled that when Podgorny was in Cairo in January he had spoken of the need to consolidate relations between the two countries. He continued: 'There is always one question I'm asked, whether in the Central Committee of the ASU, at the Higher Defence Council, or by commanders in the front line – and that is, what is going to happen if the Israelis raid us in depth again? Are we going to be able to retaliate by raiding them in depth? And to speak to you quite frankly, that is a question I can't answer. I've been to the marines. I've been to the commander of the navy, who told me all the things he lacked and all the things the Israelis had got. If I go to the front line, and if I tell the troops that now is the time to give the order for the crossing, the commanders will just tell me about the equipment they still need. So will the commanders of the airforce.

'They say that when the Soviet Union wanted to conduct an operation in Czechoslovakia it was able to completely jam the whole Nato radar system – something which took the West by surprise. We don't deny that if it hadn't been for the Soviet Union we could never have rebuilt our armed forces, and we should never have received all the electronic equipment that is coming to us. But the questions I'm being asked in the Central Committee of the ASU are still there. The tragedy for me is that we have three-quarters of a million men under arms, and yet we are in no position to cross the Canal.

'The Americans have started to contact us,' Sadat went on, 'They tell us that the Soviet Union can't help us – only the US can do that, and so we will have to trust them and follow their advice. And then they always bring up this question of the Soviet presence in our country. They don't say this to us directly, but it was implied in the letters Nixon has sent me and in his speech to Congress. The thing he is always talking about is the Soviet presence in the Middle East.

'I have made my peace initiative, including an offer to open the Suez Canal, and I've told the Americans that if they can put pressure on the Israelis to play their part I'm ready to establish diplomatic relations with the US. But this would have to be part of an overall settlement. On your advice I have gone further in my efforts for peace than any other Arab leader.'

(In his speech of February 4, 1971, which extended the ceasefire till March 7, Sadat had, in fact, stated that he was prepared to accept a peace agreement, though not an actual peace treaty, with Israel – something which took the Israeli Prime Minister, Golda Meir, completely by surprise.)

'I assure you,' Sadat continued, 'that I see our future tied to the future of the Soviet Union. I am ready here and now to sign anything the Soviet Union wants me to sign, to prove what I say. I know that my real enemy is the US and western imperialism. That is what I told ambassador Vinogradov last Friday. If I'm ready to sign anything with the Soviet Union, it is not just because I know that this is in the best interests of my country, but because when I am under pressure I don't want my enemies to think that I lack the power to hit back at them.

'So I'm going to make a complete review of my position. First, I repeat that the Soviet presence in the area is in our country's interest. Second, our mutual relations, now and in the future, must be built on a clear and well defined basis. You must be by my side to help me resist the pressures I'm facing. Third, I am prepared, just as President Nasser was, to face anything in my country or in the Arab area. Fourth, I have no specific demands, except that we should build a relationship now and for the future. If the Americans can achieve a first step according to their plans, there will be a reaction against the Soviet Union and me, because it will give the impression that the Americans were the people who succeeded after the Soviet Union had failed. It will look as if they hold the key to the situation.'

Sadat repeated his gratitude for what the Soviet Union had done for Egypt, and said that, as he had explained publicly, he had decided to afford facilities in Egypt to the Soviet Union because of their help. He said there was no need for them to worry about the internal situation in Egypt, because there were no reactionary activities there, and if there were he could crush them in five minutes. But there was a good deal of American propaganda among the people, and whispering against the Soviet Union. 'And that,' he said, 'brings me back to the question which everyone is asking – if the Israelis bomb places like Esna and Nag Hamadi again, would we be able to reply? Obviously our people want their revenge; they are mobilized for revenge. Our people are killed and wounded. The Israeli generals are arrogant. Who can believe after Czechoslovakia that the Soviet Union hasn't got a plane better than the Phantom? That is what the people are asking.'

Sadat then reverted to his peace initiative of February 4. He said his information was that the Americans had approved this initiative and were prepared to secure the return to Egypt of some of its occupied territory. But he added that he was convinced Israel would exact a price for any concessions, and that the probable price would be an end to the Soviet presence.

As for contacts with the Americans which Brezhnev had enquired about, Sadat said these were through the Spanish Embassy in Cairo (which was looking after American interests, since diplomatic relations had been broken off in 1967). He said the Israelis had tried to make indirect contacts through the Italians and Greeks, but he had refused to have anything to do with these approaches and he had told the Soviet ambassador in Cairo about them.

In reply Brezhnev and Kosygin switched to the practical problem of what was going to happen after March 7. 'Have you studied the problem?' they asked. 'Have you got a plan? Have you discussed the problem in the ASU?' Sadat said that they were working twenty-four hours a day on the problem but had not yet reached a final decision, though any further extension of the ceasefire had been ruled out. On the military side, they were working on the assumption that there would be a resumption of the fighting, but on the political side they were waiting for developments by the Americans 'and by our friends'.

This answer obviously failed to satisfy the Russians. 'We are friends here,' said Brezhnev, 'so there is nothing to prevent us from talking frankly. You say you'll refuse an extension of the ceasefire. But what is going to happen on March 8th – or on the 9th, or the 10th? Do you know what Israel's reaction will be? Are they going to attack you in depth? Are they going to attack your missile sites? If they do, what will you do? Will you take the initiative by military operations, and if so what operations? Are you going to cross the Canal?'

Sadat's answer was that the Minister of War had put forward several contingency plans – for an attrition war, for special operations, and for limited operations. 'Our people are ready to fight to ten years, and to lose one million – two million – three million people killed, just as you lost twenty million in the war. We are prepared to see our institutions destroyed, but on one condition, that if the enemy hits us in depth, we hit him back in depth.'

Brezhnev picked up Sadat's remarks about the Soviet Union's jamming of Nato radar at the time of the invasion of Czechoslovakia. 'For your information ,' he said, 'we used no non-traditional arms in Czechoslovakia. At midnight we woke up President Svoboda and told him we were crossing his borders but were not going to fire. So there was no need to jam all European radar. You musn't believe what's said in the West.'

'No, I prefer to believe what's said in the West,' said Sadat. 'Marshal Gretchko should be proud of what happened.'

'It's a nice idea,' said Brezhnev. 'The West lost face, because Czechoslovakia was occupied in only six hours. But it wasn't stricktly speaking a military operation.'

'No, no,' Sadat insisted. 'The way the West talks about it makes it a splendid achievement. In that very short time the operation was successfully completed.'

'Has it given you ideas about occupying Tel Aviv in the course of a single night?' Kosygin put in. There was general laughter; then Brezhnev brought the discussion back to reality: 'Your problem is,' he said, 'that in front of you is the desert, flat and without cover. There is no concealment, which makes an armoured attack extremely difficult.'

The discussion continued along these lines for some time, and eventually the Russians said they were prepared to send Egypt four missile-launching Ilyushin planes, but that as the crews would be Russian the decision as to whether the planes should be used would have to be taken in Moscow. 'If we don't give you all the arms you ask for,' said Brezhnev, 'it's not because we're afraid but because we think that each armament should be related to the appropriate stage of the struggle.' With that, and some more tanks, Sadat had to return content.

★ ★ ★

Sadat came back from Moscow to face a threatening situation on the home front. What later became known as the 'Ali Sabri group' had already come out into opposition over the extension of the ceasefire. Now they had found another and more significant issue on which to challenge the President in the proposal to create some form of unity between Egypt, Libya and Syria (originally the Sudan had been included, but had backed down). Sadat showed his wish for the union to go through; the Ali Sabri group fought it, and inevitably rumours of dissension within the leadership began to reach the outside world.

It so happened that all those senior Egyptian officials whom the Russians had come to know best, and so to regard as being particularly their friends, were now ranged against the President. They were men who held commanding positions in the Central Committee of the Arab Socialist Union, in Parliament, and in the intelligence – notably Ali Sabri, a vice-president; Sharawy Gomaa, Minister of the Interior and Secretary General of the ASU; Diaeddin Doaud, a member of the High Executive Committee of the ASU; Labib Shuqair, Speaker of the Assembly; Sami Sharaf, Minister of Presidential Affairs; Mohammed Faik, Minister of Information. In fact the conflict which put these men in one camp (and eventually in prison), and the President in the other, was not primarily about the union with Libya, or relations with the Soviet Union or any other specific issue. It was a struggle for power between a new president trying to assert himself and a group of his former colleagues who were determined that control of affairs should remain in their hands and who were prepared to go to almost any extreme to ensure that this should be so.

But though the real struggle was for power, the debate was decked out with some ideological clothing, and this undoubtedly helped to give the Russians a distorted idea of what was going on. The Ali Sabri group tried to present themselves as the custodians of the more radical ideas and legislation put forward by the Egyptian revolution. They failed to see that Nasser's greatest achievement as a national leader had been as a reconciler, and that in those first critical months, when Nasser was no longer there, the supreme need was to soothe the fears and heal the wounds of the nation, not to exacerbate them, and that to do this a degree of relaxation was imperative. That was why a man like Dr Mahmoud Fawzi was chosen to be Prime Minister.

But to observers in the Kremlin the scene in Egypt looked simpler and more ominous. The division between the heirs of Nasser which they had feared and warned against was unfolding and the new President seemed to be lining up against them. It was not just that they paid too much attention to the supposedly radical ideology of the Ali Sabri group; they saw a sinister implication in the proposal for union with Libya and Syria. Was not Ghadaffi still loud in his denunciation of the Soviet Union and communism, and was not the new ruler of Syria, Hafez Assad, an army officer who had forcibly overthrown a left-wing Baathist government? They failed too to appreciate that one of the reasons for the closer ties which Sadat was seeking with Saudi Arabia was the material help which the Saudis could provide.

No doubt Russian suspicions were increased by the unfortunate and probably deliberate leak in Washington of a remark Sadat had made to Kamal Adham. Adham had spoken to the President of American fears over the continuing Soviet presence in Egypt. Sadat had explained the necessity for this, but added that after the first phase of an Israeli withdrawal had been completed he would undertake to get the Russians out. This was leaked by Senator Jackson, one of the most ardent supporters of Israel and opponents of the Soviet Union in Congress, no doubt with the aim of causing as much trouble as possible to both the Soviet Union and Egypt.

★   ★   ★

The Twenty-fourth Congress of the CPSU was due to open in Moscow on March 31, 1971, and it was decided to send a strong delegation from Egypt. Inevitably the decision as to who should go became caught up in the struggle for power which was going on. I think the Soviets realized this, and were worried by it. In the end several delegations went, each trying to keep its plans and activities concealed from the others. The delegation from the ASU was headed by the secretary, Abdel Muhsin Abdul Nur; Sami Sharaf headed another delegation which carried a message from Sadat to Brezhnev, and so on. In fact it was not until after the congress was over that Sami Sharaf was able to see Brezhnev, and when the meeting did take place he took half an hour to get round to delivering the President's message; until then he was too busy giving a message on his own behalf. 'I must thank Comrade Brezhnev', he began, 'for giving me this opportunity to see him in spite of all his preoccupations. I am sure that he would not have met everybody, and that this is a special favour for me personally. I trust relations between us will be everlasting and continuous and that the coming days and the positions which we adopt will be taken as a sincere witness to the friendship which exists between the UAR and the Soviet Union, parties, peoples and governments. I hope, Comrade Brezhnev, that you will permit me to express a personal sentiment – that your meeting me today in these circumstances is to be taken as evidence of a truth in which I firmly believe, which is that, since Sami Sharaf is the son of the great leader and teacher Gamal Abdel Nasser, he occupies a special position in relation to his Soviet friends.'

Sami Sharaf hinted at the existence of rivalries inside the Egyptian leadership, talking about 'our group' and telling Brezhnev he was sure the Soviet ambassador in Cairo 'must tell him everything'. (In fact Vinogradov was always extremely careful not to give any impression of being involved in internal Egyptian politics. One of the tapes prepared by Sami Sharaf, discovered after his arrest, recorded a meeting between him and Vinogradov, which went on for nearly fifty minutes during which Vinogradov's contribution lasted at most two minutes.) Sami Sharaf was even foolish enough to treat the long-suffering Brezhnev to a long quotation from a speech by 'the great leader Lenin' to the Ninth Congress of the CPSU in 1920.

★   ★   ★

When eventually Sami Sharaf did get round to delivering the message from President Sadat with which he had been entrusted it contained at least one new suggestion – that Egyptian–Soviet relations should be formalized by the conclusion of a treaty between the two countries. So it was that on May 1 a message came from Moscow signed by all the three top Soviet leaders, Brezhnev, Kosygin and Podgorny, in the course of which they said: 'We have studied with interest the suggestion made by you, and conveyed to us by Sami Sharaf, for a treaty of friendship and cooperation between us. We think such a treaty would be of great importance and would produce a profound impression in world public opinion. It would also be a significant means of pressure on Israel and the US, who now confront the UAR in its struggle to achieve its legitimate rights and to liquidate the consequences of aggression. There is no need to emphasize the fact that such a treaty would bury for ever the desire of our enemies to break the friendship between our two countries and peoples. We are prepared to sign such a treaty any time you wish, and if you have no objection we can begin immediate consultations on the text of the treaty.'

The timing of the President's letter and of the Soviet answer is important, because it has sometimes been suggested that the treaty was insisted upon by the Soviets to make up for the damage which had been done by the dismissal of the so-called 'pro-Soviet' group. But, as has been seen, the idea of a treaty had been proposed and accepted well before the dismissals had been decided upon or put into effect.

One suggestion made in the Soviet letter of May 1 was that one of the Soviet leaders should come to Egypt on a good will mission during the first half of May. They must have been puzzled to know exactly what was going on in Cairo, because only two days before his final downfall Sami Sharaf asked Vladimir Vinogradov, the Soviet ambassador, if it was essential that the senior Soviet representative should come to Cairo then 'because this will only strengthen the President's position'. The ambassador was tactfully non-committal in his answer.

Ali Sabri and his friends were arrested on May 16, and Podgorny arrived in Cairo nine days later, bearing with him the draft text for the treaty. I was opposed to the whole idea of a treaty, which I thought would be bound to remind people of the 1936 Anglo-Egyptian Treaty of unhappy memory. When, at Sadat's request, Mahmoud Riad, the Foreign Minister, telephoned to me asking my opinion, I pointed out that the suggested duration of the treaty (20 years) was the same as for the 1936 treaty. The treaty went ahead, but its duration was altered to 15 years.

The treaty, signed on May 27, took the Americans by surprise. King Feisal was on an official visit to Washington when the news of its signing came through and was closely questioned by Nixon as to its significance. Did it mean that all the efforts Secretary of State Rogers had been making had gone for nothing? King Feisal came to Cairo in the middle of June, and the Russians were just as anxious to know how to interpret the significance of this visit, and of the growing warmth of relations between Cairo, Riyadh and Tehran, as the Americans had been to assess the implications of the treaty.

14
The Gulf Widens

SADAT HAD EMERGED truimphant from his first major test. His authority as President was now firmly established, but the rout of the Ali
Sabri group had not made relations with the Soviet Union any easier.
Now a new source of friction was to arise, this time outside the borders
of Egypt – in the Sudan.

Colonel Jaafar Nimeiry, who had led the May 1969 coup in the
Sudan, aimed to secure as broad a political backing as possible. Most
of the Sudanese Communist Party, one of the best organized in the
Arab world, at first supported him, even though he banned all political
parties and set up a single Sudanese Socialist Union, on the lines of
Nasser's Arab Socialist Union. Nimeiry would have liked the Sudanese
Communist Party to follow the Egyptian party's example and formally
dissolve itself, but this it was unwilling to do. Instead, the party leader,
Abdel Khalek Mahgoub, continued to pursue an independent line
and to maintain secret contacts with three sympathetic members of the
ten-man Revolutionary Command Council, Babikr el-Nur, Farouk
Osman Hamadallah and Hashem el-Atta.

There was evidence that the communists were working together
with some of Nimeiry's opponents at the other end of the political
spectrum, members of the now illegal Umma Party. At the time of
Sudan's independence in 1956 the Umma Party had been the more
conservative and nationalist of the two parties which more or less
divided political power between themselves. Its strength was largely
drawn from the Ansar sect, the followers of the family of the Mahdi
who, in the 1870s, started the movement of religious nationalism
which led to the death of Gordon in 1885 and the reoccupation of the
Sudan 13 years later by Kitchener's Anglo-Egyptian army.

The traditional headquarters of the Ansar sect is Abba Island, 150
miles south of Khartoum on the White Nile. In March 1970 about
30,000 Ansaris were gathered on the island. They were well armed,
with machine guns, mortars and bazookas, and a revolt seemed imminent. On March 27 Nimeiry went himself to the island in an attempt

to negotiate with the Ansaris but met with a hostile reception, and, as he told the nation in a broadcast the next day, his life was threatened.

Anwar Sadat was at the time in the Sudan, where he had been sent by Nasser to maintain personal contact with Nimeiry. In view of the gravity of the situation Nimeiry felt the need of Egyptian assistance, and sent Nasser a request for units of the Egyptian airforce to raid Aba Island. Sadat backed up his request. But Nasser refused. He did not want Egypt to get directly involved in Sudanese affairs in this way or for any Sudanese to be killed by Egyptian arms. So Nimeiry sent an ultimatum to the Ansaris, and Sudanese planes were ordered to make one strafing flight over the island. In the course of this flight and the subsequent storming of the island by government troops casualties among the Ansaris were very heavy. The Ansar leader, Imam Hadi el-Mahdi, who had been accused of leadership of the revolt, was killed in somewhat mysterious circumstances by border guards while attempting to cross into Ethiopia.

Nimeiry put Abdel Khalek Mahgoub and Sayyid Sadiq el-Mahdi, nephew of the Mahdi, who had been under arrest since June, on a military plane and had them flown to Cairo, with a letter to Nasser asking him to keep them in custody. Nasser sent me with a friendly message to Sadiq el-Mahdi telling him he should not look on Cairo as a place of exile, but that it was probably better that he should be out of the Sudan for the time being to ensure that its affairs developed in peace, without the polarization between traditional and radical forces which could only lead to civil war. Sadiq el-Mahdi reacted favourably to Nasser's message and settled down comfortably in Cairo for several years.

Mahgoub, on the other hand, went round complaining to everybody about the misery of his life as an exile. The information coming from Moscow was that the ideologists in the Soviet Union were annoyed at what they regarded as his enforced detention and anxious about what was going to happen to him. Someone from one of the institutes concerned with the Arab world even got in touch with the Egyptian embassy in Moscow and asked whether it would be possible for Mahgoub to go back to the Sudan, and what Cairo thought would happen if he did; would it mean trouble?

So eventually Nasser summoned Mahgoub and told him that the sort of talk he was indulging in was ridiculous. 'I want you to stay here,' he said, 'but I'm not making you or anyone else a prisoner. When you leave this office you will find two envelopes which will enable you to go anywhere in the world you like. It's entirely up to you.'

So when Mahgoub left Nasser's office he picked up the envelopes, one of which contained an open air ticket and the other several hundred pounds in sterling. He went to the airport and got on board the first plane going to Khartoum. As soon as he arrived he was arrested and put in prison.

During the first half of 1971 the conflict between Nimeiry and the communists moved towards a climax. At the beginning of July Mahgoub was smuggled out of prison and went underground. On July 19 the extreme left struck. A group of rebels seized army headquarters, captured Nimeiry and locked him up. At least thirty officers and men loyal to Nimeiry were murdered in particularly nasty circumstances.

In spite of their previous protestations about not wanting to come to power as the result of a military insurrection, the communists formed the most active element in the coup, which was led by Hashem el-Atta. As soon as news of the coup reached Cairo Sadat sent a special emissary by air to Khartoum asking for assurances about the safety of Nimeiry, but Atta's only answer was that the deposed president would be brought to trial and that there was therefore nothing to discuss.

Meanwhile the other two former communist sympathisers on the Revolutionary Command Council, Babakr el-Nur and Farouk Osman Hamadallah, who had been in London when the coup took place, were making arrangements for a triumphal return to Khartoum – Babakr el-Nur had been named as Nimeiry's successor as president. But while their plane, a scheduled BOAC flight from London to Khartoum, was over Libya it received orders to land. The two men were taken off the plane, put in gaol and later handed over to the Sudanese authorities.

But even without this intervention by Ghadaffi the coup was already collapsing. It received little or no backing from any section of the public, and within seventy-two hours loyal troops were in control of the capital again. Army headquarters were recaptured and Nimeiry freed.

Soviet representatives in Khartoum had been in close touch with the leaders of the coup and Moscow came out in their support. The Russians now tried to intervene on the coup leaders' behalf, both

directly with Nimeiry and indirectly through the Egyptian government. Ponomarev, who happened to be in Cairo at the time, personally
appealed to Sadat on behalf of the trade union leader, Shafi'ah Ahmed
el-Sheikh, who that year had been a joint winner of the Lenin Peace
Prize. Sadat got in touch with Nimeiry by telephone, only to be told
that the Russian appeal came too late – Shafi'ah el-Sheikh, together
with Mahgoub and about fourteen other of the ringleaders, had already
been executed. They had in fact been disposed of in great haste, with
no real trial and considerable brutality.

★   ★   ★

The Russians were extremely upset over this bloodbath involving their
friends, and started a violent propaganda campaign against Nimeiry
and the Sudan. Military and other aid was cut off, and commercial relations interrupted. The Sudanese government reacted sharply to what
it regarded as a continuing attempt by the Soviets to interfere in the
internal affairs of the Sudan. Abul Hashim Qasim, a member of the
Revolutionary Council, summoned the Soviet ambassador and handed
him a note couched in very strong language. 'The Revolutionary
Council of the Sudan', it read, 'requests the Soviet Union to put an end,
finally and completely, to the campaign being conducted against the
Sudanese government because of the execution of certain communist
and labour leaders. You must realize that a continuation of this campaign will constitute a grave threat to the future of Sudanese–Soviet
relations. The Revolutionary Command Council reserves to itself the
right to any action which it regards as necessary for the defence of the
dignity and honour of the Sudan, unless it receives a satisfactory reply
within twenty-four hours.'

The Soviets reacted in a predictably forthright manner to what
was in effect an ultimatum. The Sudanese ambassador in Moscow was
summoned to the Ministry of Foreign Affairs where he was handed a
note in the following terms: 'We are at present engaged in a study of
the message which has been sent by the Revolutionary Command
Council in the Sudan, but pending completion of this study we wish
to inform you that the ultimatum presented by the Sudanese Command Council to the Soviet Union is provocative both in its contents
and in its language, and the Soviet Union rejects it wholly. Nobody
is permitted to address the Soviet Union in this manner. Even our

enemies in the imperialist camp understood a long time ago that the times for such a communication are long past, and we are astonished that the Sudanese leadership should have reverted to it at this juncture.'

*   *   *

President Sadat had proclaimed 1971 the 'year of decision', but as the weeks went by it became increasingly clear that it was not going to be possible to launch any military operations that year. Instead of moving to a climax the outlook for Egypt was becoming increasingly confused. Political life was developing in directions which only a year or two before would have seemed out of the question. On one side bourgeois elements, encouraged by the growing influence exerted by oil wealth, were gaining strength and influence; on the other side elements claiming to be progressive (the Ali Sabri group) had been shown up as in reality more interested in power for its own sake. The gulf of misunderstanding between Moscow and Cairo was widening.

In an effort to clear the road ahead Sadat decided to go again to Moscow, taking with him Mahmoud Riad, the Foreign Minister, and General Mohammed Sadiq, the army Chief of Staff. On October 12, 1971, they had a meeting which was attended on the Russian side by Brezhnev, Kosygin, Podgorny, Gretchko, Ponomarev and Vinogradov. The discussions show the President, thwarted by his inability to move rapidly towards a battle, which would have been the catalyst to solve all his difficulties, seeking support for some new political opening, but seeking this in vain.

Brezhnev opened the proceedings by saying it was a pity that they had not met for such a long time. Their enemies were trying to drive a wedge between the two countries, so he hoped for a frank discussion without protocol.

Sadat took him at his word. 'I'll start', he said, 'with what's happened since our last meeting in March. At that meeting we talked about the ceasefire and allied subjects. Then, after we had decided on a union with Libya and Syria we had a problem in Egypt – the problem of a divided leadership. The union wasn't the real reason for the division, but I felt that our enemies might use the division, so I acted quickly. I called in the Soviet ambassador and told him there was a conflict in the leadership and that I was going to liquidate it, and was kicking out

Ali Sabri. I said I was afraid the West would use this to say that Moscow's man in Egypt was out and that Egypt was moving towards the West. Then, two days later, Rogers came to Cairo, and made new proposals, and this timing led to misunderstandings between us. But I had told you about what was happening long before Rogers came, and after I had met Rogers I called in Vinogradov and gave him full details about our meeting for him to pass on to you.

'You asked me to work for a solution,' he said. 'I agree with you. I told Podgorny in April that if there was only one half per cent of hope for a solution I would still work for it. I recall the last words I spoke to Podgorny before he boarded the plane to go back to Moscow after signing the treaty: "I'm only asking you for one thing," I said. "Have confidence in me." After May 13 I faced a conflict, made my decision and liquidated the mutiny. But the West made use of this and tried to make out that I was changing my policy, destroying socialism and reversing the Nasserist line. They exploited the fact that the Americans were contacting us about a peaceful solution. So in my speech of September 16 I exposed them. On July 6 Nixon had sent me a message – I sent you details of it – in which he asked me about our treaty with you and wanted to know whether we still had our freedom of action. I told him. But contacts with the Americans and us were broken off until four days ago when they contacted an assistant to the Minister of Foreign Affairs, Mohammed Riad.'

Sadat then turned to events in the Sudan. 'Ponomarev was with me in Cairo at the time,' he said, 'and I explained my point of view about the Sudan to him. I told him "Give me a month and I'll undertake to send Nimeiry to Moscow. He'll have found by then that he won't get any support from anywhere except the Soviet Union. Still, the weather in the Sudan is hot and the blood of the people is hot. But let's forget about that. I'll send you Nimeiry."'

Sadat then went back to the question of Soviet–Egyptian relations. 'As I've told you before,' he said, 'we share the same destiny as the Soviet Union. We have not changed our policy. More than that, I made a plea on March 23 that we should have a common strategy. I repeat this plea today. As I told Ponomarev, we are closer to you than are many Marxist countries, such as China or Cuba; we are more friendly. I always tell my people that you stood by our side as an honest friend in our times of need. I want to tell you what I really believe – this is that the target of the imperialist powers is to drive a wedge between us and the Soviet Union. This can only serve America and Zionism. As I've said, my conviction is that America has three targets, and that in this they see eye to eye with Israel. First, they want to remove the Soviet presence from the area and create misunderstandings between the Arabs and the Soviets. Secondly, they want to achieve the isolation of Egypt, because Egypt has shown how it is possible to build up a modern country, while they want it to remain a backward African country, no more important than Gabon. Thirdly, they want to liquidate all progressive regimes in the Arab world, which would be easy for them once Egypt had been isolated.'

President Sadat mentioned that Kosygin had asked him about the position of Saudi Arabia. He said he had talked frankly to King Feisal about relations between Egypt and America, and that Feisal had promised to send Prince Fahd to America two weeks later. Sadat said his request to King Feisal had been that, when the day came for Sadat to bring into the open the truth about American policy in the Middle East, he (Feisal) should, if he found it impossible to be on Egypt's side, at least remain neutral. Feisal had been very moved, and said he would stand by Sadat. President Sadat added that he had had a long talk with the Shah, whose view was that what the Americans wanted was a partial solution which would let Egypt get Sinai back on condition that it cut itself off from the rest of the Arab world. But if he (Sadat) did tell the truth about American policy the Shah's attitude would be the same as King Feisal's.

Sadat concluded by saying he asked for two things: the Americans were always claiming that they would make Israel superior to the Arabs, but he wanted the Soviet Union to put Egypt on a footing of equality with Israel. And his second wish was for the same thing as he had asked Podgorny – for confidence. 'Our friendship', he said, 'isn't a question of tactics; it's a strategic concept.'

Sadat had a second meeting with the Soviet leaders the same day in the course of which he again brought up the question of the Ali Sabri group. 'I don't want you to believe rumours about me,' he said. 'Some of those now in prison went to Ambassador Vinogradov and told him I was selling Egypt to the Americans and changing the Nasserist line. But I'm not selling Egypt to the Americans and my line hasn't changed. There was a split in the country. The President was talking one way and his associates were talking in another way. The internal situation of the country is now very good.'

Brezhnev intervened to point out that when he had asked about the internal situation in Egypt he meant things like the economic situation, and the strength of the rightist forces, not the Ali Sabri business. Sadat said the rightist forces were very few: 'I can crush them in a second. The right in Egypt has no teeth, and I won't allow it to have any teeth.'

There was a third meeting the next morning, October 13. Brezhnev began by praising Sadat and saying how glad he was to see a continuation of the good relations between their countries, built up by President Nasser. He said that the Soviet Union was giving Egypt much more than it gave some socialist countries. Soviet policy towards Egypt was not a matter of tactics, but had been fully discussed and agreed at the Twenty-fourth Congress of the CPSU in March 1971.

Brezhnev then went back to the question of the Ali Sabri group. 'I wouldn't have said anything about Egypt's internal affairs,' he said, 'if you hadn't started to discuss them. You mentioned the conflict in the leadership. These people we know, because they were emissaries of you or of Nasser. They took part in discussions with us, and as far as I can remember none came here on his own initiative. The last one I met was Sami Sharaf. I was very busy, but when they told me he had a message for me from President Sadat I saw him. The minutes of our meeting are with Ponomarev – you can see them if you want to. I recall that he said he had been one of the assistants of Nasser and was now one of the assistants of Sadat. I could not have imagined that an emissary of Sadat could have been an enemy of Sadat. That is why I tell my brother Sadat that we have no connection at all with what these people may have said. We have been told that some of those on trial said that the Soviet Union knew of their intentions, but I can assure you that this is not so.'

Brezhnev was clearly both puzzled and worried by developments in the Sudan and Libya. He said that only two months before the abortive coup the Soviets had sent Nimeiry a message of support for his policies, even at the risk of annoying the Sudanese communists. So his accusations that they had backed the coup upset them a great deal. As for Ghadaffi: 'We don't know him; we've never met him; we have nothing against him or against Libya. So I don't know why he is attacking us, and communism and the Soviet Union.' Brezhnev said they found it hard to understand that a country which was in the same federation as Egypt should attack the Soviet Union. 'We judge people by what they say. Why is Ghadaffi attacking us? We aren't attacking him, but there's no reason for us to do this. He's a gift to the bourgeois press of the world with his attacks on the Soviet Union. Obviously what Ghadaffi says can't harm the Soviet Union, and the time will come when he will repent of everything he has said against the Soviet Union. We are happy and proud about our relations with the Arab people, but there are some things that we don't understand.'

Brezhnev's main message was, as usual, the need for internal strength and vigilance. 'We have a strong party, a strong Comsomol, a strong revolution, so that no internal enemy can harm us. Our society is built on the principles of the Bolshevik Revolution,' he said, 'but in Egypt sabotage from the inside is much easier. It is not by chance that the Egyptian radio and television show tendencies that would weaken the friendship between us. We think that attempts have been made in Egypt to destroy the good relations between our two countries.' But he met at least some of Sadat's wishes by expressing his full confidence in him – 'We are happy to see our warm, sincere friend, President Sadat, here in Moscow.'

'You say that your people are sentimental and warm,' Brezhnev went on. 'Maybe our people do not have the same warmth, but we are very sensitive to truth and lies. We can tell the difference between them. Everybody in the world knows that we are helping you, but this is being done with the consent of the Soviet peasants, the Soviet workers and the Soviet people. Everybody in this country believes in the principle of aiding you.' This gave Brezhnev an opportunity to mention the questions of the debts due to the Soviet Union, now totalling six million roubles. 'This means we are exporting goods and getting nothing in return,' he said. 'I'm not complaining, but I mention this to give you an idea of the problems we face in the matter of economic aid.'

The meeting ended with fresh warnings. 'We must intensify the struggle against imperialism,' said Brezhnev. 'We must not fall into any political traps; we must not retreat one centimetre from our positions. We should never betray our people or our friendship. America is making proposals to you for the sake of its coming elections, but these are a disguised way of driving a wedge between Egypt and Egypt's friends.' Brezhnev reminded Sadat that he was due to have a meeting with Nixon the following year, and that inevitably the Middle

East would be one of the main subjects for discussion. It was very important that in the interval the Egyptian leaders should not fall into any of the traps the Americans were laying for them.

★   ★   ★

In spite of all the frank exchanges in Moscow there was no longer any real foundation of trust between the Soviet and Egyptian leaders. The first phase of Sadat's relations with Moscow were moving into the second, more acute, phase, the climax of which was to come in July 1972 with the expulsion of the experts.

Part of the trouble was undoubtedly the heavy-handedness of many Russian representatives in Egypt. There was the row over the smuggling of gold out of the country by Russian officials;[1] there were the quarrels between General Mohammed Sadiq, the Minister of War, and senior military men; there was the demand by Admiral Gorshikov for special facilities for Russian warships at Mersa Matruh and Berenice in the Red Sea; there was the Russian attempt virtually to take over Cairo West airport to the exclusion of all Egyptian authorities, and their self-isolation in Cairo, where they had bought up a lot of property in the centre of the city for the exclusive occupation of the experts and diplomats and their families. I myself was the target for bitter attacks in *Pravda* for daring to suggest in articles in *Al Ahram* that the Russians benefited from the existing state of 'no war, no peace' because it increased Egypt's dependence on them.

This particular evaluation was the result of a war game which was staged in the Centre for Strategic Study at *Al Ahram*, in which use was made of computers. But it was backed by other evidence. For example, around this time I had a talk with Luigi Longo, then head of the Italian Communist Party, at his party's headquarters in Rome. I made some remark about the 'no war, no peace' situation. 'Why are you in such a hurry to reach a solution?' he asked. 'I should have thought that a continuation of the present situation would give all progressive elements in Egypt the opportunity to intensify the class struggle and the education of the masses. This would enable you to carry out the social revolution and the national revolution simultaneously.' When I published this interview there was a row, because it appeared to show that

---

[1] See *The Road to Ramadan*, p. 160.

some communist leaders, at any rate, were not genuinely interested in a Middle East settlement.

★   ★   ★

In many ways Soviet obtuseness damaged their standing with Egyptians, and the Americans did what they could to exploit the Soviets' mistakes. But there were deeper reasons for a shift of Sadat's attention away from the Soviets and towards the Americans.

Just before Sadat's Moscow visit there had been, at the end of September 1971, a meeting in Washington between William Rogers, Mahmoud Riad and various officials on both sides, at which a final effort had been made to work out an 'interim agreement' on which the Secretary of State had set his heart. Nothing much had emerged from the meeting, and it seemed to confirm the impression which had been for some time gaining ground in Cairo that the really important foreign policy decisions were no longer being made in the State Department but had passed into the hands of President Nixon's Security Adviser, Henry Kissinger.

Kissinger's position gave him authority over the CIA, and a channel of communication had been opened between the CIA and the then Egyptian Director of Intelligence, General Ahmed Ismail. This channel was supplemented by a number of outside agencies which, with the growing economic and political strength of the oil-producing countries, were beginning to play an increasing role on the diplomatic stage and particularly in connection with American policy in the Middle East. Both King Feisal and the Shah of Iran were concerned in this, and sometimes acted as intermediaries between Washington and Cairo. King Feisal, who had always been fundamentally opposed to everything that Nasser stood for, now saw an opportunity through this intermediary role of forging the new Riyadh–Tehran–Cairo axis which, with the secure backing of the United States, would, he believed, be able to guide the Arab world back into the paths of orthodoxy and conservatism from which Nasser's dangerous radicalism had diverted it.

But the trouble about unofficial and secret channels of communication is that it is usually impossible to be sure how much importance should be attached to the information that comes through them. President Sadat began to be the recipient of a great many messages, brought to him by many different agents but almost all professing to emanate from the highest levels in Washington. Whether Nixon or Kissinger had in fact authorized or even initiated these messages there was no means of ascertaining, but the burden of them was the same – if Egypt got rid of the Russians 'America would deliver'.

*　　*　　*

Podgorny came to Cairo again on April 28, 1972 – the fifth top-level Soviet–Egyptian meeting in thirteen months – but the question of the experts did not figure prominently among the subjects on Sadat's agenda. What he mainly wanted to discuss with his visitor was what he considered the deteriorating situation in the Middle East. He felt that Soviet diplomacy had recently achieved considerable successes in Europe and South-East Asia, but could show no comparable achievements in the Middle East.

Sadat explained the position as he saw it – America was moving quickly to reimpose its control over the whole area, he said. The American navy controlled the sea approaches; its agent, Israel, was consolidating its position, and some of America's allies were liquidating the remains of the Palestinian resistance. The proposal made by King Hussein on March 15, 1972, for a federated Jordano-Palestinian state had provided America with a chance to dominate the entire area between Haifa and Bahrein. Sadat thought the Americans were engaged in a campaign directed against the Arabs in general and the Egyptian–Soviet relationship in particular. All his efforts to reach a peaceful solution had failed, and the negotiating mission of Gunnar Jarring, the UN special representative in the Middle East since 1967, was bogged down.

Sadat told Podgorny that what he particularly wanted on the military side was means to neutralize the Israeli airforce so that a crossing of the Canal might be made possible. 'I know', he said, 'that between now and your meeting with Nixon there may not be time enough to make any fundamental change in the military situation in the Middle East, but what you can do is give a clear indication of your future attitudes. Any consolidation of our military position will enable us to be flexible and firm at the same time.'

*　　*　　*

On May 26, after the Brezhnev–Nixon meeting had taken place and only six weeks before the expulsion of the experts, Sadat sent the Soviet leaders a telegram to mark the first anniversary of the signing of the Soviet–Egyptian treaty, the language of which cannot have given those to whom it was addressed any inkling of what was to come. Sadat sent congratulations 'from the bottom of my heart'. He called the treaty 'a wonderful reflection and firm confirmation of the deep and friendly ties between us', and so on.

Similar language was used in a letter from Sadat to Brezhnev which General Sadiq, the Minister of War, took with him when he went on a visit to Moscow on June 7. The President thanked Brezhnev for the way in which he had spoken up on Egypt's behalf when he met Nixon, though he had to admit that some of the things which had been said by American officials after the talks seemed to conflict with the wording of the communique issued at their conclusion. 'In my opinion,' Sadat wrote, 'there will be no settlement unless positive pressure is exerted on America and Israel. Unless Israel feels that the military balance is tilting aginst it, and that we can apply military as well as political pressure, there will be no settlement. I fear that the postponement of any movement by us, either military or political, for month after month, only helps to consolidate Israel's position in the occupied territories.' So once again he asked for the supply of arms to be speeded up.

Although a report on the Nixon meeting had been sent to Sadat through the Soviet ambassador in Cairo a little more than a week after it took place, it was not until July 6 that he received a personal letter from Brezhnev containing details of his talks with Nixon as well as assurances of continuing Soviet support for building up Egypt's defences and training the Egyptian forces. In it he again attacked 'rightists and reactionaries' and denounced the 'rumours and lies spread by some circles in Egypt'.

But by then the President's decision had been taken. It was on the same day, July 6, when Sadat was at the farm of Dr Mahmoud Fawzi, then Vice-President, that he first revealed that he was proposing to ask the Soviet Union to withdraw its military personnel from Egypt. The next day he told General Sadiq, and on July 8 the Soviet ambassador was informed. The advisers and experts would have to go.

15

Double Your Stakes or Quit

THE DECISION to expel the Russian experts was taken by President Sadat alone; whether his colleagues agreed or disagreed with it, there was nothing they could do about it. When Vice-President Fawzi read the note which the President had drafted for presentation to the Russian ambassador he suggested that one item in it, proposing immediate discussions within the framework of the Soviet–Egyptian treaty, should be moved up from the last paragraph of the note to the first. But Sadat thought this would be a mistake as in fact there was nothing to negotiate about; the decision had been made. It would be equally pointless for the Soviets as for the President's colleagues to challenge it. So the chief concern of people like Dr Aziz Sidqi, the Prime Minister, and Murad Ghaleb, who had left the Moscow embassy to become Minister of Foreign Affairs, became to contain the fall-out from the explosion of the bomb as far as was possible.

The expulsion of the Soviet experts seemed to outside observers to presage as decisive a shift in policy as had Egypt's Czech arms deal in 1955. But observers were puzzled as much by the way in which the expulsion had been ordered as by the order itself. The Russians had been publicly humiliated; how would they react? Would they seek the overthrow of the man who had snubbed them, or would they attempt to find some other Arab country and some other Arab leader to take the place of Egypt and Sadat? And, if so, where would their choice fall?

Observers also continued to speculate on what had been Sadat's 'real' motives. Was this a quick decision, made on impulse as the result of some genuine or imagined slight, or did Sadat feel some more deeprooted antipathy to the Soviets, dating back to the early days of his presidency (over the Ali Sabri business, perhaps), or even beyond? If so, what other long cherished and still secret initiatives might he be preparing?

Perhaps the main cause for surprise was that Sadat had apparently made no effort to extract some concession from the Americans for his action. Surely, it was argued, if he had told Washington that he was seriously contemplating getting rid of all his Soviet advisers the Americans would have been eager to offer him something in exchange. It soon became known that Kissinger himself shared this surprise.

Both the National Security Council in Washington and the Politburo must have spent many hours in an attempt to analyse the real meaning of Sadat's move and the effect it was likely to have on the training and equipment of the Egyptian armed forces, on their ability to conduct defensive or offensive operations and on what exactly it implied for superpower rivalry in the Middle East.

There was, in fact, one dominant assumption underlying the President's decision. From the outset, the Egyptian calculation had been that the Middle East conflict had to be seen as operating on two levels – the international and the local. As a result of the 1967 war the balance at local level had tilted strongly in favour of the Israelis, so the only option to Egypt was to lift the conflict onto the higher, international level, where the balance was more equal, until the time came when Egypt was in a position to match Israel's strength with her own. Thus it was that the Soviets had been encouraged to negotiate on Egypt's behalf with the Americans; this, it was felt, would not only show them the virtual impossibility of achieving any positive results but would also involve their interest and their prestige directly in the outcome of the conflict. Gradually the Soviet Union did in fact become more and more involved, the agreement to send a large number of experts to every branch of Egypt's armed forces being a notable stage in that process. This was originally welcomed, in the belief that a greater Soviet presence in Egypt would mean greater Soviet interest in Egypt's future, and that greater Soviet interest would mean more Soviet aid.

But by 1972 the disadvantages of having so many Soviet experts in the country had become at least as apparent as the advantages. Most of the retraining and re-equipping of the armed forces to which first Nasser and then Sadat had devoted themselves in the aftermath of the 1967 war had been completed. The current quality of the experts was uneven, and many commanders, junior as well as senior, found their continued presence irksome. There was widespread but unjustified belief that the Soviet leadership wanted their men to stay in Egypt in force and growing mistrust over their reasons for doing so. When, for example, it had been put to Marshal Gretchko in May 1972 that some of the Soviet missile crews should be replaced by Egyptian crews, who were now fully trained – a move which had in fact been part of the original missile agreement – he objected on the ground that this would create a bad impression on the eve of Nixon's visit to Moscow. His objection was upheld by the Politburo, but failed to convince Cairo. So some change in the position of the experts was probably inevitable.

★   ★   ★

The Russians withdrew in good order. Twenty-one thousand experts had to be sent home by air, and each day General Okunev, head of the Soviet military mission, presented the Egyptian Minister of War with the evacuation programme for that day. So efficiently was the operation carried out that it was completed in seven days instead of the ten days which had been Sadat's target.

Neither Cairo nor Moscow wished to see the incident escalate into a major public quarrel. There was a considerable degree of dignity and restraint on both sides. Yet in private the Russians continued to show a good deal of understandable resentment.

On July 13 Dr Aziz Sidqi, who had taken over from Dr Fawzi as Prime Minister in January, was sent to Moscow with instructions to do what he could to soothe the Russians' ruffled feelings and, if he could, arrange for the purchase of more equipment. In neither aim was he able to achieve much. But at the beginning of August Brezhnev sent Sadat a personal letter. Its opening was bleak enough: 'Dear Mr President,' he wrote, whereas the usual style of address had come to be 'brother' or 'friend' or 'comrade'. The letter continued:

> 'Over a long period we have exchanged opinions on matters affecting Egyptian/Soviet relations on a basis of mutual friendship. In the course of the last few weeks we received from Prime Minister Dr Sidqi some reflections on the latest developments in Egyptian–Soviet relations. We too would wish to explain our point of view, especially in the light of the events connected with the withdrawal of Soviet personnel from Egypt.
>
> 'In the first place we have to confirm that our friendship for Egypt and the other progressive Arab states is based on principles laid down by the party. This is something which we have often proclaimed; it is not a short-term objective but an essential element of our international policy. Neither in the Middle East nor anywhere

else does the Soviet Union pursue the policy of a superpower, as some circles in Egypt maintain. Such a policy belongs to the imperialist forces and is wholly alien to our nature. It is in our nature as a socialist state to have developed a specially friendly attitude towards the Arab nation, and other socialist states have cooperated in the development of this attitude.

'It has been the imperialist states which, in recent years, have endeavoured to place obstacles in the path of newly developing countries in Africa and Asia. It is they who have continually tried to control, suppress, enslave and exploit these countries, and this is something of which the Arab nation has had direct experience.

'Our policies are completely different. The aim of our policies is that the Afro-Asian countries should, through their strengthening friendship with the Soviet Union, ensure that their independence is consolidated along an increasingly progressive path. This was the situation in the days of the leadership of Gamal Abdel Nasser, the great son of the Egyptian people, after the Egyptian revolution had broken free from the restrictions imposed upon Egypt by the imperialists and had marched firmly forward to build up its relations with the Soviet Union.'

Brezhnev then described at some length the various fields in which Soviet assistance had been made available to Egypt, and continued:

'Yet, Mr President, we should not be true to ourselves if we were to pretend that nothing had happened to affect relations between our countries. The questions raised by your decision to request the withdrawal of Soviet personnel still await an answer. These questions are not simply a matter of the withdrawal from Arab territory of Soviet officers and men, who were there on a temporary basis at the request of Gamel Abdel Nasser, a request which was confirmed by yourself on numerous occasions. It is rather that the speculation aroused by your decision has given encouragement to our enemies who are ignorant of the true nature of Arab–Soviet relations. We believe that this weakens our friendship and damages relations between us. It does not conform to the true interests of Egypt. We cannot be indifferent to the policy which has been adopted by the Egyptian government, which is objectively and subjectively contrary to the interests of our two peoples. It is a policy resulting from the intrigues of rightist elements directly or indirectly allied with imperialism to halt Egypt's march along the progressive road and turn it back. Where is Egypt going? Where is it being driven by forces inside and outside its borders? What is the relationship between us to be in the future? These are the questions which are causing anxiety to your friends and giving encouragement to your enemies. We look forward to receiving an answer to these questions and hope that it will be made in all frankness.

'You have asked for a meeting at a high level, and we agree that such a meeting is necessary. It would be consistent with the text and spirit of the Soviet treaty. We agree with you that such a meeting could take place either in Cairo or in Moscow. That would be easy to settle, but first there are many points which will have to be the subject of further discussion.'

Brezhnev had asked for an answer to his questions 'in all frankness'. As has been seen, the demand for frank speaking had been made by both sides on many occasions and at many meetings in the past. There can be no doubt that it was sincerely made, and that both Sadat and Brezhnev had done their best to explain their thought processes to each other without deceit or reservation. Yet neither ever managed to persuade the other. Brezhnev's letter shows him again convinced that the Soviet Union's behaviour had been beyond reproach, that its concern for the Arabs and the Third World as a whole had always been disinterested, that its policies were free from superpower calculations, and that therefore what had gone wrong must be the fault of the imperialists and 'the intrigues of rightist elements' inside Egypt. He writes more in sorrow than in anger; Sadat has not yet been abandoned as someone irredeemable, but he is going to have to do a lot of explaining if he hopes to be restored to anything like the favour which he had once enjoyed.

*   *   *

Parts of Brezhnev's letter caused Sadat considerable annoyance. It would have been tempting to return an angry answer, but the temptation had to be resisted if the quarrel was to be kept from getting out of hand. Drafts for a reply to Brezhnev were prepared by the Minister of Foreign Affairs and Hafez Ismail, the President's Adviser on Security

Affairs, but eventually Sadat sat down and wrote his own text. It was a long letter, and took him seven hours to complete, but it is worth giving more or less in full as the clearest evidence of his thinking at the time.

'My dear friend, President Brezhnev, First Secretary of the Communist Party of the Soviet Union – I am writing to you confidentially, and in the spirit of those friendly sentiments which I have felt in the course of our meetings, since my wish is that a way may be found out of that vicious circle in which our relations now appear to have become trapped. This continues to create misunderstandings and will grow worse if nothing is done to clarify matters. It is for this reason that I propose to write in complete frankness, so that you should be given full information concerning my point of view on all subjects.

1. We are continually mindful of the Soviet Union's role in World War II. The Soviet people resisted the Nazi occupiers, fought them heroically, and made every sacrifice to ensure the liberation of their territory and the safeguarding of their national dignity. It should not therefore be surprising that the Egyptian people should in their turn have been ready to make all sacrifices necessary for the recovery of their territory. This is the real point of departure.

2. In order to safeguard our friendship I think it desirable that I should begin this letter at the point where our discussions broke off during our last meeting, in April 1972. It is essential that, as friends, we should understand what has taken place in the interval and so continue the dialogue between us.

3. I think you will agree, my dear friend, that I have always been deeply concerned about the friendship between us. That accounts for the four visits which I have paid to Moscow over the past two years – in March and October 1971, and in February and April this year. The main subject for discussion on all these occasions has been Israel's aggression, and what we should do about it. May I remind you of the points relating to this problem which I tried to outline to you at our meetings? I explained that we were animated by two main principles – first, that we wished our battle to be fought by nobody except our own forces; second, that we did not wish our battle to be the occasion for a confrontation between the Soviet Union and the United States, knowing well that this

would mean a disaster for the whole world. I have always insisted that only a madman would seek this.

4. We agreed at our meetings, and particularly during our meeting last February, that Israel and the US will take no action to solve the problem, by peaceful or any other means, unless Israel feels that our military strength is in a position to challenge the superiority at present enjoyed by Israel. Only then will Israel and the US feel it is in their interest to reach a solution. In our discussions I have constantly pressed on you the necessity for a deterrent arm which would make the enemy hesitate before raiding our territory in depth. This will only be when he appreciates that we are equally capable of raiding his territory in depth. But it is clear that we are still without this deterrent arm, and that without it we are incapable of taking any military initiative. There is, consequently, no reason for Israel to alter its attitude towards a settlement.

5. It was these considerations which prompted the message which I sent you by Marshal Gretchko in May 1972 some days before your meeting with Nixon in Moscow. I did my best to make the Marshal's visit a success. I agreed to issue the statement which he had brought with him from Moscow to the effect that Egyptian pilots had flown planes flying at three times the speed of sound, and that these new fighters [X–500s, later known as Mig–23s] were in service in Egypt. None of this was true, but I agreed to the statement's being issued in order to ensure the success of the visit. I knew that the Marshal's visit to Cairo was related to Nixon's visit to Moscow, and I wished, as a friend, that you should be able to talk to Nixon from a position of strength. But at the same time I gave Marshal Gretchko a clear message to you concerning what I believed should be our situation following your meeting with Nixon. It was not difficult for us to forecast what the outcome of the Nixon meeting would be as far as our problem was concerned. I fixed October 31, 1972, as the date for what should be achieved in this period, though this hardly gave time for completing our efforts in the aftermath of the American election. I told Marshal Gretchko that we needed every hour and every minute of that period so that we could do what was necessary to embark on the new phase from a firm foundation.

6. When your ambassador gave me the message reporting the

result of your meeting with Nixon, ten days after the meeting took place, the information it contained was neither new nor surprising. The same day I sent you a seven-point message, in which I recapitulated my message to Marshal Gretchko, and urged that no further time should be lost. In that message I specifically asked for a solution to the problem of command and control, since I regarded it as inconceivable that Soviet units should be stationed in Egyptian territory and not under Egyptian command.

7. After a further month's interval, and following reminders by my Prime Minister and Minister of Foreign Affairs, I eventually received your letter to me of July 8 – and this in spite of the fact that I had previously told you that I regarded every day, every hour, and even every minute as vital. I found this letter disappointing, since it totally ignored the points which I had conveyed to you, both through Marshal Gretchko and in my letter of June 6. It confirmed my impression that the attitude from which we have suffered over the past five years since Israel's aggression, which neglects the needs of our battle, still persists. I have tried for a year and a half to draw attention to this attitude, but my efforts have been in vain. I was consequently obliged to reject both the content and the tone of your letter. It became necessary for me to seek an interval during which I and my friend might attempt to clarify our positions. I want, my friend, to give you my impressions of this interval because I believe that you, as my friend, have a right to know the reasons for my decisions. The situation at the moment is frozen. No way forward is open to us. The Americans claim that as a result of Nixon's talks in Moscow it is they alone who hold the key to a solution. In the absence of any deterrent Israel is behaving with increasing irresponsibility, yet the communique issued at the end of the Moscow talks spoke of a relaxation to follow a solution of the problem. Your letter of July 8 totally ignores our earlier agreement on the measures required to render us capable of making a military move, following the American elections, should this become necessary. America is now in the process of equipping Israel with an entirely new airforce. The attitude reflected in your latest letter shows that for five years a partial arms embargo has been imposed on us, and that this covers the deterrent arm which I wrote to you about and which you have

completely ignored. These are the considerations which led to my decision to terminate the experts' mission, which was intended to mark the ending of one phase and the opening of another.

8. Allow me, my friend, to give you some examples of what is happening to our armed forces and to our people – and the armed forces are, after all, only the sons of the people. These are matters about which your experts should have informed you before they got out of control.

i. The Navy. For four years the commander of the navy has been asking for an apparatus to detect submarines, since the existing apparatus at his disposal has a range of only half a kilometre. He has been told that the Soviet Union has nothing suitable for his requirements. But all the officers in our navy are aware that your ships are equipped with a device which can detect submarines as far as the horizon. The West too has this device, so there is nothing secret about it. We are not a backward country. We can read; we know what weapons you and the West possess. The whole world knows. But unfortunately your navy operates side by side with ours. In the West there are devices with twenty times the efficiency of any we possess. Can you imagine the comments that are made by our naval officers?

ii. The Airforce. All our airforce pilots (and they are graduates of your colleges) know that you possess advanced planes, like the M-500, which we had until recently. But with you everything is secret; nobody is allowed to go near them. [Then followed technical comparisons between Phantoms and the latest available Migs, greatly to the disadvantage of the latter.]

iii. The Army. Our officers know that you have much more powerful guns than the Americans have, but as usual all this is kept secret, and your experts deny that they exist. Can you imagine the comments that are made by our artillery officers on all this? The infantry. In the infantry every officer, NCO and private soldier knows that the most dangerous part of an operation is forcing an opening in the enemy lines. At this stage every minute means a life. Yet we still lack so many things we should have for this operation. You deny that you have any more advanced equipment. Is this what should be understood by cooperation between friends?

We are in need of so many things, though we pretend the contrary to our own people and to the world. We say that we have received from you all we require. But what I wish to discuss with you is not so much our specific requirements as the attitude of mind responsible for holding up the delivery of them. You treat us as if we were a backward nation which knows nothing about anything. Yet our officers have undergone in your schools exactly the same training as your own officers. We follow all that is going on in the world, East and West. There can be no secrecy, since the arms are described in books published everywhere in the world. Yet when we enquire about these matters from Soviet experts they either remain silent or deny that such weapons exist in the Soviet Union. But we know perfectly well that the Soviet Union possesses everything.

9. I appreciate, my dear friend, that we are facing a very difficult period in our relations. The most dangerous aspect of it is the likelihood that it will leave a legacy of bitterness against the Soviet Union. You have a perfect right, following my decision on the experts, to take any steps which you regard as necessary for the safeguarding of your interests. But I do not believe that it is in your real interest to increase the feelings of bitterness among our people. Your decision to withdraw the four M-500 planes, after the communique issued during the visit of Marshal Gretchko and the statement that these planes had been flown by Egyptian pilots, was, in my opinion, calculated to do more than anything to increase the feelings of resentment among our armed forces and our people. Another almost equally disastrous decision was the one to withdraw the jamming equipment on the grounds that it was secret and so could not be operated by our people. All this adds up to one thing only – the imposition of conditions on us by the Soviet Union. In 1955 together we broke the West's arms monopoly. We have to face an enemy who is equipped with all the latest weapons. What do you suppose the ordinary citizen in Egypt makes of this? I leave it to you to answer, but I should betray our friendship if I did not state all the facts to you in perfect frankness.

10. There is one final point which I would like to make clear. I have on a number of occasions informed you that I have set October 31 as the target date for settlement of relations between

us. I hope that, in all friendship, you will understand that in holding to this date I have no intention of trying to blackmail you or to present you with ultimatums, as some people have suggested. That is something which we would never do. This date has been fixed with two considerations in mind, one political and one military. Politically, we shall face a situation after the American elections in which we may expect joint American–Israeli pressure to force a solution favourable to Israel unless we have achieved the solid foundation which we have agreed on. Otherwise we shall face the familiar roundabout of Security Council resolutions, Jarring missions, ever increasing Israeli demands, and so on. From the military angle, you have only to ask your own people the extent which Israeli preparedness is likely to be reached by November or December. By then Israel will have received and absorbed all its new airforce hardware. The large addition to its stock of Phantoms and Hawks will have made the gap between them and us even wider than it is now. You must, therefore, my friend, appreciate that this date has indeed a special significance for me. Ultimately all of us in Egypt are going to be grateful to you for your help to us. When I announced the termination of the experts' mission I was careful to remind the Egyptian and Arab people of the part the Soviet Union has played in helping us. But it remains my duty to tell you, in all honesty, that the only thing which we looked for out of the cooperation between us is the chance to liberate our territory. We wish to have good relations with you, but this will be determined by the extent to which our friends in the Soviet Union are prepared to assist us in the solution of our first and last problem, namely the liberation of our territory.'[1]

*   *   *

President Sadat's letter was received in the Kremlin shortly before the celebrations marking the anniversary of the October Revolution, which is always a time (the May Day celebrations being another) for the Soviet leadership to take stock of the international situation. They

---

[1] A text of this letter has been given by President Sadat in Appendix I of his autobiography, *In Search of Identity* (Harper & Row, 1978).

must, I think, have felt that, as far as the Arab world was concerned, the situation was extremely bewildering. Delegates from a number of Arab communist parties were arriving in Moscow – people like Khaled Bakdash, those who had escaped massacre in the Sudan and Iraq, and others – all now claiming that their analysis had proved correct, and that the policy of dependence on the bourgeoisie had proved a failure. I think they found many elements inside the Soviet Union prepared to agree with their point of view. But, as always, the Soviet leadership had to take into account its role as a superpower as well as its role as headquarters of world revolution. As a revolutionary power no doubt the wisest course for the Soviet Union would have been to minimize the significance of the debacle over the experts, to assert that they had been stabbed in the back by ungrateful Arab governments, and to adopt the easy alternative which presented itself – that is to say, switching to support of local communist parties.

But there were plenty of those in the leadership, especially among the military, who were much less concerned with ideology than with the Soviet Union's responsibilities as a superpower. These felt that the position in the Middle East must be maintained at all costs, because of its military significance, the importance of the sea routes and, possibly, of the oil supplies, as well as, of course, for reasons of political prestige. The result was that, like a gambler who has lost a throw, the Soviet Union decided to double its stakes. The military, and in particular Marshal Gretchko, argued repeatedly in the Politburo that there was no easy way out, and that the flow of military aid to the Arabs must be stepped up. They feared that the Arabs were contemplating the abandonment of their alliance with the Soviet Union and were in favour of direct talks with the Americans. Let the Arabs have sufficient arms to enable them to risk a battle, the argument continued. Should this happen, and should the Arabs win, their victory will have been achieved thanks to Soviet arms. Should they be defeated, or the fighting reach a stalemate, it is still to the Soviet Union that they will have to look for rescue in the aftermath of the battle.

These arguments prevailed, and so at last Egypt began to receive some of the equipment for which Sadat had been so earnestly pleading and for which he had waited so long, a large part of it being due under agreements which Nasser had made when he was in Moscow shortly before his death. Sam–3 and Sam–6 missiles, the latest anti-aircraft and anti-tank weapons (Strellas and Molutkas), tanks with infra-red ranging devices, bridging equipment, all started pouring into Egyptian ports in vast quantities. It was, as Sadat said, as if all taps had been fully turned on. 'It looks as if they want to push me into a battle,' he added.

I think they probably did. Certainly I believe that the military, backed by Brezhnev, wanted to make it possible for Egypt to embark on a limited war. By the beginning of 1973 the Soviets realized that, having lost the political battle, they might be able to recoup their losses in the military field. They were not instructing the Arabs to fight, but they were providing them with sufficient arms to make the idea of fighting extremely tempting, particularly since all advance in the political and diplomatic fields seemed to be blocked.

★   ★   ★

It was, moreover, at this time that the shift in the balance of political forces inside the Arab world in favour of the traditional forces, and in particular of Saudi Arabia, became even more pronounced. This was a development for which nobody was really prepared. During most of the fifties and sixties it had appeared to be merely a question of time before the Arab world saw the last of its traditional regimes vanish into history. Monarchies had toppled in Egypt, Iraq, Yemen and Libya. The young kings of Jordan and Morocco hung onto their thrones by the skin of their teeth. Elder conservative politicians like Nuri Said, Shukri Kuwatly, Ismail el-Azhari and Ferhat Abbas had disappeared from the scene. Everywhere it was the young radical leaders who were in command, or who seemed destined soon to take over. If in the Arabian peninsula traditional dynasties and traditional forms of government still survived this could be explained by their geographical isolation. They were regarded as being outside the main stream of events, and it was assumed that, once the real forces of the twentieth century caught up with them, the days of these regimes would be numbered.

By the beginning of the seventies these assumptions were being shown to be manifestly wrong. The twentieth century had caught up with countries like Saudi Arabia with a vengeance, since they had become one of the main sources of supply for the mineral on which the whole life of twentieth century civilizations depended – oil. But so far from causing the disintegration of the traditional regimes which ran these countries, oil wealth was proving their salvation. More than that –

it was providing them with the means by which they were able to extend their influence into other Arab countries. This did not necessarily mean that they could dictate policy outside their own borders – some early and rather crude attempts to do so had proved disastrous failures – but they were clearly now in an excellent position to make their views on any subject listened to with attention.

While Nasser was still alive the Saudis had said that they could not do more to help him because he had accepted UN resolution 242. 'If you had rejected the resolution and declared a general *jihad*,' King Feisal told him, 'we would have given you everything.' But now they were all in favour of a negotiated settlement, and often seemed to echo the arguments for this which were heard from Washington. The main complaints coming from both Washington and Riyadh continued to be connected with the Soviet presence in Egypt. The Saudis in particular manifested an almost obsessive detestation for anything to do with communism. No doubt, in their eyes, Sadat had, by the expulsion of the Russian experts, a considerable achievement to his credit, but it was not enough.

The American position was explained to Hafez Ismail when he met his opposite number, Henry Kissinger, for secret talks at a private house in Connecticut at the end of February 1973. Egypt, he was told, was not going to be allowed to play off the Russians and Americans against each other.'We have ways of finding out what you tell the Russians,' Kissinger said, 'and if we find you are deceiving us it will have a very harmful effect.'

The Americans had important links with Israel, but they also had vital interests in the Arab world. Should the Arab–Israeli conflict flare up it would place the US in an almost intolerable dilemma. The only way in which to avoid this eventuality was to see the conflict settled. That was easier said than done. But the first step towards a solution was to make it impossible for war to break out. For this, the expulsion of the Soviet experts would have to be followed by the removal of Soviet arms. There is no doubt that during 1973 the flow of Soviet arms to Egypt and Syria caused Kissinger as much anxiety as the presence of the Russian experts had ever done.

So the scene moved on to the October war.

16

The October War

FEW LIMITED WARS in recent years have had such far-reaching repercussions as the October War of 1973. It altered the balance of forces in the Middle East, and by provoking the first use of the 'oil weapon' it had a profound impact on the economies of the western world and of most countries in Asia and Africa. It might, of course, have had much more decisive consequences had the initial successes of the Egyptian and Syrian armies been maintained. But military victory eluded the Arabs, and once that had happened the political victory which they were also seeking became more elusive too.

However, after the October War nothing would ever be the same again for Israel and the Arabs, either by themselves or in their mutual relations; nothing would be the same again for the Soviet Union as far as its relations with the Arab world were concerned.

This last was the most surprising development of all, and one which, when the war broke out, it would have been almost impossible for anyone to predict. I think the Soviets were as much astonished as delighted by the results of the first days' fighting. They had naturally known that an attack across the Suez Canal was almost certain to be launched – many of the training exercises for the crossing had taken place while Soviet experts were still attached to the Egyptian armed forces – but they had not known (and had not wished to know) any details of the operation or its timing. They had supplied the up-to-date arms and equipment which made the attack possible, but they knew that, even so, the undertaking was bound to be a hazardous and dangerous one.

In their estimate of the Arabs' prospects for a military success the Russians, like so many others, failed sufficiently to take into account both the overconfidence of the Israelis and the fighting spirit of the Egyptian and Syrian troops. For six years these armies had had to live with the shame of defeat. They had trained as few armies had trained before, performing the same operations scores of times, month after month, year after year. Now they had a chance to prove not just their courage but their skill, and it was a chance which each officer and man seized almost with rapture. Other factors which made the October War different from previous Arab–Israel encounters, and which, consequently, came as a shock to the Russians as well as to everybody else, were the meticulous planning over a long period between the staffs of two Arab armies for a coordinated attack on two fronts, the successful use of the element of surprise, and the employment on the battlefield for the first time anywhere of defensive weapons such as Strellas and Molutkas for offensive purposes.

So when news of the successful crossing of the Canal and of Syrian advances in the Golan Heights reached the Russians their delight knew no bounds. It was their arms, in the hands of their friends, which were winning the day. 'Tell Brezhnev that it is Soviet arms which achieved the miracle of the crossing,' Sadat told the Soviet Ambassador in Cairo, Vladimir Vinogradov, who had been the first person he called up from his secret command post at Centre Number Ten to report the Canal crossing and the assault on the Bar-Lev line. Vinogradov's own congratulations on this achievement, as well as those he quickly passed on from Moscow, were generous and sincere. Past differences were forgotten, wiped out by present victories.

Because their initial hopes had been raised so high, Russian fears that victory might be allowed to slip from Arab hands, or even be turned into defeat, were correspondingly acute. As early as Tuesday, October 9, three days after the start of the war, the Russian embassy in Cairo was expressing anxiety about the military situation, particularly the situation on the Syrian front, being afraid that the Israelis might succeed in knocking out the Syrians and so be free to turn the full weight of their attack against Egypt. The Russians would have liked to see the Egyptian army pressing on to the Sinai passes, to take some of the pressure off the Syrians. They were also giving a great deal of attention to the political side of the war.

★ ★ ★

The Russians had, from the first moment of the war, a clear conception of its political implications. It would, they believed, rehabilitate them in the Arab world, and do this without endangering their relations with the US. For by now detente was the key to Soviet foreign policy.

In Moscow the common interests of the superpowers had come to be emphasized as much as their ideological or territorial rivalries.

Kissinger, newly promoted to be Secretary of State, had at first been angered by the Egyptian–Syrian attack, feeling that he had been deceived by both the Arabs and the Soviet Union. But after the initial shock the mechanics of detente had worked remarkably well. The 'hot line' was brought into service, Kissinger and his team were welcomed in Moscow and eventually a resolution was jointly worked out by them with the Russians for presentation to the Security Council.

The Moscow negotiations were conducted with remarkable smoothness because, though neither side may have openly admitted as much, both the Russians and the Americans were pursuing the same objectives. The Russians wanted an Arab victory, but not one so absolute that it would compel American intervention on behalf of Israel and so bring about direct superpower involvement in the area. The Americans wanted to assist Israel, but not so effectively that she would be able to counterattack and inflict another 1967 humiliation on the Arabs. Neither side wanted to let down its protege, but neither wanted the other to have an excuse to get more deeply committed in the Middle East. Americans and Russians therefore had a joint interest in working for a stalemate war and a compromise peace.

There was of course the moment of peril, when it seemed that superpower collaboration had broken down and a Cuba-style confrontation might be on the point of developing. This came three days after the ceasefire with the American order for a nuclear alert. I have described elsewhere[1] some of the calculations – or rather miscalculations – which brought this about. What is not generally known is that one of the main instigators of the alert was King Feisal of Saudi Arabia.

The ceasefire was supposed to come into effect on October 26, but the Israelis had no intention of observing it and continued to improve their military position on both sides of the Canal by every means available to them. The Syrians were also dangerously situated, and both Sadat and Assad were appealing to all friendly nations for help.

The explanation for the alert given at the time was a note sent by Brezhnev to the American government on the evening of Wednesday, October 24, in which he urged that, if the Israelis were not prepared to observe the ceasefire, America and Russia should work together to im-

---

[1] *Road to Ramadan*, p. 243.

pose it, if necessary by force. If the Americans were unwilling to do this, said Brezhnev, the Russians might have to act alone. This was certainly tough talking, but there were other factors influencing the American decision. One was the exchange of messages between Sadat and Assad which, intercepted by the Americans, may have given the false impression that the Syrian government was asking Moscow for the dispatch of combatant troops.[1] Another was an intervention by King Feisal.

A special line of communication had been set up between the presidency in Cairo and the royal palace in Riyadh. One of the Saudi liaison officers in Cairo, in a moment of panic, used this line to report to Riyadh that the Russians were about to descend on the Middle East *en masse*. When he received this message Feisal immediately got in touch with Nixon, warning him that seven Russian divisions were on their way; the Soviets, he said, were coming back to the Middle East in undreamed of strength. It was this scare report which encouraged Nixon to go to the extreme of the nuclear alert, and which justified Brezhnev's later reference to the responsibility of 'fantastic rumours' for causing the alert.

★   ★   ★

It must be said that throughout the October War the Soviet attitude towards the Arabs was impeccable. They identified themselves wholeheartedly with the Arab cause, and did what they could to bring assistance to Egypt and Syria both at the local and at the international level; at the local level by the air-lift of arms and supplies, and at the international level by acting as the Arabs' advocate with the Americans and at the UN.

An example of their practical concern came after the ceasefire, when General Sharon's crossing of the Canal had been identified. President Sadat was then informed through the Russian ambassador in Cairo that the Central Committee had agreed to make Egypt a present of 250 tanks and was encouraging other governments to make similar contributions. In fact, of course, many Arab countries were offering the combatants material aid of every description. The Algerians sent a brigade of tanks with their crews, and the Libyans also a tank brigade,

---

[1] *Road to Ramadan*, p. 253.

but without crews. Nor was it only the Arab countries which provided assistance. Yugoslavia sent a tank brigade to Egypt, though naturally this came without crews. But the close links between Russia and Egypt which had been restored thanks to the fighting were not to survive long after the sound of battle had faded away.

17

Double Your Stakes and Lose

EVEN BEFORE the fighting stopped oil had taken over from tanks and aircraft as the main weapon in the Arabs' armoury. Few people, the Soviets included, had thought that when it came to the point the often talked of embargo would be so unanimously agreed on or so drastically put into effect. But now the implications of the oil weapon seemed almost limitless. Everywhere people were speculating, often in highly fanciful terms, about what the Arabs could do, both by manipulating supplies of their oil and by channelling the vast profits they were going to make from selling it to an oil-hungry world. Commentators began to talk about 'the Arabs' almost as if they were a new superpower. They were rumoured to be about to buy their way into every branch of industry in America and western Europe. What was to prevent their gaining control of General Motors or the City of London? It seemed nothing.

All this speculation found its way back to the Arab world. Combined with the over-optimistic way in which the war had generally been presented in the Arab media it encouraged ordinary Arab men and women to feel that all was over bar the shouting. They had been prepared to make the sacrifices necessary for battle, but in the new state of euphoria, when all the talk was about victory and wealth, sacrifice was made to sound out of place.

People saw, too, how power in the Arab world was passing to new men. For a generation the men who directed the course of events in the Arab world had been ideologists or officers from the armed forces – or sometimes officers who turned into ideologists or ideologists who tried to behave as if they were officers. Such were Sadat, Assad, Ghadaffi, Boumedienne, Michel Aflaq, Sadam Hussein and many others. Many of these were still there, but they were now being joined by the first instalment of a new breed of power brokers, the middlemen, the arms dealers, the wealthy merchants who flitted between East and West, between royal palaces and the offices of oil companies – men like Kamal Adham, Mahdi Tajjir, Adnan Khashoggi and others – and by royalty itself, for who in the Arab world now exercised more power than Prince Fahd or Prince Sultan of Saudi Arabia? Could not individuals such as these, it was argued, achieve more for the Arabs than mass movements and radical revolutions?

It is not surprising if in this changed atmosphere men and women in Egypt and Syria felt that the time had come for them too, to see some improvement in their material circumstances. They had known hardship; now they looked for their reward – for more to eat and for better houses to live in. Of course money would have to be found to pay for this, but who would dare to suggest that the Arabs were short of money? It was being said that the Arabs possessed the power to bring the rest of the world to starvation; surely they must have the power to feed themselves? So eyes turned to the oil-producing countries. Oilfields began to loom far bigger in the public mind than battlefields; *tharwa* (riches), it was said, had begun to take over from *thawra* (revolution).

Those who thought along these lines had little time to spare for the Soviet Union. As they saw it, the Russians could provide the weapons but not the cash, and if, as everyone seemed to be assuming, neither side was going to start up the war again, at any rate in the immediate future, the Russians' usefulness seemed to vanish. Better results for the Arabs, the argument went on, could only be won through diplomacy, and that meant that the Arabs would have to be in a position to influence the only people who could put pressure on Israel – the Americans.

The new men in the Arab world were vigorous expounders of this doctrine. Why, they asked, was America reluctant to pressure Israel? The answer must be because the Arabs had brought the Russians into the Middle East. So the Arabs must ensure that all Russian influence was removed from the area, whereupon they could present themselves as guardians of American interests there, making America's dependency on Israel no longer necessary.

★   ★   ★

Ismail Fahmi, Egypt's Foreign Minister, was sent to Washington and arranged that Kissinger should come to Cairo. Before the Secretary of State's arrival President Sadat consulted some of his senior officials and advisers over who should represent Egypt at the forthcoming negotiations. My own feeling was that the President should not take direct part in the negotiations himself, on the grounds that he was head of state and commander-in-chief of the armed forces, and that as such he would be expected to produce instant decisions. Golda Meir would, on the other hand, be able to haggle and procrastinate, claiming that she would have to consult her cabinet colleagues or take into account the Opposition's objections and so on. Sadat would have no such excuses or delaying tactics available to him. I thought the best arrangement would be for him to be the nominal head of the Egyptian team, but not to take part in any of the negotiating sessions. These could be left to three of his closest associates – Dr Fawzi, Assistant to the President, Hafez Ismail, Security Adviser to the President, and Ismail Fahmi, or, if three was too many, any one of these could be designated sole negotiator. In either case the President would of course make the final decisions.

However, Sadat was very clear in his own mind that this was not the way to do things. What he wanted was a *tête-à-tête* with Kissinger, and he could argue that, if Brezhnev could talk to Kissinger *tête-à-tête*, so could Sadat.

Kissinger came to Cairo on November 6. He and Sisco met President Sadat, Hafez Ismail, and Ismail Fahmi at about ten o'clock the next day. The photographers did their work and then withdrew. All the others withdrew too, and for almost three hours Sadat and Kissinger talked alone.

I believe it was in these three hours that the fate of the Soviet Union in the Middle East was sealed. Soon after the meeting started Kissinger opened his briefcase and began to pull out some documents. 'What are you doing?' asked Sadat. 'No, no. Put them away. I don't want to discuss those details, But look – I know you are a man of strategy, and and so am I. Let us see if we cannot agree on a common strategy.'

And this is precisely what they did, the common strategy being to get the Russians out of the Middle East. When, at about one o'clock, Hafez Ismail and Sisco were called back into the room Kissinger once again opened his briefcase and drew out the six-point ceasefire agreement which he had brought with him from Washington. Sadat accepted the typewritten draft without changing a word.

According to Abba Eban, Israeli Foreign Secretary at this time:[1]

---

[1] *Abba Eban: An Autobiography* (Random House, 1978), p. 538.

'Mrs Meir [Israeli Prime Minister] proposed a six-point programme which would satisfy Egyptian requests for an Egyptian–Israeli meeting and for an immediate implementation of the prisoner exchange. Kissinger and Mrs Meir parted in an atmosphere of some coolness, with the American Secretary of State sceptical about the prospect of these points ever being accepted in Cairo . . . [After the six points had been accepted by Egypt] As Kissinger magnanimously conceded, Israel had shown a clearer perception of Egyptian attitudes than the United States.'

The fact is that for Sadat such a document as the Meir–Kissinger 'six points' was of relatively minor importance. What really mattered was that he should have created a good new working relationship with Henry Kissinger, whom he correctly saw as the key figure in the negotiating process. As he said to me: 'This man is the only person alive who can say to this woman [Golda Meir] get out, and she will have to get out.'

I was not so convinced of Kissinger's ability to produce the desired results. Even though the crisis had by now without question moved from the level of armed conflict between local powers to that of a diplomatic struggle between the superpowers, it did not necessarily follow that the local powers had lost all influence over the conduct of events. I could not help recalling that most of the rest of the world had believed Egypt to be under Russian control at the very moment when Sadat himself was preparing the summary expulsion of all Russian advisers. It would, I felt, be easier for Israel to resist American pressure now that Nixon was bogged down in Watergate and the whole administration had lost so much of its authority.

★   ★   ★

Kissinger was astonished but delighted by Sadat's attitude, but he could not openly proclaim the common strategy which Egypt and the US were now to pursue; to do so would be to risk a collision between the US and the Soviet Union. It would be much better to leave the practical application of the strategy to the Arabs, and this is what happened at Geneva, where the peace conference on the Middle East opened on December 21, 1973. The Russians of course were there, as joint co-chairmen with the Americans, but they found that instead of acting as participants they were relegated to the role of spectators.

As one of their delegates said bitterly: 'We went to Geneva to act as witnesses to a marriage. What we in fact witnessed was not a marriage but an affaire!'

In Geneva American headquarters were the scene of constant coming and going, with the American delegation talking all the time to both Arabs and Israelis. The Russians were there too, but nobody talked to them. All the time the Americans remained extremely correct. They protested that they welcomed Russian participation and were eager for them to play a useful role – but, alas, it was the Arabs who insisted on keeping them at arms length. The whole business took on elements of farce when a Russian colonel announced that he was going to attend meetings of two committees – which in fact he was perfectly entitled to do. The Americans said that they would not themselves be attending because the Arabs had intimated that they wanted no outsiders there. The Russian colonel insisted, and forced his way into the meeting, but as long as he sat there none of the Arabs said anything of any substance, confining their remarks to trivialities.

The Russians sensed that the Americans were ultimately responsible for what was going on, but found it hard to produce evidence with which to convict them. In fact the Kissinger strategy was quite clear. He was pursuing two parallel aims. In the first place he saw the Middle East as still the most likely area for superpower confrontation, and thought the best way to avoid any risk of that was for the Russians not to be there. In the second place he was the guarantor of Israel's security, and thought this could best be achieved by making certain that Israel was involved in no more wars like the October one. The key lay in the supply of arms. If the Arabs continued to draw their arms from the East they could again get into the position where they could threaten Israel with extinction; but if their arms came from the West they could be controlled at a less dangerous level. Kissinger wished to achieve a situation in which both the Arabs and Israel looked to Washington for material aid and political support. As in the case of Greece and Turkey, now so situated, there might still be quarrels which could at times get out of hand – the two parties might even fight each other – but there would be no danger of their quarrels again escalating into an American–Russian confrontation. In pursuit of both these aims it was Russia's influence in the Middle East that became Kissinger's target.

So the Russians went to the final ceremony at Geneva on November

11 to sign an agreement in the framing of which they had played no part at all. Their arms had made the battle possible; their friends had been robbed of military victory, but all the same everybody was talking about the political power which the Arabs were now in a position to wield. Yet the Arabs' benefactors were left out in the cold. It must have been extremely difficult for the Russians to understand the calculations in the Arab world which had led to this result. Certainly the tone of the first message which Brezhnev sent Sadat after the Geneva conference was a mixture of anger and conciliation. He said, in effect, that if only the Arabs and the Russians had maintained close cooperation after the war, the outcome of Geneva would have been far better for both of them. However, he did not want to waste time in mutual recrimination, but he sincerely hoped that the lesson would have been learnt, and the mistakes that had been made would not be repeated on a future occasion.

18

No Way to Treat a Superpower

ON OCTOBER 1 1977 the American and Russian governments issued a joint statement on the Middle East, calling, among other things, for a renewed Geneva conference by December. Henry Kissinger, now out of office, disapproved of the statement. His view was that it was a good thing to have the Russians present at the beginning of negotiations, and at the end, but not in the middle. In other words, he liked to have their help in defusing an immediate crisis and in putting the seal on a settlement, but he did not want them interfering in the actual course of negotiations. It must be conceded that after the October War he managed to arrange things pretty successfully according to this formula, manipulating the players with an artistry which it would have been a pleasure to watch had it been possible to forget the stakes for which the game was being played.

His success in keeping the Russians out of the Egypt–Israel ceasefire negotiations has been seen, but when it came to the matter of a ceasefire between Israel and Syria he found the going more difficult. The Syrians had boycotted the Geneva conference, and the Russians were continuing to give them political and military support. But now came a striking example of how much more subtly Kissinger played his cards than the Russians did theirs.

Kissinger saw that one of the keys to the stand taken by the Syrians was the attitude of the Iraqis. The Russians had dealt with the Iraqis in a pretty straightforward manner. While the fighting was still going on the Iraqis had wanted to send a part of their army to fight on the Syrian front, but they were afraid that Iran, with whom their relations were at the time extremely tense, might take the opportunity to create trouble. So a member of the Iraqi Revolutionary Command Council was sent to Moscow to ask the Russians to use their influence in Tehran to see that this did not happen. He had a meeting with Podgorny, who was not normally known as an enthusiastic supporter of an active Middle Eastern policy; Iran agreed to stay its hand. But by this time the whole Soviet leadership was in a state of great excitement over the war, almost mesmerized by the possibilities it seemed to be opening up. 'Why are you wasting time?' Podgorny shouted. 'Why haven't you sent your troops to the Syrian front long ago? What do you think your arms are for? Of course the Iranians won't be allowed to do anything.'

By contrast Kissinger was a great deal more devious, appreciating that here was a situation where local powers could be neatly played off against each other by a superpower. The Iraqis were opposed to the idea of any ceasefire with Israel, and their hostility made it harder for the Syrians to move forward towards one. So, with the connivance of Iran, Iraq's large and chronically disaffected Kurdish minority was called in to make a diversion. In March 1974 the Kurdish insurrection flared up again, the Iraqi government found itself otherwise occupied and the pressure was taken off Damascus. The Syrian disengagement agreement was signed two months later.

During 1974 there was some improvement in relations between Egypt and the Soviet Union. The Egyptian Foreign Minister, Ismail Fahmi, paid two vistits to Moscow, at the first of which in October, arrangements were made for Brezhnev to undertake a journey to Arab capitals in January 1975 which would include Cairo as well as Damascus and Baghdad. But when Fahmi was in Moscow again in December it was anounced that the visit was cancelled. However, to demonstrate that cancellation was genuinely due to Brezhnev's ill health and not intended as a snub, Ismail Fahmi and General Gamassy, the Minister of War, who was with him, were taken to see Brezhnev in his bedroom. They were allowed five minutes talk with the invalid, and left convinced that the Soviet leader's illness was a real one.

* * *

The autumn of 1974 had seen the dramatic appearance of the PLO chairman, Yasser Arafat, before the General Assembly of the UN. There was some comfort for the Russians in this development, and by then they were badly in need of comfort. Hitherto they had not paid a great deal of attention to the Palestinians, but by 1974 the Palestinian movement had largely recovered from the shock of its suppression by King Hussein's army in September 1970. More and more the PLO was being treated as the embryo of another Arab state, and not by Arabs only. Palestinian leaders were, moreover, trying to overcome the suspicions they had aroused among conservative Arab regimes and in the West by showing a more flexible political approach. Some of them talked openly of a Palestinian and an Israeli state living peacefully side by side with each other. They were learning the lesson that international support was not the automatic byproduct of a just cause but something that had to be worked for, and they saw in the Soviet Union their most powerful potential backer.

For the Soviets the Palestinian movement offered certain very real advantages. It could well turn out to be the time-bomb which would upset the prospect of a *pax Americana* for the area. Neither America nor Israel, after all, had a place for the Palestinians in their plans. There might be some talk of them as refugees, but no serious backing for the idea of allowing them to have a state of their own. Besides, as far as social and economic matters were concerned, the Palestinian revolution had now begun to speak in a language which Moscow found more understandable and to address itself to the dispossessed everywhere. This was something which might have a considerable impact in the emerging pattern in the Arab world, where huge gulfs were yawning between the very rich and the very poor. And compared with some of the other forces which the Soviets had backed in the area, the Palestinians could be a remarkably economical investment. They would not be asking for steel mills and dams and supersonic planes, but for small arms, mines, and perhaps some anti-tank missiles. Backing the Palestinians would not bring the Russians back to the position of authority in the Middle East they had enjoyed before 1972, but it might at least provide them with a power of veto over what went on there.

* * *

Nothing, however, could prevent Egyptian–Soviet relations from moving to their destined climax. The second phase of President Sadat's post-1973 strategy had to be concluded, and this meant demonstrating to the world that, as far as he was concerned, the Soviets no longer had any role to play in the Middle East. On May 5, 1976, he told the Egyptian Parliament that he had abrogated the Soviet–Egyptian treaty which he and Podgorny had signed only four years earlier.

Before President Sadat took this step it had been suggested that, if he was determined to do something about the treaty, three options were open to him: he could threaten cancellation, suspend operation of the treaty for a period, or cancel it outright. He chose the third and most drastic course. There were probably a number of reasons for his choice. The Ali Sabri affair had strongly influenced Sadat's thinking, he still suspected that the Soviet ambassador in Cairo had been in touch with the Ali Sabri group before the final showdown. The timing of his move was also determined by his conviction that the problems of the Middle East were moving towards a solution and that in this process the Russians had nothing to offer. They had been of great assistance when a solution could only be sought through war, but now the President saw ahead a period of peace. This would, moreover, be a period in which the greatest political and economic power in the area was going to be wielded by those Arabs who were allies or friends of the US. The further therefore he succeeded in removing himself from the losing Soviet side the nearer he would come to the winning American side. As he told a group of visiting American senators, headed by Abraham Ribicoff, 'I have proved myself.'

I do not think the Russians ought to have been surprised at the cancellation of the treaty – there had been too many signs that something like this was in the wind – but they were. They felt they were victims of a conspiracy. They might, they admitted, have made mistakes, have played some of their cards badly, but, as they saw it, only a conspiracy involving the major powers and the conservative forces in the Arab world could explain so total a rebuff.

★   ★   ★

Two days after the cancellation the Soviet ambassador asked for an interview with President Sadat. The President was not available, so he was referred to the Vice-President, Husni Mubarak, who received him in one of the salons in Abdin Palace. The ambassador said that he had a message for the President from the Soviet government, and placed an envelope on the table between them. The two men talked for a while on a variety of subjects, and as the ambassador got up to go Husni Mubarak asked him what was in the envelope. He was told it was a message from the Soviet government. 'I think you had better deliver that to the Ministry of Foreign Affairs,' said the Vice-President. So the ambassador went round to the ministry, where he saw the

Head of Protocol to whom he gave the envelope. That afternoon the Minister of State for Foreign Affairs, Mohammed Riad, saw the letter and decided that it could not be accepted but must be returned to the Soviet embassy immediately. So the Head of Protocol spoke to the ambassador on the telephone, telling him that the letter was going to be sent back. The ambassador said he would be unable to receive it; his instructions had been to deliver the letter, and this he had done. Then Ismail Fahmi instructed the ministry that the letter should not be accepted, but should be returned to the Russians – who, however, again refused to take it back.

The next day Cairo papers announced that the Egyptian government had rejected a note sent by the Soviet government. Again the ambassador was called to the ministry and asked to take back the letter. 'How can I today take back a letter, which, according to the papers, you refused to receive yesterday?' he asked. So the ministry put the letter in the post, addressed to the Soviet embassy. The Soviet embassy readdressed it, and sent it back to the ministry. For all I know it is still shuttling backwards and forwards.

The offending letter was couched in fairly strong language. It accused President Sadat of taking a one-sided step for which there was no excuse whatever. This was the consequence, it said, of a redirection of Egyptian foreign policy which amounted to a retreat from the policy of friendship and cooperation with the Soviet Union which had characterized recent years. The letter accused some politicians and the press of waging an ugly campaign against the Soviet Union, doing their best to denigrate everything that the Soviet Union had done for the Egyptian people, and to give the impression that the treaty of 1971 had been forced on Egypt. President Sadat himself had told parliament that he had signed the treaty for the benefit of future generations.

The letter then went on to attack the disengagement agreements, saying they meant that Egypt was withdrawing from the struggle for the liberation of Arab territory. According to the treaty there should have been continuous consultation between the Soviet Union and Egypt, but 'instead the Egyptian leadership has constantly endeavoured to slander the Soviet Union, trying to make excuses for dealing with the aggressor and those who back him, even going so far as to assert that the Soviet Union had wished to see the Arabs defeated in 1973, and so had given insufficient help to the Egyptian armed forces.' This was to ignore the airlift mounted by the Soviet Union, and much more besides. It was untrue to suggest, as had been done, that the Soviet Union had made demands on Egypt which Egypt was unable to fulfil; on the contrary the Soviet Union had agreed to Egyptian requests to reschedule its debts. 'World opinion', the letter concluded, 'is correct in condemning the actions of the Egyptian leaders as being against the Soviet Union, against the Egyptian people, and against the Arab nation.'

*   *   *

The breach was not complete. Diplomatic relations were maintained. The two foreign Ministers, Ismail Fahmi and Andrei Gromyko, met in Sofia at the beginning of November 1976, but their discussion largely consisted of recriminations, Ismail Fahmi complaining about the non-delivery of spares and replacements for Egyptian arms and Gromyko about the way in which the Soviet Union was being excluded from everything. Restore the treaty, he said, and then we can discuss other matters.

I think the Russians would have preferred to let things lie fallow for a time. They must have been aware of the pitfalls with which the attempt to impose a *pax Americana* on the Middle East was surrounded. The search for a solution was bound to run into difficulties, and though oil wealth might have reduced the prospect for revolution in the immediate future, in the long run the social complications and disparities which followed in its wake were bound to create an explosive situation. So their best course would have been to sit tight, swallow their humiliations, and wait for the Americans and their friends to make their inevitable blunders.

But the Soviets were denied even the dignity of silence. At the beginning of 1977 President Sadat began publishing his memoirs in an Egyptian magazine, and practically all that appeared concerned his dealings with the Russians. This was something that could not be ignored. On February 19 *Pravda* published a long editorial called 'Anwar Sadat's "memoirs" are a blow at Soviet–Egyptian Friendship'. It described the memoirs as being 'based on lies, slander, and falsification. Lies about the Soviet Union's policy in questions of the Middle East settlement. Slander against the many years of friendly Soviet–Egyptian cooperation. Rude distortion of the Soviet Union's position in respect of Egypt and its people's vital problems. Falsification of the history of the heroic struggle by the Egyptian people, under the leadership of President Nasser and after his death, for its freedom and independence, for restructuring society according to new principles. Anwar Sadat's "memoirs" are misinformative on every question that the author takes up. These are not political memoirs but political libel.'

The *Pravda* article recapitulated, as the various Soviet notes had already done, the assistance which had been given to Egypt, particularly towards its recovery after the defeat of 1967. It quoted from Sadat's own speeches expressing his gratitude for the work done by the Soviet experts, for the Soviet airlift in the 1973 war and his warm endorsement of the Soviet–Egyptian treaty. 'In his striving to exaggerate his own role in every way Sadat goes so far as to smear the outstanding Egyptian leader, Gamal Abdel Nasser. He tries to cast aspersions on Soviet–Egyptian relations during Nasser's presidency, whereas it was precisely then that they were characterized by a spirit of friendship and mutual trust.'

'Lies and slander,' the article concluded, 'even if repeated many times, cannot eradicate from the minds of the Arab peoples the truth about Soviet policy which is invariably directed at supporting their struggle for freedom and independence, and for a really just Middle East settlement. The course of developing equal and friendly relations with Egypt, as with other Arab states, is an inseparable part of this policy. This, however, requires reciprocity.'

But even this bitter exchange was not the end of the story. Early in June Ismail Fahmi went to Moscow and even managed to see Brezhnev, who told him that he wanted to make two things absolutely clear. First, he would like to start a new page in Egyptian–Soviet relations. The past was the past; but it was up to the Egyptians not the Russians to make the first step. And when the new page had been turned he, Brezhnev, would be watching very carefully every development. Secondly, the Egyptians must understand that what they had done was quite outrageous and beyond the bounds of normal relations between states. If Egypt, or any other country in the world, thought it could treat the Soviet Union with contempt, and then expect the Soviets to come crawling back, it was making a very big mistake indeed. Egypt's behaviour had necessarily had repercussions everywhere. 'We have dealings with 120 governments,' said Brezhnev, 'and we give aid to more than half of them. If any of these countries think that, because of the Egyptian precedent, they can heap daily insults on us, unilaterally cancel their agreements with us, and renege on their debts to us, the whole reputation and authority of the Soviet Union would be destroyed, and we are not going to allow that. So all I can say is – if you want a new start we are ready, but we shall be watching you.' Brezhnev added that any improvement in relations between their two countries would be a slow process, because the dispute with Egypt was now out of the hands of the Central Committee – it had been passed down to the party cadres. 'Don't' number two in Nasser's manual of advice was coming home to roost.

19

Inquest and Forecast

BY 1975 the great Soviet offensive, which had begun in 1955, was a spent force. Over a period of twenty years it had had its successes and failures; there had been moments when those who welcomed it had felt it almost triumphant and when those who opposed it were panic-stricken; but now there could be no two opinions – the offensive was in a state of total collapse. By the time Henry Kissinger completed his mission as almost single-handed arbiter of the destinies of Middle Eastern countries, one chapter for those countries and their relations with the Soviet Union had closed and a new chapter had been opened.

The reasons for this spectacular collapse were many. In the first place, the offensive had originally been undertaken without any prior calculation on either side, by the Russians or by the Arabs. After 1945, broadly speaking, two political designs for the Middle East had emerged, competing with each other to fill the vacuum left by the old colonial domination of Britain and France. On the one hand there was the design, sponsored by the US, for a Middle Eastern system to cover the area which would meet the needs of American cold war strategy in the same way that NATO was supposed to meet the needs of Europe and SEATO and other bilateral alliances the needs of Asia. It was a design based purely on geography; all the countries in the area were to be included in it it just because they were there, regardless of their feelings about Russia, the West or each other. The planners in Washington foresaw a Middle Eastern bastion against Russian expansion in which the Arabs, Turkey, Iran and even Israel stood shoulder to shoulder.

On the other hand was an Arab system. This concept, which was advocated by the growing ranks of nationalists who, like Nasser, rejected the American design, was based not on geography but on historical realities and the genuine interests of the peoples of the area. If that Arab system had an enemy, it was Israel, not the Soviet Union. The whole of the post-1945 struggle in the Middle East can be seen in terms of a conflict between the West-sponsored Middle Eastern system and the Arab system.

The nationalist leaders, while turning their backs on all proposals for pacts and alliances, which they felt to be simply old colonialism in new clothing, realized that they would not be able to stand entirely on their own. They needed allies, and the natural direction for them to look was towards the Soviet Union. This was not just because the Soviet Union was innocent of a colonial past in the area, but because, if a new independent system was to achieve any credibility, it would have to be strong. This meant finding a new source of arms to replace the niggardly and conditional supply from the West, and that new source could only be the Soviet Union.

So the Arabs turned to the Soviet Union for arms, and the Soviet Union agreed to supply them. The immediate advantages of this development must have seemed clear in Moscow. It halted the hostile wall being built on Russia's southern borders, and destroyed the effectiveness of the West's main instrument in the area, the Baghdad Pact. But though the Soviets answered the Arab request with unusual alacrity, they did so without making it the basis for any clear long-term strategy. They seized an opportunity that was offered them, but had neither the time nor the ability to consider the wider implications of what they were doing.

★   ★   ★

How, in fact, was the Soviet Union to define its objectives as it moved into this new partnership with the Arabs? Was its main aim to seek a position from which to bargain with the West? All Russian thinking in the mid-1950s was, after all, dominated by the problem of relations with America. The Russians wished to be able to negotiate with the West, yet feared and mistrusted their principal antagonist. In the game of global chess which they were then playing the centre of the board was occupied by Europe, and most of the other major pieces were in Asia, but the Middle East might at least be worth a few pawns. To achieve parity with the US was the goal for which they constantly strove – to be recognized by the rest of the world as America's political and military equal. Might not replacing the West in the Middle East provide the most convincing evidence that parity had been won?

Or was the real Russian objective to communize the area? Or was it to make available to themselves the Middle East's resources? This had always been a tempting area for the expansion of Russian interests, and now, with its huge oil reserves and the access it provided to the world's sea routes, the temptations of the Middle East were greater than ever.

But no sooner were these possible objectives listed than doubts and dangers began to present themselves. The Russians were aware that, however fiercely the Arabs rejected political domination by the West, whether in an old or a new guise, they were still linked to the West by ties of language and culture. The Soviet Union could only be a substitute for the West, and probably a poor substitute at that. Nor could the Russians really in their hearts expect the Middle East as a whole to embrace quickly the self-evident truths of communism. There may have been moments when some leader seemed a hopeful prospect for conversion, but always there were the nagging obstacles of nationalism, religion, culture, custom and so forth. As for the economic and strategic attractions of the area, these could prove a trap as well as a bait. The Russians were aware that any real threat to the oil supplies of the Middle East could be for the West, including America, the occasion for war. True, they intended to step up their competition with America in every field and in every area, but at the same time they wanted this competition to be controlled by political realities, whether of the cold war or of detente. So the Soviet Union remained uncertain what exactly it was trying to do in the Middle East. Its hopes were frustrated by doubts and hesitations.

The Russians failed to identify their objectives clearly, but their failure went much further than this. Of course, other great powers have gone still more disastrously astray in their dealings with what is now called the Third World. The death-throes of the British and French empires in the Arab world and Africa, and American involvement in South-East Asia, for example, showed incomprehension on a far greater scale and a ruthlessness in pursuit of national aims which the Russians never sank to or even contemplated. The Russians were not trying to hold on to something out of date or to hold back something irrepressible; they were trying to accommodate themselves to people and circumstances that apparently needed them. They stood, it seemed, on the threshold of a great historical opportunity. But the opportunity was missed. Why? This is the question to which they and we must try to find the answer.

★   ★   ★

In the first place, as has so often emerged in the course of this narrative, the Russians were unable to comprehend the dominating role of nationalism in the Arab world. They could not appreciate that these were nations still in the process of formation, still in active conflict with the imperialist forces to which they had been so long subjected, and that, this being so, the solution of many social problems to which the Soviet Union gave priority had inevitably to be deferred. Nor were the Russians really happy when they saw that the leaders of the national independence movements in the Arab world came almost exclusively from the middle class, and that it was in fact this class which still played a predominant role in such movements. They could not help noticing that these middle-class national leaders were capable of conducting a dialogue with their counterparts in the West, with whom culturally and linguistically they had so much in common, whether they agreed or violently disagreed with them. For the people of Western Europe, North Africa and the Middle East, the Mediterranean had been a bridge as well as a barrier. Present quarrels might prove to be only an interlude in a long and enduring partnership.

Then there were the innate contradictions in the Soviet Union's own attitudes to the outside world. It has been obliged to speak and act on two levels, as the bastion of world revolution and as a superpower. Speaking as representatives of the motherland of the revolution the Soviets will talk with a smaller power, such as Cuba or Egypt, on a basis of equality. They will encourage this; it is, they will say, as equals that we must discuss our affairs. But if a friendly country tries to argue with them when the Soviets are playing their role of superpower, they are not pleased. It is as equal to equal that they give advice, but as a superpower instructing a local power that they expect to be listened to.

Another stumbling-block was the extreme rigidity of Soviet institutions. The Communist Party may have left a profound impression on mother Russia, but mother Russia has also left a profound impression on Soviet communism. Bureaucracy and party in the Soviet Union are the reincarnation of Tsarist bureaucracy and the orthodox church, power spreading out from the centre down to parish priest or party functionary. But in the newly independent countries of the Arab world there has usually been one man – a Sadat, a Boumedienne, an Assad – in whose hands the power to make decisions is concentrated. These men expect the same rapidity of decision from their friends and helpers in the Soviet Union which they exercise in their own countries, and when, instead, they are confronted by a creaking bureaucracy they become disillusioned.

It is not just the Soviet bureaucracy which is slow, but the men at the top who present the impression of frozen immobility – what Sadam Hussein of Iraq, who had many dealings with them, once called their 'Siberian mentality'. Whatever the shortcomings of the American system may be, it at least provides variety. If a Third World leader finds his relations with, say, Nixon, turning sour, there is always the probability that within two or three years he will find a new face in the White House, whereas if he gets on bad terms with the men in the Kremlin his fate is sealed for ever. And each new face in the White House means a whole new team of decision-makers recruited from the best brains available in the business world, the universities, the law and anywhere talent is to be found. But whereas Nasser dealt in turn with Truman, Eisenhower, Kennedy, Johnson, Nixon and their teams, and Sadat with Nixon and Kissinger, Ford, Carter and Vance, for 25 years between them they dealt in Moscow only with Khruschev and Brezhnev, and with the same Gromyko coming back year after year to lecture them in the same manner and in almost the same words.

* * *

The Arabs first found themselves in direct contact with the Soviet Union in the period immediately following the Twentieth Congress of the CPSU, at which Stalin's tyranny was exposed to the world by his successors. The fallibility of revolutionary leaders was thereby admittted. No longer could the heirs of Lenin claim, with any plausibility, a monopoly of the truth. Yet this is precisely what they often appeared to be doing. In 1955 the Soviet Union was still at loggerheads with Marshal Tito. But when the Arabs started looking around for allies with whom to face the importunate demands of the West, a man like Tito seemed to them hardly, if at all, less worthy of respect than the Russian leaders. Here was another man who had refused to be dragooned into a great power system, and just because the system which he had rejected was the Warsaw Pact, this did not make him any less admirable in Arab eyes than Nehru when he rejected SEATO or Nasser when he rejected the Baghdad Pact.

Then China took the place of Yugoslavia as arch-heretic to the Soviets and the Arabs were expected to pick a quarrel with China, for which they felt the greatest respect as an oriental country which had stood up to the West and which was embarking on new and exciting political and social developments. There was no conceivable Arab interest which could be served by quarrelling with Peking. Nor, later, was there any Arab interest which could be served by the invasion of Czechoslovakia – an event which the Arabs were invited to approve of but which instead profoundly shocked them. If, they felt, the Red Army and its allied armies had to be sent to crush a country where a communist government was in power, this had to be taken as further evidence that the communist system was not only fallible, but more probably fundamentally wrong in some respects. It reinforced the strongly held conviction that Russians and Americans were equally at fault in insisting that their brands of communism and capitalism were the only alternatives open to the rest of the world. Some systems superior to both must surely exist.

*   *   *

The Soviet Union frequently showed a surprising inability to understand the realities of power in other parts of the world. Because they regard themselves as custodians of the only true interpretation of history, the Russians have always tended to see events elsewhere in terms of their own experience. When discussing the Arab–Israel problem they were liable to draw parallels from the treaty of Brest-Litovsk and the partition of Germany, which in fact were quite irrelevant. It took them a long time to relate the problem to broader American designs, and they continued to underestimate the expansionist element in Zionism. They confused the problem of Israel with their own still unresolved Jewish problem. They would argue that, when the requisite degree of social development had been reached, and when working-class solidarity had been recognized, not only would the Jewish problem in the Soviet Union be solved, but the Histadrut and the Arab labour unions would advance side by side in proletarian solidarity. In 1966 Kosygin, flushed with the success of the Tashkent meeting which had concluded the Indo-Pakistan war, could even suggest to Nasser that he might care to consider an 'Arab–Israel Tashkent' to conclude this other vexing problem. He did not appear to grasp that, if such a meeting ever took place, it would be in Texas not in Tashkent, since the only people who could conceivably bring it about would be the Americans.

The case of Somalia illustrates the Soviet Union's most recent failure to understand the nature of its commitments as a power with global responsibilities. The Soviet leaders did not appreciate that when Siad Barre, a military man and a Somali, approached them for aid he must have had only one aim in view – to secure arms with which he could reunite the five regions under different sovereignty into which the Somalis were then divided. As his part of the bargain Siad Barre dedicated Somalia to what he called 'scientific socialism', put the hammer and sickle on government posters, and asked for Soviet experts to come and give advice. Once again the Soviets thought they could see the preferred roads for influencing a young country – arms and industrialization – opening before them, and as on previous occasions they rushed headlong in, provoking the maximum alarm among Somalia's neighbours and in the West by doing so. This time, however, they were determined not to repeat their mistakes in Egypt. There was to be no High Dam, but something much more modest; a meat-packing plant and a fish-processing fleet would provide this nation of shepherds with profitable industries and the nucleus of an industrial proletariat. The Soviet Union would benefit too. But the new industrial proletariat numbered no more than a few hundreds, and most of the fruits of its labour seemed to go in canned meat for the Russian market. Most of the fish that was processed seemed also to go direct to the Soviet Union, and there were grave fears that the waters off Somalia were being drained of their stocks of fish.

Then Somalia's neighbour and adversary, Ethiopia, started asking the Soviet Union for arms, and this appeared to offer much more attractive possibilities. So the Soviets switched their support, and their proteges, the Somalis, found themselves deserted. Having recently joined the Arab League, they turned for aid to the Arabs. An Arab mission was sent to see what could be done. Its report showed that Siad Barre had taken steps to liquidate Soviet influence: the word 'scientific' had been dropped from the description of Somali socialism; the hammer and sickle had been removed from Somali government posters and the Russian experts had been kicked out. From being Somalia's greatest benefactor, the Soviet Union had become Somalia's public enemy number one. So easily assumed, and so easily shrugged off, was Soviet influence in an area of the world about which they knew too little.

It is, of course, true to say that, at any rate in the short term, the Soviet Union gained considerably by its switch of support from Somalia to Ethiopia. In the first place, it was able to appear as the champion of legitimacy, and the sanctity of existing frontiers is very precious to the Soviet Union itself, as well as to most African states. Secondly, it was able to mount a large-scale military operation, involving complicated problems of logistics, in a difficult African terrain, which the Americans could not have bettered. But the Soviets gained above all by being successful. They achieved the object which they had set themselves – the creation of an effective Ethiopian military force and the expulsion of the Somalis from the Ogaden. This is something of which all those who have cause to look on Russian involvement in Africa with hope or with fear will have taken careful note.

In other parts of the world besides the Horn of Africa the Soviet Union has plunged into disputes stemming from old colonial frontiers which wiser heads might have felt reluctant to become involved in. Iraq and Iran, Iraq and Kuwait, Algeria and Morocco, Ethiopia and Kenya, are other cases in point, where an outside power will have to walk with extreme circumspection if it is to avoid taking sides and where any side taken is likely to prove the wrong one. This is a danger which the Soviet Union has not always been able to recognize until it has been too late.

★   ★   ★

It is not only in its dealings on a government to government basis that the Soviet Union has often shown an astonishing insensitivity. Almost all representatives of Third World countries who have had dealings with the Russians have found it virtually impossible to achieve any real personal relationship with them. The problem in hand could be discussed, but that was all. Beyond that, oratory and an exchange of slogans had to take the place of conversation or argument. This applied not just to those Third World leaders who had to negotiate at the highest levels, but to the lower ranks who came into contact with Soviet officers, bureaucrats, party leaders and politicians.

Thus by now there have probably been more than 200,000 Arabs, students and servicemen, who at one time or another have gone to live in the Soviet Union, and perhaps 120,000 Soviet citizens who have spent some time in their professional capacity in the Arab world. But there has been no mixing. No Arabs have been able to visit Russian homes; no Russians have visited Arab homes. Friendship may have sprung up between individual Russians and Arabs working side by side on a particular job, but it has hardly ever blossomed into a more personal relationship. The wish to communicate may have been there; the capacity to do so has been lacking.

One statistic is particularly revealing in this connection. Of the 200,000 Arabs who have been to the Soviet Union – from the armed forces, or for training as engineers and other specialists, or as negotiators for trade and other bilateral agreements – fewer than a hundred have married Russian girls, while of the 15,000 Arabs who went to the United States as students in the late fifties and sixties 7,000 – almost half – married American girls. And those Arabs who did marry Russian girls found life hard for them. It was made abundantly clear by the Soviet authorities that their matrimonial alliances were not welcome.

The Soviets have proved particularly inept in cultural exchanges and, indeed, in the whole field of public relations. There was, for example, a time when the Soviet Ministry of Cultural Affairs hired the Odeon cinema in Cairo for the showing of Russian films. But at each showing there were perhaps no more than two or three people in the audience. This was not because of any hostility to the Russians or to the language barrier (how many in an Arab audience, after all, can follow the dialogue in an American film?), but because of the films' content. The Middle East is one of the great story-telling areas of the world; its people love stories – they love to make them up and to listen to them. No doubt the Russian people do too, but, if so, this weakness is not allowed to be shown in the face presented to the rest of the world. A privileged leader like Khruschev may entertain his hearers with stories, but Soviet films remain a string of predictable clichés. Nor is their literature more inviting. The Arabs are eager to read the works of Tolstoy or of Dostoevsky, but these are not what they are offered. They would find at the Soviet Publishing House in Cairo the collected works of Lenin for as little as 30 piastres, but this is not what they want to buy. In the same way, the classical Russian ballets are superb; the new ballets are just boring.

The trouble arises from something which I have already mentioned

– the different concept which the Soviet leaders have of public opinion. They see it as something to be moulded by education and propaganda, not as something that has to be watched, listened to and humoured. Because of this they are unable to give much thought to the cultivation of public opinion in other countries. It has been said that the ruler of every newly independent country in Africa feels the immediate need of two things – a television station (colour, if possible) and a beer factory. These are the means by which he can reach the mass of the population. But it is no use his looking to the Soviet Union for either of them, whereas America, Germany, France or Britain will be only too happy to oblige. The same is true of the next step in communication between ruler and ruled – a news agency.

An experience of my own illustrates this Soviet shortcoming. When Kosygin came to Cairo for Nasser's funeral I was, being at that time Minister of Information, delegated to look after him. This was at a moment when the Americans were making a great deal of noise over the accusation that Egypt had moved some of its rocket installations after the ceasefire along the Suez Canal had come into effect. Reports of American annoyance had got into the Egyptian press, and Kosygin taxed me with them. Why, he asked indignantly, did we give publicity to such charges? We were playing into the hands of the Israelis. But I had a reason for not stopping the reports. I was aware that the ceasefire was not generally popular with public opinion in Egypt, or the rest of the Arab world, and thought that if people knew that there was some controversy about the way in which the ceasefire was being observed, this might give some satisfaction. I tried to explain this to Kosygin, but failed to make my point. Arab public opinion was irrelevant; all that mattered was that reports coming from the other side were being allowed to circulate.

*　*　*

In spite of all these failures and shortcomings it must be emphasized that the achievements of the Soviet Union since the revolution in the fields of education, health, employment, technology, scientific research and much more have been tremendously impressive. Unfortunately they have not been able to present these achievements abroad in an easily recognizable form. Indeed, sometimes these very achievements have been turned to their disadvantage.

The Soviets' role as a supplier of arms is a case in point. They fully appreciated the influence they derived as a source of armaments, but they did not want attention to be focussed on this particular role. Yet their contribution has been of almost staggering proportions. Over the years they have supplied the various Arab countries with 25–30,000 tanks, with 7–8,000 military aircraft and with 15–17,000 guns. From nowhere else could a fraction of these have been obtained. During the October War the Arabs and Israelis lost between them over 2,000 tanks – more than the total tank production of western Europe for a period of two or three years. There was a time in 1975 when President Sadat has arranged a ten-year agreement with France for the supply of Mirage fighters. This was after his quarrel with the Soviets over the expulsion of the experts. But during a brief lull in this quarrel the Soviets resumed the despatch of Mig-23s to Egypt, and in one month more Migs arrived from the Soviet Union than Mirages were due to arrive from France in three years.

Recent technological advances have done nothing to help the Russian position in the Middle East. On the contrary, since most Arab governments are opposed to communism they now, thanks to new surveillance techniques, find it easier to keep their opponents under control. And because the content of Soviet information services is so poor they still make no impact on the Arab world. A recent survey of which foreign radio stations were listened to by Egyptians showed Radio Monte Carlo at the top, followed by the Voice of America and the BBC. China came at the bottom, because its programmes are so remote and hard to receive, but Moscow's Arabic service, though put out on a powerful medium-wave transmitter, was almost equal bottom. Even the Iraqi, Libyan and Israeli services commanded a wider audience than it did, and simply because its programmes show as little consideration for the tastes of listeners as *Pravda* does for the tastes of readers. There is no entertainment, and practically nothing that anywhere else would pass as news. Instead there is comment and exhortation. There is little market in the Arab world for either.

★   ★   ★

Soviet policies towards the Arab world are in disarray, and so in consequence are Arab communist parties. In most Arab countries they are illegal. One communist sits in the Iraqi cabinet, but he is well aware that the real decisions are taken outside the cabinet and that he is not a party to them. There is, indeed, a little reason why the young in any Arab country should be attracted by the old men and antiquated slogans which they see in Moscow. The paradox is that the country which is supposed to represent the future goes on repeating the slogans of the past, while the so-called reactionary countries seem capable of absorbing new ideas. Except on ceremonial occasions American leaders do not normally pad out their speeches with quotations from Washington and Jefferson, but every Soviet leader must cite Lenin, Marx and Engels to prove his orthodoxy. The only surprising thing about the growth of Eurocommunism is that it took so long to develop and that its sincerity should still be in question.

Signs of a movement comparable to Eurocommunism are to be detected in the Arab world. As has been seen, communism in the Arab world since the end of World War I has passed through three fairly distinct phases. First came the generation of theorists, who showed an almost total inability to communicate with the masses, and so were quickly relegated to the obscurity from which, except in the files of the police, they had never really emerged. Next came the generation which was active in the years leading up to World War II. This generation also failed almost completely to reach the masses, but what mainly accounted for its lack of success was the fact that its leadership was almost entirely foreign and Jewish. The post-1945 generation of communists was of more account than the preceding two but, weakened by official suppression and internal bickering, only on one or two occasions did it become a force to be reckoned with.

Now a fourth generation of communists is coming to the fore, emerging from the preceding generations but including also some entirely new elements. Apart from the so-called 'new left' – Maoists, Trotskyists and so on – these are people who have taken an active part in the national struggle, and who have a clearer, personal knowledge of what that struggle has been about. Like the Eurocommunists they will be concerned to maintain their independence, and will not be prepared to bow to the supposed superior wisdom of Moscow. This new breed of communists is also to be found among the Palestinians – men who have a lot of experience of working among the people and who understand, from personal knowledge, how to handle problems like religion or the role of the bourgeoisie. These people certainly give advice to Moscow, and may even be respected by the

Soviet leadership, which, however, is probably not altogether happy with them because of their independence of mind. They know that this new generation has close contacts – perhaps too close – with the communist parties of France, Spain and Italy – contacts which have, as has been seen, in some cases a tradition going back to the early days on both sides.

These Arab communists continue to treat Moscow as a head-quarters – they have more or less regular meetings, twice a year, in the institutes attached to the Central Committee of the Soviet Union – but they also meet each other in the Middle East, often, for obvious reasons, in places outside the Arab world, such as Cyprus or Athens. Their general view, as might be expected, is that short-cuts to revolution and social progress are to be avoided, as is dependence on one man, however charismatic. Slow but sure is their motto.

It is possible to see a time when individual communists and local communist parties will play a useful part in the political life of their countries, though I do not expect ever to see them take a leading role. I remember putting this point of view to one of the leading old guard communists of the Arab world, Shafi'ah Ahmed of the Sudanese Communist Party, a very intelligent man, a winner of the Lenin Peace Prize and one of the victims of the abortive left-wing coup in Khartoum in July 1971. 'There are excellent ideas in Marxist thought,' I told him, 'but if you come to me with Marxism as preached by Marx, applied by Lenin and Stalin, talked about by Khruschev, and tell me that that is the road we must follow, I'm bound to tell you that I'm sorry, but in our part of the world it's not going to work. For you to think that the communists will one day be in a majority is absurd. You'll never be the seed or the tree, though, if you participate with the national elements in a dialogue, you may be the fertiliser.' The only answer from Shafi'ah, who had a good sense of humour, was: 'What sort of fertiliser? Chemical or manure?'

But, though orthodox communism may have little or nothing to offer, the social tensions and injustices that exist in the Arab world make it certain that radical ideas will continue to flourish. Admittedly Arab governments do as little to encourage new ideas as does the Soviet Union, but in the Arab world as a whole there is a constant cross-fertilization of ideas. All Arabs discuss the same topics; they all face the same problems. There may be no dialogue inside Egypt, or inside Iraq or Libya, but ideas do get exchanged between Cairo and Beirut, between Beirut and Baghdad, between Baghdad and Damascus, between Damascus and Riyadh, and so on. That is the true Arab dialogue.

★   ★   ★

For the present the Soviets have probably come to the conclusion that the only way open to them is to sit and wait for the inevitable processes of history to take their course. Naturally, if there was a change in the Kremlin – if the old men were replaced by a younger generation more open to new ideas, more ready to take risks and experiment, more able to learn about the men and movements outside their borders, the story would be different. But there is no sign of this.

What looks inevitable is that the coming period in the Middle East will be a period of ferment – even of chaos. The scene there is dominated by two factors – oil wealth and Israel. Oil wealth puts more power into the hands of the traditional elements – the tribes, merchants, bourgeoisie, landlords – and in most Arab countries these still have the machinery of state in their hands. Even countries like Egypt, where direct benefits from oil are limited or non-existent, are indirectly conditioned by the rich conservative regimes on which they depend for financial support. Never has the power of the state machine been greater; never have its armed forces and surveillance networks been better equipped. The continuing struggle against Israel has provided an excuse for postponing change. It has absorbed the energies of politicians and the revenues of states.

Recently Arabs have been offered the prospect of a negotiated settlement with Israel. I myself think this prospect is illusory, but even if this proves to be so there is another possibility that has to be taken into consideration. This is that some Arab regimes will become so frustrated by the incubus of confrontation with Zionism that they will prefer peace at almost any price. Should this happen – should the struggle of the last thirty years be ended, even by exhaustion – the Arab world will pass into a new era.

Arab governments are moving to the right, and apparently consolidating themselves. But below the surface all sorts of tensions are building up. Education, industrialization, technology, contact with the world at large all play their part in this process. The necessity for change everywhere grows greater; the ability of the regimes to adapt to change grows less. An explosion is inevitable.

When the explosion takes place the Soviet Union is bound to be involved. No *pax Americana* is going to be able to prevent that. The closeness of the Arab world and the Soviet Union to each other, the genuine commercial and strategic interests which they have in common, are enough to ensure that. Once again we are likely to see the Soviet Union being sucked into the Middle East by the imperatives of the moment, just as it was in 1955. Another offensive will be begun. Whether this second offensive turns out to be more successful than the first will depend on how well the Soviet Union and local communist parties have learned from past experience. If the Soviet Union has by then come to realize that the future cannot be organized by means of quotations from the past – that history provides guidelines, not a book of rules – and if local parties have managed to rid themselves of the taint of being agents of a foreign power, we may find the next chapter of Arab–Soviet relations full of surprises. A second chance will be offered, and this time it may not be missed.

Index

differences with Russia, 104; Iraq prints forged Nasser directive, 105; discusses High Dam with Novikov, 110; 'criticism' of Khruschev's family, 117; five-hour speech (May 21, 1962), 117; in Russia (1965), 143–7; on Russia's quarrel with China, 150; discussions with Kosygin (1966), 162–5; talks with Gromyko in Cairo on arms, 169–70; USA turns against him, 173; proclaims state of emergency, 175; accepts U Thant's moratorium, 176; leaves negotiations to Russia, 190–92; hopés Russian arms supply will not fluctuate, 194; secret visit (Jan. 1970) to Moscow asking for missile (SAM-3) wall, 197; accepts Rogers Plan on ceasefire, 198; receives advance warning of Russia's intervention in Czechoslovakia, 205; his answer, 206–7; Sudan asks advice about Russia, 208; death, 214; effect on Arab world and Russia, 215–16; steps he took after ceasefire, 218–9

NATO, 56, 167, 275
Neguib, General Mohammed, clash with Nasser, 54
Nehru, Jawaharlal, 50, 57, 108–9, 114, 279
Neto, Agostinho, 24
New Dawn Group, 47
Nimechenko, Colonel V., 59
Nimeiry, Jaafar, 20; ousts Mahgoub in Sudan, 208; conflict with communists, 229; arrests his opponents, 230; captured by rebels, 231; freed, 231
Niporozhny, 19, 126
Nixon, President Richard, 215, 234; meeting with Brezhnev, 241; nuclear alert in October war, 258–9, 264, 279
Nkrumah, Kwame, 20, 154, 160
Nokrashy Pasha, Egyptian Prime Minister on declaration of Arab–Israeli war (1948), 52; assassinated, 53
Novikov, Ignatiy, discusses High Dam with Nasser, 110
nuclear arms, effect on Russian policy, 56
Nur, Abdel Muhsin Abdul, 226

Pakistan, Russian toast to, 69–70
Palestine, creation of Israel (1948), 49; Fateh's first communiqué, 149; 174; Russia's attitude to Palestinians, 209–11; embryo state, 268–9
Patolichev, Nicholai, 208
Perides, Theodosis, 44
Pilz, Dr Wolfgang, 151
Plisetskaya, Maya, 26
Podgorny, N., visit to Egypt (1968), 144, 161–2, 174; 189–90; 190–2; on request for loan to Sudan, 208; 227, 233; in Cairo (April 1972), 240
Ponomarev, Boris, Politburo meeting, 11–15, 185, 211, 233–4
Pravda, 138; attacks Heikal, 84–5; on Sadat's memoirs, 272–3
Problems of Peace and Socialism (Bakdash), 157–8